ST. ANDREWS UNIVERSITY PUBLICATIONS, NO. XLIII

NATURE IN GREEK POETRY

NATURE IN GREEK POETRY

STUDIES PARTLY COMPARATIVE

BY

GEORGE SOUTAR, M.A., D.Litt.

SOMETIME READER IN ENGLISH, UNIVERSITY COLLEGE, DUNDEE,
UNIVERSITY OF ST. ANDREWS

Published for St. Andrews University by
HUMPHREY MILFORD
Oxford University Press
AMEN HOUSE, LONDON, E.C. 4

1939

JOHNSON REPRINT CORPORATION
New York • London

1971

This reprint has been authorized by
The Oxford University Press

61282

First reprinting 1971, Johnson Reprint Corporation

Library of Congress Catalog Card Number: 74-178220

Johnson Reprint Corporation
111 Fifth Avenue
New York, N.Y. 10003, U.S.A.

Johnson Reprint Company Ltd.
24/28 Oval Road
London, NW1 7DD, England

Printed in the U.S.A.

CONTENTS

PREFATORY MEMOIR

WHEN the University Court decided to include Dr. Soutar's *Nature in Greek Poetry* among their St. Andrews University Publications, they asked me to preface it with a short memoir of the author. It was a request that I could not refuse after sixty-five years of unbroken friendship, however unequal I felt to the task.

George Soutar was born on 28th December 1864, at East Leys of Dun, a small farm on the Braes of Angus of which his father, another George Soutar, was at that time tenant. He was the younger of two brothers. Their father, I believe, was a new-comer to the district, but their mother, Susan Nicol, came of a family long connected with Dun, so that George had his roots struck very deep in that soil. And he had a faithful memory: that nook of earth, in Horatian phrase, smiled on him beyond all others to the end of his days: he seldom let a summer pass without a visit to Dun. Later in life a common love of Dun brought him the friendship of Violet Jacob, a daughter of the historic house of Erskine, who has found her best inspiration in the Braes of Angus and the Howe o' the Mearns. 'When I next came to Scotland,' Mrs. Jacob writes, 'we met and spent an unforgettable afternoon sharing our recollections. The Den of Dun had been a very land of romance to us both, and we went over in memory the bits of it we had loved, or feared, or peopled with the

vii

knights and giants and goblins of imaginative children.'

George received his early education at Dun Public School under Robert Spalding. It was Spartan fare that our rural Board Schools provided in those days, but George had got a good grounding in the three R's and a little Latin before, in 1879, his family removed to Montrose to let him attend the Academy there. At that time Montrose Academy, like most Scottish Secondary Schools, was in effect a congeries of independent departments; but much of the teaching was excellent. David Campbell was a prince of English teachers, and the Rector, James Stobo, who taught Classics, was a scholar of remarkable linguistic gifts. In these subjects George excelled; but he had no gift for Mathematics, and his struggles with Algebra and Geometry distressed his sensitive mind.

In 1882 he went to the University of St. Andrews, where he spent four happy winters. The St. Andrews of the 1880's differed considerably from the St. Andrews of to-day. The town was smaller, the University much smaller—some 170 men in Arts and perhaps 30 in Divinity. There were no women students, and no halls of residence. The students 'bunked' in private lodgings, often in pairs. It was a simple, frugal life; not so frugal as it had been in the days when Sydney Smith said of the Scots that they cultivate the Muse on a little oatmeal, *tenui Musam meditantur avena*, but still frugal. The students no longer used Meal Monday to go home and replenish their meal-pocks, but most of them were poor. Bursaries, however, if small, were numerous, and living was very cheap: a man could live comfortably on ten or twelve shillings a week.

George entered St. Andrews with a University Endowments Association bursary, which he bettered next year by winning a Bruce bursary. At college as at school his favourite subjects were English and Greek, and he was fortunate in his professors—Thomas Spencer Baynes ('Tommy' to his affectionate students) and Lewis Campbell. Mathematics still afflicted him, but in the Humanities he proved one of the best men of his year: he was first in Rhetoric and second in Logic, Latin, and Greek, and crowned his career in 1888 by graduating with First Class Honours in Classics. Perhaps the distinction that pleased him most was a prize that he won for a poem on 'Immortality.' It was not his only adventure in verse.

St. Andrews gave him something even better than book-learning and the cultivation of the Muse; its small and friendly society gave a unique opportunity to his genius for friendship. Then and thereafter he made many friends, and kept all that he made. His closest friend in student days was George Ritchie Croll, with whom he 'bunked' for several winters; then there were R. F. Murray, the poet; David Kay, afterwards Professor of Hebrew in St. Andrews; R. D. Mackenzie, George Harper, W. G. MacAndrew, and others. In July 1937, while motoring in Devon, he visited the churchyard of Ilminster, and laid on R. F. Murray's grave a wreath composed of flowers arranged in the form of a St. Andrew's Cross. The action was typical of that steadfastness in friendship which was one of his most endearing qualities. It was no less typical of him that in the note which he affixed to the wreath he ascribed it to the piety of the After Many Days Club, which took its name from one of Murray's poems. In November 1938 he contributed a charming account of this visit to the Club's Year-book.

I have said that he spent four happy winters in St. Andrews. His summers, I fear, were less happy. His father had been dead for some years, and his mother died early in his College course, so that for a long time he was homeless. He stayed sometimes with his brother David, or with one of his aunts, or with friends, or in lodgings, solacing his loneliness with reading and composition. Most of his verse belonged to these solitary summers. At the end of this Memoir I have given a few specimens of his translations from the Greek poets, as being germane to the treatise that follows.

In those days he dreamed of proceeding to Oxford; but by the time he had finished his St. Andrews course he was over scholarship age, and had to think of making a living. He put in short spells of teaching at private schools in Banff and Ramsgate, and at Dundee High School. He used to tell with a chuckle how the Head of the Ramsgate seminary gave him the whole mystery of discipline in a nutshell: '*Suaviter in modo*, Mr. Soutar, but *fortiter in re*!' In 1890 he went as principal teacher of English to Elgin Academy, where he found a congenial Head-master in George Smith: the two became life-long friends. In 1893 he left Elgin for a similar post in Hermitage School, Helensburgh.

He was now in a position to make a home of his own, and in 1894 he forged a new link with St. Andrews by marrying Janet Aitken, a daughter of the old grey city. The years at Helensburgh were years of quiet happiness and industry. Here his three children were born—Margaret, Ritchie (named after George Ritchie Croll), and David. Here too he published his first book, a volume of selections from Pope with a learned and witty introduction ending with an epigram which damned the barrenness of the Popian school in seven words: 'Pope has written nothing since his death.' It was at Helensburgh also that he completed the first draft of the present work, for which, in 1898, the University of St. Andrews conferred on him the Degree of Doctor of Letters. His appointment as External Examiner in English in 1896 made another link with St. Andrews, and the connection became permanent when in 1907 he was appointed to the staff of University College, Dundee, where, first as Lecturer, after 1927 as Reader, in English, he served the University till he retired in 1935. The official connection did not end even then, for the University showed its gratitude by appointing him External Examiner in English for a second time—an unusual compliment. The Senatus designed yet another honour for him; they meant to present him at this year's graduation for the Degree of LL.D., but his death frustrated their intention.

Dr. Soutar came to Dundee in a happy hour. After fifteen years of independent existence, University College had recently been incorporated into the University of St. Andrews, and it was very fortunate that in an institution devoted mainly to Science and Medicine the subject of English should at this juncture be in the hands of a man who represented the humanistic tradition of St. Andrews at its best. From the first he was on excellent terms with Professor Lawson, his 'opposite number' in St. Andrews; and his relations with Professor Blyth Webster were equally cordial. Both Professors had complete confidence in his scholarship and judgment. He took a personal interest in all his students; all of them were invited to his house every session: 'tea at the Doctor's' was a regular institution. He took special pains to guide the reading of his Honours students, for whose benefit he accumulated in the College Library a collection of English classics which before he retired amounted to three or four thousand volumes.

Dr. Soutar had no great liking for administrative work, but such duties as fell to him on the Education Board, the Library Committee, the Faculty of Arts, or the Senatus were faithfully and efficiently discharged. Moreover, he was at one time President of the Scottish Branch of the English Association and represented the University for many years on the Provincial Committee for the Training of Teachers, of which body he was Chairman when he died. In point of fact this modest, self-effacing scholar had considerable gifts for Committee work; he had humour, and (what is rarer in Scotsmen) he had wit; he had an equable temper and a conciliatory manner; but he had backbone too, and could snub an offender if need were with a sharpness which his habitual gentleness made all the more biting.

He had not many recreations, in the physical sense. He was a golfer, though never a good one. He disliked motoring at first, but he got over his aversion when his boys grew up, and latterly he and his wife enjoyed many motor tours with one or other of their sons. But his favourite recreation was walking, an exercise for which his length of limb and spare frame adapted him admirably. Country-bred, he loved country sights and sounds, and his sight and hearing were remarkably acute. Though he looked wiry he was really of a delicate constitution, nervous and sensitive to a degree. After his retirement he suffered much from gastric trouble, and finally underwent an operation, from the effects of which he did not recover. He died on 9th February 1939.

His students knew his great gifts as a teacher, but he published very little. The volume of selections from Pope which I have mentioned and a *Book of Ballads* in which I collaborated were all the books that appeared in his life-time, though he also contributed two articles on Sir George Mackenzie and one on 'Scot or Wyatt?' to the *Scots Magazine*. But he left behind him the MSS. of two important works. One is the treatise now printed, which grew out of his thesis for the Doctorate of Letters. He worked over it at intervals for the rest of his life, remodelling it and enriching it as his knowledge of literature increased. Chapter VIII. as here printed was re-written four times, the last time within a few weeks of his death. The last two chapters never received his final touches. The other manuscript is of a different kind. For thirty years Dr. Soutar spent much of his leisure in wandering about in Angus and the Mearns, picking up Scots words and phrases, out of which he meant to compile a Glossary of Angus and Mearns Scots. When the project for a Scottish National Dictionary took shape he put his material at the editor's disposal; but all his slips, carefully docketed, are now in safe keeping in University College Library, and I hope that local patriotism will some day make it possible to carry out his intention. The result will be a unique contribution to Scots lexicography, for many of the words and phrases that he collected are already ceasing to be heard on the lips of men. But whatever be the fate of his books, George Soutar will long be re-

membered by all who knew him as a gentle scholar
and a steadfast friend. 'His learning,' Mrs. Jacob
writes, 'sat lightly on him, and he had a gracious
gentleness of manner that made one forget his great
attainments and think only of his charm.'

J. C. SMITH.

TRANSLATIONS FROM GREEK POETRY

(1) TO THE CICALA.   From Anacreon

Drunken with a drop of dew,
Happy, happy as a king,
We can hear thee twittering;
Everything within thy view
From the tree-top, in the fields,
Everything each season yields,
O cicala, is thy dower;
Dear to everyone thou art,
Dearest to the farmer's heart,
Prophet sweet of summer's hour!

Darling of the muses nine,
Phoebus' love is also thine,
For he gave thee that clear song;
Age can never do thee wrong,
Skilful lover of thy part;
Nought know's thou of suffering,
Bloodless, fleshless, earth-born thing,
Almost as the gods thou art!

(2) From Pindar, *Oly*. II.

Wealth is a star far seen whose certain light
That man may soothly trust who knows aright
What yet shall be,
How guilty souls must endless penance pay,
For all the sins done in life's little day,
How by unloved decree
One in the nether world pronounceth penalty.

But there, day reigns, the night hath no command,
The sun in splendour aye illumes the land
Where rest the glorious dead;
No toil-cursed hands the vexèd fields annoy,
No selfish cares their anxious thoughts employ,
No tears are shed;
For with the loved ones of the gods they dwell
Who in the ways of truth their trust accomplish'd well.

Whoso, in life, refrained their souls from ill,
Whoso, death past, thrice stood unfaltering still,
Travel to Kronos' towers;
There round the Happy Isles for ever blow
The western Ocean-winds, there all aglow
Are golden flowers
On trees of grandeur or by waters fed,
Whereof they twine them wreaths to bind the hands and
    head.

While, to other realms allotted, an unsightly load of woe
Bear the erring souls of sinners—
Rhadamanthus orders so,
Loved of Zeus, the lord of Rhea, throned above all gods
    below.

(3) From Euripides

O land of my birth and my home,
Ne'er be it mine, is my prayer,
Houseless and helpless to roam
Leading a life of despair,
A sorrowful lot alway;
Rather, O death, for thy prey
Take me, and darken the day
Of my life in the light of the sun;
Hardship of earth is there none
Like to the loss of one's land.

This do I know of a truth;
Not from report is the tale
That I ponder; pity nor ruth
For thy burden of bale
From city and friend hast thou
To solace thy suffering now.
Perish the ingrate, I trow,
Who never at friendship's behest
Flings back the bars of his breast,
Friend is he none for me.

(4) THE FISHERMEN.   From Theocritus

Years gone two aged fishers shared their rest
Where, in a wattled cabin, on a bed
Of dry sea-moss beside the rush-lined wall
The twain had laid them down; around were strewn
The instruments of their laborious hands,
The creels, the rods of reed, the hooks, the sails
Yet weedy from the wave, lines, nets and weels,
Traps framed of wicker, there a pair of oars
And, on the props, a weather-beaten craft;
Spare plaited mat-work, coats and caps
Served as a pillow for their sleeping heads;
This told the story of their days of toil,
This was the sum of all their worldly wealth:
Nor door nor watch-dog guarded them from harm:
In their eyes all things seemed superfluous
Who knew no sentinel save Poverty:
They dwelt remote—still 'gainst their narrow home
Rolled up the gently-breaking waves of sea.

(5) THE LAMENT FOR ADONIS.   From Bion

While on the lonely hills Adonis lay,
In silent anguish travailing with death,
And all around the wilding-flowers flushed red,
Or in sad clusters hung their woeful heads,
Lo, through the shivering oak-woods, sable-stoled,
Her feet unsandalled and her hair unbound,
Fair Cypris came to look upon her lord.
And when she spied the mortal wound unstayed
And marked the scarlet river coursing down
His snow-white side, her arms abroad she cast
And called aloud, ' Stay, stay, Adonis, stay,
That I may have thee for my own at length,
May round thy body fair my own entwine,
And lip with lip commingle for the last!
Wake, O Adonis, for a little while,
One moment wake, and kiss me once again,
Long as the life-time of a lingering kiss,
Till through those lips from which the rose hath fled
Out from thy soul to mine the life-breath ebb,
And I have drained the fountains of thy love!
Dear as thyself that kiss shall ever be,
For thou, ill-fated, soon must flee me far,
Too soon must fare to fearful Acheron ;
While I, a goddess, born to endless days,
All-wretched live and may not follow thee.
But thou, dark queen of Pluto's dreary realm,
Take to thyself my leman and my lord,
Since I am weakling when compared with thee,
Since in the end thy hateful house shall hold
The perished flowers of all earth's loveliness.
Now thou art dead, Adonis thrice-desired,
And, dream-like, my desire hath with thee sped,
With thee too gone my beauty's strength and stay
And left me widowed in Cythera's halls—
Why didst thou, fond one, in thy hardihood,
Essay to match with thine the wild-beast's might ? '

CHAPTER I

LANDSCAPE IN HOMER

HOMER—if one may use the name as a convenience, without discussion, and without necessarily assuming unity of authorship for *Iliad* and *Odyssey*—is the mouthpiece of an age and a race. He throws the glamour of poetry over an early stage of Hellenic life, the life heroic. His audience is gathered in public assembly, and its interest is centred on the deeds of men of mark. The audience determines and limits the nature of his recital, which must make an immediate social appeal. Action and character, the scenic and other accessories of the poems are seen through heroic eyes. The society depicted, however, shows no great gulf fixed between noble and common man. In the *Iliad* the daily out-of-door life is that of a camp and a battle-field. The poem abounds in exploits of warriors, genealogies of heroes, descriptions of their arms, details of fighting and of wounding, of death and funeral. It is in the similes that we make the acquaintance of the shepherd, the farmer, the carpenter, the hunter, the sailor. But in the *Odyssey* Odysseus is a Jack-of-all-trades and proficient in all. He fells tall trees, builds his own ship, and acts as his own captain. He can plough and wield the scythe. He is a judge of soil, of cattle, and of sheep. He ascends Parnassus, not to break a record or to admire the view, but to hunt a boar.

Thus the two Homeric epics do not offer equal

opportunities for the introduction of landscape scenes. The action of the *Iliad* is confined to the place of battle round Ilium, and the phenomena of the larger areas of land and sea are utilised mainly to supply analogies to the actions of gods and heroes on the field. For this reason still nature is rarely presented to our view. The *Odyssey*, on the other hand, is an epic of personal adventure. It describes the wanderings of a man who has travelled far and suffered much, who has seen the towns and marked the ways of many peoples. In the company of this hero, then, we may hope to learn something about Greek landscape. So we begin with the *Odyssey*, setting out without prepossession or theory to suit which facts must be bent and twisted, but content to draw what seem reasonable deductions from the poet's words.

At the beginning of the Fifth Book, Hermes is sent by Zeus to the island Ogygia to inform the nymph Calypso that she must send Odysseus home. Hermes speeds over land and sea, and comes to the place. ' But now when he reached that distant isle, then he came up from the sea of violet blue and went into the land until he came to a great cave, where dwelt the nymph of the fair tresses; and her he found within. A great fire was burning on the hearth, and from afar through the isle was smelt the fragrance of split cedar and citrus blazing: and within she was singing with sweet voice, and walking to and fro before the loom, and weaving with a golden shuttle. And round about the cave a wood grew in bloom, alder and poplar and fragrant cypress. There were wont to roost long-winged birds, owls and falcons and screeching cormorants, whose business is with the waters. And on the spot, round about the hollow cave, there trailed in luxuriance a garden vine, rich with clusters.

2

Four fountains in order were running with clear water, near to one another, turned to their several courses; and around soft meadows of violet and parsley bloomed. Even an immortal coming there would wonder at the sight and be glad in his heart. Standing there, the messenger, the slayer of Argus, wondered. But when he had beheld all with wonder in his heart, at once he went into the wide cave' (v. 56-77).

As landscape this is eclectic and orderly, simple and unperplexing. Gradation of distance is scarcely perceptible, it is deficient in background, everything seems near our feet. It lacks atmosphere, light and shade, and colour. There is sound, but it is that of the sweet voice of Calypso. Ruskin remarks, rather facetiously, that he does not know whether the screeching cormorants are to be considered as part of the ideal landscape.[1] They need not be there at all at the moment—εὐνάζοντο. The place is low ground, probably marshy, for parsley grows there. The presence of the violet is 'unjustifiable from a botanical point of view,' we are told.[2] Be that as it may, we are glad to see this flower, for we shall never again meet with it in the *Odyssey*. Homer has drawn a picture, material for sense-perceptions, to please the eye, for 'pure organic pleasure,' to use a phrase of Wordsworth's. It is almost a pattern for a worker in plastic art as it lies before us, cold and dumb, nearly independent of time, soulless and apart from humanity. No auxiliar light from the poet's mind sheds a

> 'Glory beyond all glory ever seen
> By waking sense.'

[1] Ruskin, *Modern Painters*, Part IV.
[2] Miss Agnes M. Clerke, *Familiar Studies in Homer*.

3

The spectator is as tranquil as the scene. The thoughts and emotions of the man-god, the passion of the moment, are left in the main to our imagination. We hear no lyric raptures; naïvely Homer holds on his epic way:

αὐτὰρ ἐπειδὴ πάντα ἑῷ θηήσατο θυμῷ,
αὐτίκ᾽ ἄρ᾽ εἰς εὐρὺ σπέος ἤλυθεν.

Like Hermes, like Homer, let us reconcile ourselves to realities and waste no sentiment.

In passing we may glance at a modern counterpart. A perusal of the *Aventures de Télémaque* of Fénelon is full of interest for the student of comparative literature. Homer's simplicity does not suit the taste of the sophisticated age of Louis XIV. Founded on Homer, the scene in Fénelon is embellished and gains in perspective. The grotto is there, but it is now partly of shell-work. It is set on the slope of a hill commanding a view of the sea. Gentle zephyrs temper the fierce heat of the sun's rays. The vine is there, just as in Homer. The meadows are there gaily metamorphosed. The trees now put forth wondrous blossoms and bear marvellous fruits. The cormorants give place to song-birds. In the distance there is a range of mountains, which lose themselves in the clouds.

Following in the wake of Odysseus we come to the land of the Phaeacians. Nausicaa indicates to the hero the conspicuous landmarks on the route from the river to the city—a harbour on each side of the town, the place of assembly, a grove, a park and gardens, a splendid palace. 'Thou shalt find a fair grove of Athene, a grove of poplars, by the wayside; in it a spring is welling, and round it lies a meadow.' Probably these words suggested to

4

Ruskin the remark that when Homer's landscape is intended to be beautiful, it consists of 'a fountain, a meadow, and a shady grove.' When Odysseus has reached this spot, he prays to the presiding deity. As he proceeds on his way, guided by the goddess in disguise, he has to pass by the havens. Now his sailor soul is touched, and we are told: 'Odysseus marvelled at the havens and the goodly ships, the assembly-places of the heroes too, and the long high walls, fitted with palisades, a wonder to see' (vii. 43-45). He is again full of wonder when he sees the palace. Last come the gardens. Phaeacia is a fairyland, and to describe it Homer may work to plan but not to type; he has to exert his highest powers of invention, and the wonders of the gardens must match those of the house and household. 'Outside the courtyard, near the door, is a great garden of four ploughgates, and round it on all sides runs a hedge. There grow tall trees blooming, pear-trees and pomegranates, and apple-trees with goodly fruit, and sweet figs and olives in bloom. The fruit of these neither falls nor fails, winter or summer, but it lasts all the year. Evermore does the west wind breathe and form some fruits, while it ripens others. Pear on pear grows old and apple on apple, grape-cluster on grape-cluster, and fig on fig. There also has he a fruitful vineyard planted, of which one part, a warm spot on level ground, is dried by the sun; other grapes again men are gathering, others too they are treading. In front there are unripe grapes shedding their blossom, and others are colouring. There again, alongside the last row, grow trim garden-beds of all kinds of herbs, always fresh. Therein are two fountains of water, of which one is scattered all through the garden, while

5

the other runs opposite to it beneath the threshold of the court, and from this the citizens draw water' (vii. 112-131).

This is perfect gardening under ideal conditions. Even the west wind, which normally in Homer brings rain and storm, is here, as in the Elysian plain, the beneficent wind. In Scheria all things are beautiful, but nothing is useless. Alcinous is supplied with abundance of succulent fruits and kitchen vegetables all the year round. That is one of Homer's ways. He never overlooks the claims of the body, and he stints neither god nor man of his meals. Looked at as landscape, this appears too trim and tame to twentieth-century eyes—'truly Dutch in its quadrangular proportions,' as Gladstone says.[1] With its succession of orchard, vineyard, and herb garden, it is a long description for a Greek to give; and probably it troubled Lessing more than he cared to say. Dew-cool and fresh, it contrasts with the glare and sultriness of Renaissance counterparts. Whether the passage be early work or late, whether or not Scheria be an actual country known to Homer, whether or not the poet is here indulging in satire and the sport called leg-pulling, let others decide, if they can. Alcinous may be a ' bounder,' but he is not made responsible for the account of his gardens. It must be admitted that the grape-clusters are mentioned out of order. Yet it is just at this point in question that the poetry is of a vintage no connoisseur can mistake, fine old Chian. The ascetic, half-etherealised, Wordsworthian side of us may not be moved, but the persisting unregenerate boy—Homer's share in us—

[1] Hegel approves of such uniformity and symmetry in gardens, because thus human beings are allowed to dominate the scene (*Aesthetik*, Part I. 3).

makes instant and glad response to the crooning of
the lines:

ὄγχνη ἐπ᾽ ὄγχνῃ γηράσκει, μῆλον δ᾽ ἐπὶ μήλῳ,
αὐτὰρ ἐπὶ σταφυλῇ σταφυλὴ, σῦκον δ᾽ ἐπὶ σύκῳ.

'These were the splendid gifts of the gods,' says the
poet. As he views them Odysseus shows the same
baffling, simple, childlike wonder as Hermes in
Ogygia:

αὐτὰρ ἐπειδὴ πάντα ἑῷ θηήσατο θυμῷ,
καρπαλίμως ὑπὲρ οὐδὸν ἐβήσετο δώματος εἴσω.

There is in the Homeric epics a strong utilitarian
garden instinct, as it may be called. Orchards would
seem to have been prized possessions, and there is
frequent mention of them. Penelope speaks of her
slave Dolius keeping her garden of trees (*Ody.*, iv. 737).
Achilles thus twits Aeneas, who has come out against
him: 'Have the Trojans chosen out for thee some
plot of ground more excellent than all the rest, fine
arable land, or orchard, that thou may'st dwell
there, if thou slay me?' (*Il.*, xx. 184-86.) Even men
of royal birth did not think it beneath them to perform
manual labour in an orchard. Achilles captured
Lycaon when busy in his father Priam's orchard
(*Il.*, xxi. 35-38). When contrasting Greek and mediaeval ideas of landscape, Ruskin points out that the
mediaeval knight did not, like Laertes, prune vines.
That is true. But neither did the wealthy Athenian
in classic times. There are many striking contrasts
between Homeric manners and those of the fifth
century B.C. From such homely incidents in Homeric
story, we have no right to assume, that the cultivation of a garden was an ideal occupation in the
historic age of Greece. Dandy Alcibiades did not

7

plant cabbages, and those who associated Euripides with vegetables were lying.

Ruskin, however, introduces a legitimate point of contrast when he says, 'Leeks are not now (in the Middle Ages) the most important objects in the garden, but lilies and roses.' The modern student notes with surprise that Homer has not included a flower-garden among the possessions of Alcinous. Such an omission is the rule, not the exception, in this poet. A famous simile in the *Iliad* might seem to prove that Homer knew of flower-gardens:—'As a poppy in a garden droops its head to one side, being heavy with fruit and the spring rains, so he bowed his head made heavy with his helmet' (viii. 306-8). But it has been said that in all probability the poppy (μήκων) had its place among herbs and vegetables, being artificially cultivated 'for gastronomic purposes.' [1] Nor do later classical Greek poets show any marked advance on Homer in this respect. Greek love of flowers was perhaps due less to their cultivation in gardens than to their presence in field and meadow. In fact, the word κῆπος was probably never used in the restricted sense of our *garden*. While we read of gardens of the nymphs, we know that they were in many cases planted with fruit-trees. The name κῆπος is often applied to any fertile spot, and generally associated with deity.[2] It is thus difficult to determine the precise nature of the gardens mentioned in the *Electra* of Euripides:

κυρεῖ δὲ κήποις ἐν καταρρύτοις βεβώς,
δρέπων τερείνης μυρσίνης κάρᾳ πλόκους.

(777-8.)

Nor is the reference to κήπους εὐώδεις in the *Birds*

---

[1] *Familiar Studies in Homer.*
[2] See Pindar, *Oly.*, iii. 24; ix. 27; *Pyth.*, v. 22; ix. 53.

of Aristophanes (1067) more conclusive. It must be remembered, however, that the loss of so much non-Attic lyric poetry may have robbed Greek literature of many garden references.

Ismarus, the country of the Cicones, yields no landscape features. Nor do we fare better with the land of the lotus-eaters, and to satisfy our curiosity we must have recourse to Tennyson's voluptuous music. So the land of the froward Cyclopes receives us next. Here the hero, who now tells his own story, for the most part, rather keeps up a running commentary on physical features than sketches a landscape. These men, he tells us, neither plough nor plant; yet barley and wheat and vines grow in plenty. They do not meet together for council or for law-making, but dwell in caves on the crests of the high hills. The waste island off the coast is wooded and desolate of men, given over to wild goats; the soil lies always untilled and unsown, for the Cyclopes have no ships wherein to voyage to the towns of others and so make their own island a goodly settlement. 'Yet it is by no means a poor land, but would bear all things in their season; for therein are meadows soft and moist by the shores of the grey sea, there vines wither not, and the plough-land is level. Ever as the seasons come round men might reap a fine deep crop there, for surely there is fat soil beneath. And there is a good harbour, where is no need of moorings, of casting anchor, or of fastening hawsers; but after running the ship on the beach men may wait till the sailors think of going and breezes begin to blow' (ix. 105-139). There is considerable 'excitement of emotion' here, but it is that of the good citizen, the farmer, and the merchant-sailor. The landing-place at the head of the harbour

9

combines utility and ornament—a cave and a spring
'edged with poplar pale':

αὐτὰρ ἐπὶ κρατὸς λιμένος ῥέει ἀγλαὸν ὕδωρ,
κρήνη ὑπὸ σπείους· περὶ δ᾽ αἴγειροι πεφύασιν.

(140-41.)

When contemplating this spot, Odysseus thinks
mostly of what it might become under the hand of
man. If he had his way, he would, like Tennyson's
Northern Farmer, soon 'stub Thurnaby waste'; he
would build a town and begin an era of commerce.
Yet who can forget those meadows set to music by
the old enchanter! Hear him:

ἐν μὲν γὰρ λειμῶνες ἁλὸς πολιοῖο παρ᾽ ὄχθας
ὑδρηλοὶ μαλακοί· μάλα κ᾽ ἄφθιτοι ἄμπελοι εἶεν.

(132-33.)

With the above contrast Fitz-James's exposition
of mediaeval sentiment in Scott's *Lady of the Lake*,
Canto 1. He surveys a wild country of mountain
and lake, and he too would play the part of improver:

'From the steep promontory gazed
The stranger, raptured and amazed,
And "What a scene were here," he cried,
"For princely pomp or churchman's pride!
On this bold brow, a lordly tower;
In that soft vale, a lady's bower;
On yonder meadow, far away,
The turrets of a cloister grey.
How blithely might the bugle-horn
Chide, on the lake, the lingering morn!
How sweet, at eve, the lover's lute
Chime, when the groves were still and mute!
And, when the midnight morn should lave
Her forehead in the silver wave,

10

How solemn on the ear would come
The holy matin's distant hum,
While the deep peal's commanding tone
Should wake, in yonder islet lone,
A sainted hermit from his cell,
To drop a bead with every knell—
And bugle, lute, and bell, and all,
Should each bewilder'd stranger call
To friendly feast, and lighted hall."'

So much of Greek poetry was written from the purely heroic point of view that the agricultural and pastoral spirit, the tendency to regard the land as the sustainer of human life and not merely a scenic stage, is much in evidence during the whole classical period. It is very prominent throughout the Homeric poems. It comes out, in a very telling manner, in Athene's description of Ithaca. 'In truth, it is rough, and not fit for the driving of horses, but it is not a very poor island though it is narrow. In it is corn in abundance wonderful, and wine too, and the rain and the refreshing dew fall ever thereon. It is good for feeding goats and kine. Here is wood of every kind, here are watering-places that never fail' (xiii. 242-47). When Menelaus tells Telemachus of his roaming and gain-getting in many lands, he says of Libya merely that there lambs are born with horns, there ewes yean thrice in the year, there neither master nor shepherd lacks cheese and flesh and milk (iv. 85-89). But more of this anon.

The situation of the cave of Polyphemus is very briefly sketched. 'When we came to the land that is near by, there saw we a cave on the border near the sea, lofty and overhung with laurels, and there many flocks, both sheep and goats, were wont to rest.

Round about a high-walled yard was made with deep-bedded stones and with tall pines and oaks of lofty foliage" (ix. 181-186). Inside the cave are found a farmyard and a dairy—lambs and kids, pens, milk-pails, bowls, baskets laden with cheeses. There is an idyllic touch when Polyphemus talks to his ram, and his affection for this four-footed creature is the sole redeeming feature in the character of the big blackguard.

The isle of Aeolus presents to our view nothing but a wall of bronze and a sheer cliff, so we pass to Laestrygonia, a Land of the Midnight Sun, where

'The midsummer, midnight, Norway sun
Sets into sunrise.'

Homer states the situation thus: 'There, as he drives in his flock, shepherd hails shepherd, and the other, driving out his flock, answers him. There a man who could live without sleep could earn two sets of wages, one by herding cattle, the other by pasturing white sheep, for the outgoings of night and day are quite near' (x. 82-86). Odysseus is interested in the harbour. 'When we came to the splendid (κλυτόν) haven, round which on both sides goes a steep cliff unbroken, and jutting headlands project over against each other at the mouth, and narrow is the entrance, into that all the others steered their curved ships. Now the ships were bound near to one another within the hollow haven, for therein no wave ever swelled, great or small, and all around was a white calm' (x. 87-94). Somewhere I have read that these lines show a feeling for nature in general and for rocks in particular. They do; but it is a seaman's feeling, in the first intention at least, indicating the love of a good harbour, a land-locked haven. Much depends on how one understands κλυτόν, the root meaning of which is 'heard of,' 'worth hearing about.' Translate it 'fair,'[1] and a reader ignorant of Greek is apt to think it refers to the beauty of the surrounding scenery. The meaning of many ornamental epithets is far from fixed, and κλυτός is a most elusive word. In this same episode it is applied to the house of the Laestrygon Antiphates and to Antiphates himself, who in all probability was not a beauty. The practical Greek liked a rock when there was a convenient cave in it, and Gilbert Murray tells us that 'a good cave was probably more comfortable than many a Greek house.'[2] Apart from harbours and caves, the Greek view of rocks is often unfavourable enough. Aeschylus calls Salmydessus 'step-mother of ships':

> τραχεῖα πόντου Σαλμυδησσία γνάθος
> ἐχθρόξενος ναύταισι, μητρυιὰ νεῶν.
>
> (*Prom.*, 726-7.)

And English writers seem to have held similar opinions about rocks until quite modern times. In *The Franklin's Tale*, Chaucer regards rocks as blots on creation:

> 'But, Lord, thise grisly, feendly, rokkes blake,
> That semen rather a foul confusioun
> Of werk than any fair creacioun
> Of swich a parfit wys God, and a stable,—
> Why han ye wroght this werk unresonable?'
>
> (868-72.)

In Laestrygonia Odysseus could find no trace of 'the labours of men or of oxen'—no ploughed land and no gardens. He has the same ill fortune in

---

[1] Butcher and Lang's translation. What of 'the fair havens'—Καλοὺς Λιμένας—in *Acts* xxvii. 8?

[2] *Euripides and his Age.*

Aeaea, the island of Circe, 'ringed round with endless sea':

νῆσον, τὴν πέρι πόντος ἀπείριτος ἐστεφάνωται.

(x. 195.)

From a place of outlook he sees ruddy smoke rising, through a thick coppice, from the halls of the goddess. These 'sacred' halls, built of polished stones, are situated in a 'sacred' glade. Circe keeps greater state than Calypso. 'Shining doors' are opened to admit unhappy strangers.

The episodes of Calypso, Circe, Polyphemus, and others, are generally regarded as excrescences—invasions, so to speak, into epic by romance. But it is Greek romance, brought within the Aegean zone, made reasonable, and limited in certain directions; the tone is entirely Greek. Homer has not painted a detailed voluptuous picture of Circe or of Calypso. Circe is εὐπλόκαμος, δεινὴ θεὸς αὐδήεσσα. Calypso is εὐπλόκαμος and δῖα θεάων. Circe is a greater power for evil, but the two have the same matronly and housewifely qualities. Polyphemus is a man of monstrous size, but he is not said to be deformed. Homer makes no mention of his one eye, though we can infer it from the incident of the blinding. Circe's abode is set in a framework of external nature neither much inviting nor much repelling. The surroundings of Calypso are of a somewhat sombre kind. The country of the savage Cyclopes is wilder of aspect and less easy of access, a sort of brigand stronghold; but it is quite true to nature and within Greek ken. Round none of the three has Homer drawn a landscape of mystery and marvel, a forest of Broceliande, or a circle of echoing and conspiring scenery, as in Ariosto's Island of Alcina, Tasso's

14

Gardens of Armida, Spenser's Bower of Bliss. Homer's characters are not, like Spenser's, personified abstractions, and he does not invent pageantry and scenery to suggest and sustain character. In the story of Polyphemus the Greek poet has not made a landscape effort like that of the author of *Beowulf* when he describes the desolate mark-land and mere haunted by Grendel and his dam. In that instance, the Teutonic writer may be said to become romantic in the midst of an epic. But Homer, so far as scenery is concerned, remains epic. To a Greek audience the Celtic *Voyage of Maildun* would have seemed intolerable silliness.[1]

When Circe is instructing Odysseus how to proceed to the dwelling of Hades, she says: 'But when thou hast sailed in thy ship across the stream Oceanus, where is a waste shore and the groves of Persephone, tall poplars and willows that cast their fruit, there beach thy ship by Oceanus of the deep eddies, but thyself go to the murky house of Hades' (x. 508-12). What induced Homer to plant poplars and willows here? We moderns at once think of the willow 'worn of forlorn paramours' and of all its dismal associations. But the willow had no such significance for Homer or for classical Greek poets. Nor had the white poplar as yet any connection with Hades. It has been suggested that, as both the poplar and the willow were accounted sterile, they may have been regarded as of evil omen.[2] The one funereal tree in the *Iliad* is the elm.[3] The mountain nymphs planted elms

---

[1] With the country of the Cyclopes compare the description of the cave of Cacus in *Aeneid*, viii. 190-97.

[2] Hayman's *Odyssey*; Pliny, *Hist. Nat.*, xvi. 46; *Familiar Studies in Homer.*

[3] Virgil has an elm—*ulmus opaca*—at entrance of Orcus—*Aeneid*, vi. 283.

round the burial-mound of Eëtion (vi. 419-20). Homer often plants poplars round fountains, to be near water. He even calls poplars 'water-nourished' (ὑδατοτρεφής), and in this he is followed by Theocritus and Virgil. Willows grow by the Scamander, beside tamarisks and elms (*Iliad*, xxi. 350). Homer is a judge of soil, he knows what to sow and what to plant; and so poplars and willows flourish at the world's end, by the banks of Oceanus. Those who prefer a sentimental explanation will welcome that suggested by Ruskin, who says, 'It is with exquisite feeling that it (the poplar) is made the chief tree in the groves of Persephone; its light and quivering leafage having exactly the melancholy expression of fragility, faintness, and inconstancy which the ancients attributed to the disembodied spirit.'

The wanderers pass by the island of the Sirens, who sit and sing in a flowery meadow—'Aνθεμόεσσα, which the son of Cronos gave them' (Hesiodic *Catalogues*). They then come to the two rocks, Scylla and Charybdis. That of Scylla reaches up to heaven and is never clear of cloud. No mortal may scale it. 'It is smooth as if it were polished, and in the midst of the rock is a dim cave, turned to Erebus and the region of the dark' (xii. 73-81). According to Homer's wont, no epithets of feeling are applied to the rock; these are reserved for Scylla herself, an ultra-Greek monstrosity. On the other rock Homer sets a fig-tree in full leaf; beneath Charybdis sucks down and again spouts up the water three times a day.

On another day, at evening, they came to Thrinacria, 'the fair island of the god,' where the marvellous herds and flocks of Helios Hyperion graze. They stayed the ship in a haven, 'near to sweet water.' At dawn they dragged the vessel up into a hollow cave, ' where were

the beautiful dancing-places and seats of the nymphs'
(xii. 260-318). Here natural characteristics are
interpreted in the light of the genial Greek religion;
there is nothing of awe or mystery in keeping with
the coming catastrophe.

Our last two scenes are in Ithaca. Homer thus
describes the landing-place as the Phaeacian ship
draws near the land: 'In the land of Ithaca there is a
haven of Phorcys, the old man of the sea, and there
are two steep jutting headlands, sloping towards the
harbour, which keep off the great wave raised by evil
winds outside, while inside the well-beached ships
remain without mooring - cable when they have
reached as far as the landing. Now at the head of the
haven is a long-leaved olive-tree, and near by it is a
cave, pleasant and shadowy, sacred to the nymphs
called Naiads. Therein are bowls and jars of stone,
and there too bees store their honey. There are tall
looms of stone where the nymphs weave webs of sea-
purple, a wonder to behold; and there are waters
ever welling. The cave has two doorways, one looking
to the north, for men, but the other towards the
south-west is rather for the gods; by this men may
not enter, for it is the way of the immortals'
(xiii. 96-112).

The rocks here, serving as breakwaters, remind us
of the similar scene in Laestrygonia. The poet does
not describe the interior of the cavern with personal
feeling. In associating the stalactite forms with the
life of the minor divinities he is the interpreter of
popular sentiment. The φάρεα ἁλιπόρφυρα have
probably no reference to any actual colour in the
cave, for the same epithet is applied to the yarn of
Queen Areta (vi. 306). 'The way of the immortals'
seems to imply greater inaccessibility. At the

harbour head Homer has set a single olive, though, as we shall see, there are other trees at hand. Virgil, however, in a passage supposed to be, partly at least, founded on this (*Aeneid*, i. 159-168), has pictured an overhanging grove, and behind on the height a wood of waving trees; thus suggesting contrast, light and shade, and a feeling of gloom, which are absent from Homer's picture:

Tum silvis scaena coruscis
Desuper horrentique atrum nemus imminet umbra.

This landscape of Homer's lies colourless in the light of the morning star, which comes up as the ship approaches the haven; it can gain no interest, as yet, from any words of the hero, who is laid by the sailors on the sand asleep. When he awoke, 'all things seemed strange to the master':

ἀτραπιτοί τε διηνεκέες λιμένες τε πάνορμοι
πέτραι τ' ἠλίβατοι καὶ δένδρεα τελεθόωντα.

(xiii. 195-6.)

In the company of Eumaeus, Odysseus has set out for his home. 'Now, as they walked along the rugged way, they came near to the town, and reached a fair-flowing spring, with a basin made by hand, from which the citizens used to draw water. This had been fashioned by Ithacus and Neritus and Polyctor. Round it was a grove of poplars that grow by the water, all in a circle; and the cold water ran down from on high, from a rock. Above was raised an altar to the nymphs, at which all travellers were wont to make offering' (xvii. 204-11).

A grove, a well, and water falling from a rock may go some little way to satisfy modern taste for the picturesque. It is a pleasant spot for the tired bodies

18

and pious souls of wayfarers. It has a history, old as the days of Ithacus, who gave his name to the island. What it meant to the lord of the land returning after twenty years inexorable Homer leaves us to imagine. Let us neither exalt nor depreciate the scene unduly, but make an offering to the nymphs, by subscribing the motto, 'Rest and be thankful.'

When we turn to the *Iliad*, we find no extended descriptions of still nature; an epithet, a phrase, or a clause is all that Homer can spare in his rapid march. His profusion of similes is not now in question. Mention of a hero and his home often suggests to the poet a genealogy, a local legend, or a short topographical note. But in the *Iliad*—especially in the Catalogue of Book II.—and in the *Odyssey* as well, Homer makes use of a system of fixed epithets as a means of summing up in shorthand fashion the most striking characteristic of a town or a district. Some are realistic and such as would be in all men's mouths; others are ornamental and conventional counters; all are of a communal cast and of general appeal to a heroic audience. One class specifies characteristics of climate, situation, or configuration—'windy,' 'rocky,' 'sandy,' 'full of ridges,' 'wide-lawned,' 'white' (chalky). The sunken site of Lacedaemon, surrounded by mountain heights, has gained for it the double epithet κοίλην Λακεδαίμονα κητώεσσαν. Another class denotes economic advantages—'horse-pasturing,' 'mother of flocks,' 'deep-soiled,' 'deep-meadowed,' 'abounding in vines,' 'rich in wheat,' 'grassy': special richness or a shot at a venture gives rise to 'flowery.' Some denote sacredness and connection with deity—ἱερός, ἠγάθεος, ζάθεος, δῖος— the last shading into the idea of 'noble,' 'splendid,' 'bright.' Others would seem to have some aesthetic

19

import—ἐραννός, ἐρατεινός, καλός.[1] In some cases
the reference may be to scenery; more often the
meaning may be no more than 'pleasant' or 'desirable' in an indefinite way. Thisbe and Messe are
distinguished by the unusual epithet πολυτρήρων,
'frequented by doves' (ii. 502, 582), a fact which
Matthew Arnold called to mind when writing
Empedocles on Etna.

In this respect Homer set a fashion which was
followed all through Greek poetry, the epithet and
the phrase being the descriptive norm, in accordance
with the general method of Greek art. Homer's
Catalogue suggested, but only suggested, to Virgil
the pageant of Italian tribes in Book VII. of the
Aeneid. Virgil writes, not merely as a Roman for
Romans, but as an Italian for Italians. 'He achieves
the feat of keeping Rome and her solemn destiny in
our minds while he shows us the bloom and vigour
of Italy in a series of splendid pictures. . . . The poet
does all he can to secure variety, to make this city
or that, with its surrounding region, stand out clearly
in the picture, and take the right colouring for the
delectation of its descendants.'[2] Homer is disinterested, sometimes even uninterested; pride and
affection often warm Virgil's verses. The following
line might be called Homeric:

Ereti manus omnis oliviferaeque Mutuscae.

(711.)

[1] ἱμερτός is used only of a river (*Il.*, ii. 751). ἐρατός is not used with
names of places: Pindar applies it to physical beauty—παῖδ᾽ ἐρατόν
(*Oly.*, x. (xi.) 120). ἐπήρατος is used of Ithaca in *Ody.*, iv. 606:
πολυήρατος is attached to a place-name only in the phrase ἐν Θήβῃ
πολυηράτῳ (*Ody.*, xi. 275).

[2] Dr. W. Warde Fowler's *Virgil's 'Gathering of the Clans,'* a little book
of great interest. He refers to the Catalogue in the *Punica* of Silius
Italicus. One might compare also the lists, more or less vapid, in the
Argonautica of Apollonius Rhodius, the Orphic writer, and Valerius
Flaccus, respectively.

The following personification is in his own manner:

Et quos maliferae despectant moenia Abellae.
(740.)

Here he both personifies and apostrophises:

Et te montosae misere in proelia Nersae,
Ufens, insignem fama et felicibus armis.
(744-45.)

These lines are a combination of all his characteristics:

Quique altum Praeneste viri quique arva Gabinae
Iunonis gelidumque Anienem et roscida rivis
Hernica saxa colunt, quos dives Anagnia pascit,
Quos, Amasene pater. (682-85.)

Among moderns who treat of similar episodes Milton is generally much nearer to Virgil than to Homer, though there is a touch of Homer in the last line of the following:

'In Hesebon
And Horonaim, Seon's realm, beyond
The flowery dale of Sibma clad with vines.'
(*P.L.*, i. 408-10.)

Sir Walter Scott's Homeric treatment of local names has often been commented on—'Ulva dark,' 'the wild Tiree,' 'the sandy Coll,' 'verdant Islay,' 'lonely Colonsay.' In Book III. of *The Life and Death of Jason*, William Morris is neither Homeric nor Virgilian, nor does he recall his more immediate model, Apollonius. He is just Morris, simple, limpid, leisurely, pictorial:

'From the grassy plain
Anigh Pellene, where the harvest wain
Scatters the grazing sheep, Amphion came.'

21

'Next from Tegea, where the long green grape
Grows yellow in the dewy autumn night,
There came Ancaeus, stubborn in the fight.'

'Erginus, son of Neptune; nigh the sea
His father set him, where the laden bee
Flies low across Maeander, and falls down
Against the white walls of a merchant town
Men call Miletus.'

Again and again in the *Iliad* we meet with a few
words, a line or little more, in which a natural feature
or a whole landscape is flashed before us and made to
stand out in almost preternatural clearness; sound
and sight being, as it were, one and inseparable,
and the result a charm unforgettable. In his quarrel
with Agamemnon, Achilles declares that he did not
come there to fight by reason of the Trojan spearmen,
who had never harried deep-soiled Phthia, for
'very much lies between, shadowy mountains and
roaring sea':

$$\mathring{\eta} \ \mu\acute{a}\lambda a \ \pi o\lambda\lambda\grave{a} \ \mu\epsilon\tau a\xi\grave{v}$$
$$o\mathring{v}\rho\epsilon\acute{a} \ \tau\epsilon \ \sigma\kappa\iota\acute{o}\epsilon\nu\tau a \ \theta\acute{a}\lambda a\sigma\sigma\acute{a} \ \tau\epsilon \ \mathring{\eta}\chi\acute{\eta}\epsilon\sigma\sigma a.$$

(i. 156-7.)[1]

On the shield of Achilles there is represented a herd
of lowing kine hurrying from the farm-yard to the
pasture, 'along by a sounding river and beside
waving reeds':

$$\pi\grave{a}\rho \ \pi o\tau a\mu\grave{o}\nu \ \kappa\epsilon\lambda\acute{a}\delta o\nu\tau a, \ \pi a\rho\grave{a} \ \dot{\rho}o\delta a\nu\grave{o}\nu \ \delta o\nu a\kappa\mathring{\eta}a.$$

(xviii. 576.)

When, in the eighth year of the siege, Odysseus is
trying to persuade the grumbling host, he says: 'It
was, as one might say, but yesterday or the day

[1] Quoted by F. T. Palgrave in *Landscape in Poetry*.

before that the ships of the Achaeans were gathered in Aulis, bearing trouble for Priam and the Trojans; and we round a spring were offering on the holy altars unblemished hecatombs to the immortals, beneath a fair plane-tree, whence bright water flowed':

καλῇ ὑπὸ πλατανίστῳ, ὅθεν ῥέεν ἀγλαὸν ὕδωρ.

(ii. 307.)

'Perfectly finished'—*recht abgerundet*—Woermann calls the scene. It may be more to us than it was to Homer's audience. For the argument of Odysseus the chief point of the reminiscence lies in the portent of the serpent and the swallows, which is to follow. We dwell upon a pleasant vignette conjured up for us during a noisy debate in a camp assembly. Perhaps we make sentiment out of what was almost a necessity in the situation—water and shade. Sentiment, however, is not sentimentality. They say Homer was blind: I have not read that he was deaf. Something of the same haunting charm is exercised on us by a few words in the Old Testament, peeping out of a bald matter-of-fact account of the journeyings of the Israelites: 'In Elim were twelve fountains of water, and threescore and ten palm-trees; and they pitched there' (*Numbers*, xxxiii. 9).

CHAPTER II

LANDSCAPE AFTER HOMER

PASSING by elegiac and iambic poets and writers of monodic lyric as negligible in the meantime, we come to choral lyric and Pindar. Pindar is interested to obsession in blue blood and family trees and myths. The victors he celebrates are of those

$$\tau\hat{\omega}\nu\ \dot{\epsilon}\nu\ {}^{\prime}\mathrm{E}\lambda\lambda\dot{\alpha}\delta\iota\ \tau\epsilon\rho\pi\nu\hat{\omega}\nu$$
$$\lambda\alpha\chi\acute{o}\nu\tau\epsilon\varsigma\ o\dot{\upsilon}\kappa\ \dot{o}\lambda\acute{\iota}\gamma\alpha\nu\ \delta\acute{o}\sigma\iota\nu.$$

He is a lofty traditionalist, who would not let 'the grace of old time sleep,' and he uses the past to irradiate a present already glorious. By means of myth after myth he links city to city and traces cunning lines of association between man, hero, and god; drawing parallels and contrasts, and pontifically exhorting, warning, and prophesying. When we consider that no fewer than eleven of his winners are natives of Aegina, his resource and variety seem marvellous. Even his periphrastic references to the scene of the contest are evidence of this—'in the rich corn-lands of Pylades'; 'in the deep meadow stretching along under Cirrha's cliffs'; 'in the pastures of the Pion'; 'beneath the dark-shaded immemorial mountains of Phlius'; 'leafy Nemea'; 'in the tree-clad precincts of Pisa by the Alpheus'; 'sunny Kronion'. He is not insensible to natural beauty, but landscape fills small part of his dazzling entablatures. He does not

detail, but with epithet or phrase, often with magnificent compounds, he stamps out a scene, and sometimes with another stroke associates it with some high
moment in the story of humanity. Primarily, a land
is fair in Pindar's eyes in proportion to its fatness and
its power of contributing to the sum of material
blessings (ὄλβος), and the splendour of a well-built
and well-ordered city or its local myth counts for
more than picturesqueness of situation. Aetna is
'the forehead of a very fruitful land'—εὐκάρποιο γαίας
μέτωπον (*Pyth.*, i. 30). Rhodes is 'child of Aphrodite
and bride of the sun'—παῖδ' Ἀφροδίτας Ἀελίοιο τε
νύμφαν, Ῥόδον (*Oly.*, vii. 14); but it is also πολύβοσκον
γαῖαν ἀνθρώποισι καὶ εὔφρονα μήλοις (*Oly.*, vii. 63).
Cyrene is 'a well-built city,' 'the sweet garden of
Aphrodite,' 'excelling in beauty and glorious in the
games.' Neoptolemus reigns in wide Epirus, 'where
high cattle-pasturing lawns (βουβόται πρῶνες) slope
onwards from Dodona as far as the Ionian strait'
(*Nem.*, iv. 51-53).

Three of Pindar's preludes, each fine in its own
way, show almost the full cycle of his interests on this
head. *Pythian*, ii., in honour of Hieron, has this
martial opening, suitable to a time of stress and
impending war:

Μεγαλοπόλιες ὦ Συράκοσαι, βαθυπολέμου
τέμενος Ἄρεος, ἀνδρῶν ἵππων τε σιδαροχαρμᾶν
δαιμόνιαι τροφοί.

Contrast *Nemean*, i., which opens on a note of peace
and rest, typified by the myth of Alpheus, who took
breath and gained repose in Ortygia:

'Divine Alpheus, who by secret sluice
Stole under seas to meet his Arethuse.'

The home of the victor Chromius was in the Ortygian quarter of Syracuse:

Ἄμπνευμα σεμνὸν Ἀλφεοῦ,
κλεινᾶν Συρακοσσᾶν θάλος Ὀρτυγία,
δέμνιον Ἀρτέμιδος,
Δάλου κασιγνήτα.

Pythian, xii., is in honour of Midas of Acragas, a city set in a strong and commanding position, with fertile surroundings, a holy and beautiful habitation:

Αἰτέω σε, φιλάγλαε, καλλίστα βροτεᾶν πολίων,
Φερσεφόνας ἕδος, ἅ τ᾽ ὄχθαις ἔπι μηλοβότου
ναίεις Ἀκράγαντος ἐΰδματον κολώναν, ὦ Ϝάνα.

Pindar's tribute to Athens soon became hackneyed:

αἵ τε λιπαραὶ καὶ ἰοστέφανοι καὶ ἀοίδιμοι,
Ἑλλάδος ἔρεισμα, κλειναὶ Ἀθᾶναι, δαιμόνιον πτολίεθρον.
(*Frag. Dith.*, 46.)[1]

Pindar's poetry is permeated with his personality, and there has been no more self-conscious poet. But his art was conditioned. He spoke through a chorus, on a public occasion, at a religious ceremony, among a people whose holidays were holy days. The games themselves were a religious institution, they were held in honour of gods—Zeus, Poseidon, Apollo— and the place of contest was sacred. There might be virtue in a trainer, a victor might be born and not made, blood might speak, but if a man were to win a weight of glory (πελώριον κλέος), a god must 'mingle in the game' (θεοῦ σὺν παλάμᾳ), and the gods must be thanked in the hearing of all. The fame of a victor was reflected on his family, his clan, and his

[1] See also *Oly.*, xiv (Orchomenus); *Oly.*, xiii. (Corinth); *Nem.*, x. (Argos); *Oly.*, xii (Himera).

city, that city's founder and tutelary deity. Thus the victory and the place of victory, the victor's home and lineage, all conducted the poet along the route, long or short, of myth and legend, which was fundamentally a common possession and a national inheritance. And so the odes of Pindar are steeped in communal sentiment, and his treatment of nature is conditioned in so far as it must be of general appeal and not the product of individual and wilful fancy.

Between the tragedians and this fascinating but puzzling writer there are striking differences. They show a deeper knowledge of the heart and a consciousness of the need of reinterpreting tradition to an age of intellectual speculation and ferment. They are broader as well as deeper than Pindar. Emancipated from caste feeling and sacerdotalism, they are more human. They are more of their age and they are more for all readers and all times. But for our present purpose the likenesses are more important than the differences. In drama the artistic conditions and conventions are in some respects similar to those in choral lyric. We find there too a religious atmosphere and the use of mythology and heroic story for moral and spiritual ends. These serve as weighty counteractions to individualistic vagaries and excesses.

A form of drama so concentrated in its action as the Greek, with its paucity of actors, its general fixity of place, its lack of secondary plots and digressive episodes, would seem to give less scope for landscape description than the loose romantic plays of Shakespeare and other Elizabethans. Even in Shakespeare's tragedy the description of Dover Cliff in *King Lear* is something unique. Greek tragedies have little or no background, and at the outset attention is rarely focussed on details of local scenery. The following lines open the *Prometheus Vinctus* of Aeschylus:

Χθονὸς μὲν ἐς τηλουρὸν ἥκομεν πέδον,
Σκύθην ἐς οἶμον, ἄβατον εἰς ἐρημίαν.

The *Philoctetes* of Sophocles opens thus:

Ἀκτὴ μὲν ἥδε τῆς περιρρύτου χθονὸς
Λήμνου, βροτοῖς ἄστιπτος οὐδ᾽ οἰκουμένη.

The *Helena* of Euripides thus:

Νείλου μὲν αἵδε καλλιπάρθενοι ῥοαί,
ὃς ἀντὶ δίας ψακάδος Αἰγύπτου πέδον
λευκῆς τακείσης χιόνος ὑγραίνει γύας.

The abrupt opening of the *Choephoroe* contrasts with that of Sophocles' *Electra*, where the Paedagogus, standing with Orestes on some spot in the near neighbourhood of Mycenae, points out conspicuous landmarks—the Argive plain to the south; the agora and temple of Apollo Lyceus in Argos, six miles away; the Heraeum, two miles distant. Travellers maintain that the last-mentioned could not have been in view; but that does not matter at all. In the *Bacchae* Dionysus refers to the springs of Dirce and the water of Ismenus. He is looking upon the tomb of Semele, now enclosed as a hallowed place and embowered with the clustering greenery of vine planted by the god's own hands. In Euripides' *Electra* the Peasant addresses Argos and Inachus, whence Agamemnon set out on the expedition to Troy.

In the course of a tragedy, the surrounding scene, even when it plays a dramatic part or is an emotional element in the action, is seldom more than indicated in words. In Sophocles' *Ajax* the scene is laid on the coast of the Troad, near Cape Rhoeteum, before the tent of the hero, at the inland end of the Greek camp. At line 654 Ajax says he will go 'to the baths and the meadows by the cliffs.' Tecmessa sends the chorus to search for him, part along the western, part along the eastern bay (805). The scene changes to a lonely spot on the sea-shore overgrown with bushes at one part (815). The body of Ajax is found by Tecmessa in this copse, whence the chorus hear her cry:

$$\tau\acute{\iota}\nu\text{os } \beta o\grave{\eta} \ \pi\acute{\alpha}\rho\alpha\upsilon\lambda os \ \grave{\epsilon}\xi\acute{\epsilon}\beta\eta \ \nu\acute{\alpha}\pi o\upsilon s;$$

(892.)

More important, in fact almost indispensable, and a means of heightening the pathos of the hero's situation, are the landscape features in the *Philoctetes*. In defiance of Homer, who calls Lemnos 'well-peopled,' Sophocles makes the island uninhabited, as the part of it to which Philoctetes was confined by reason of his infirmity might very well have been. The scene is laid on the north-east coast, near Mount Hermaeum, the modern Cape Plaka. The cave of Philoctetes is situated in a steep cliff. Odysseus describes it as open at both ends, one doorway looking seawards, we may suppose, so that the inmate has 'a double opportunity of sitting in the sun,' morning and evening. A little below, to the left, is a spring of fresh water. The volcano of Mount Moschylus is within sight of the cave, for during a paroxysm of pain Philoctetes implores Neoptolemus to carry him to be burned 'in yon famed Lemnian fire' (800). It is referred to again in line 986. When bereft of his bow, Philoctetes addresses his cave and pictures it as a less inviting home than the words of Odysseus had implied. It is 'now hot, now icy-cold' and infected with his pain (1081-87). His farewell invocation to the island gives a calendar of the sights and sounds that had been his daily familiars for so long—wind-dashed spray filling the cavern, the moist meadows of the plain, the headland beaten by booming waves, the Lycian spring, the Ἑρμαῖον ὄρος which had echoed his cries.

The scene of the *Oedipus Coloneus* is best known to readers by reason of the First Stasimon. It is a grove sacred to the Eumenides, where laurel, olive, and wine flourish abundantly, and where a choir of nightingales are singing (14-18). To the south-east, a mile away, are seen the walls and πύργοι of Athens, including probably the Acropolis. Oedipus sits down on an un-hewn stone—ἐπ᾽ ἀξέστου πέτρου—perhaps just within the sacred enclosure (19). Whether the spot called 'The Brazen Theshold'—χαλκόπους ὁδός (57)—is to be applied to the whole region and to be distinct from the καταρράκτης ὁδός of line 1590 need not be discussed here. Passing through the grove, the blind man is discovered by the chorus (138) and finally seated outside the precinct on a ledge of natural rock—αὐτοπέτρου βήματος (192).[1] But the Stasimon is the glory of the piece, and it is so well known that it will bear neither transcription nor attempt at translation. As Patin says: 'Comment rendre ces épithètes homériques, moins générales cependant, moins vagues, en rapport plus direct avec le sens particulier de la phrase, que celles d'Homère, ces épithètes qui, selon l'esprit de l'ancienne poésie, peignent seulement par un trait sur lequel travaille, qu'achève, que complète l'imagination? Comment reproduire cette musique des paroles qui en même temps qu'elle enchante l'oreille, amuse l'esprit par un harmonieux écho de la pensée? C'est dans la texte qu'il faut lire ce morceau aux riches couleurs, fond éclatant sur lequel

---

[1] I have followed Jebb here.

se dessine la mélancolique composition de Sophocle.' ¹
This patriotic outburst is not a specimen of landscape composition; it is addressed to a blind man. But
it is remarkable as a fine sample of Greek sentiment
and of Sophocles' artistry. The sentiments are fore-
shadowed by the words of Antigone (16-18), of the
Athenian Stranger (53-63), and of Oedipus (84-110).
It is not fantastic to find in ἔπαυλα (669) an echo of
παῦλαν (88). Dr. Makail has remarked that the lines
on the nightingale recall a simile in the Nineteenth
Book of the *Odyssey*.² The mention of the stainless
waters of Cephisus, the Muses, and Aprodite, connects
the ode with one almost equally famous in Euripides'
Medea (824-865). The first two stanzas are in praise
of Colonus mainly, with hints of Attica as a whole and
the neighbouring Academy; the second strophe
and antistrophe treat of Attica mostly, with references
to the Academy and Colonus. The opening word,
εὐίππου, strikes a note thoroughly Greek. Compare
Pindar's praise of Orchomenus as καλλίπωλος ἕδρα
(*Oly.*, xiv. 2). In this inviolable spot the music of
birds charms the ear and floral beauty delights the eye.
The whole land is under the care of gods, who have
watched over it from of old, who visit it, and bless it.
Sleepless fountains of pure water bestow fertility, a
miraculous plant defies all enemies and fosters generation after generation of sure defenders, a breed of
horses never fails, and there is 'the sea to friend and
comfort.' Yet the utilitarian features are treated with
Sophoclean delicacy, and the notes of proper pride
are so tempered with a sense of divine protection and
the ministry of deity to a favoured land as not to
disturb the air of 'softness still and holy' that seems

¹ *Études sur les tragiques grecs.*
² *Lectures on Greek Poetry.*

31

to brood over the picture. Utility is clad in beauty, and beauty is consecrate. The ode never palls; it gains rather by familiarity. In the poet's own words:

τοιαῦτά σοι ταῦτ' ἐστίν, ὦ ξέν', οὐ λόγοις
τιμώμεν', ἀλλὰ τῇ ξυνουσίᾳ πλέον.   (62-3.)

In one respect Greek tragedy offers opportunities for description not found in modern romantic drama. A messenger or other actor, or sometimes the chorus, has to indicate a place of action outside the immediate scene. Sometimes the merest reference, a word or two dropped as if by chance, rouses the imagination of the reader. There is an example in the *Trachiniae*. The messenger informs Deianira that a herald is proclaiming the home-coming of Heracles to a crowd of people 'in a meadow where oxen feed in summer':

ἐν βουθερεῖ λειμῶνι πρὸς πολλοὺς θροεῖ
Λίχας ὁ κῆρυξ ταῦτα.   (188-9.)

As Campbell says, 'the epithet brings before us the picture of a warm sunny field, where men might gather round Lichas.' An instance even finer, because our curiosity is satisfied after having been again and again baffled, is found in the *Phoenissae*. A messenger announces that the brothers, Eteocles and Polynices, are ready for mortal single combat in mid-space between the hosts—ἐν μεταιχμίοις (1240). Antigone is informed of what is toward, and she says to Jocasta:

ἡγοῦ σὺ πρὸς μεταίχμι', οὐ μελλητέον.
          (1279.)

The chorus picture the two:

δίδυμοι θῆρες, φόνιαι ψυχαὶ
δορὶ παλλόμεναι.   (1296-97.)

32

Another messenger tells how the pair took their stand εἰς μέσον μεταίχμιον (1361). He tells how mother and sister arrived too late to prevent the tragedy, and how Jocasta seized a sword and drove it through her neck. A procession enters with corpses. Antigone utters a θρῆνος, in the course of which she lights up the scene of the catastrophe with the words—'She found her sons at Electra's gate, in a meadow of clover'—λωτοτρόφον κατὰ λείμακα (1571).

In the *Helena*, the chorus, who are servants of the palace, respond to Helen's monody and explain how they were washing the royal garments and drying them in the golden rays of the sun, by the dark water, on the twining grass and the shoots of reeds, when they heard her piteous lament. There is a passage remarkably similar in *Hippolytus* (121 ff.). In the *Iphigeneia in Tauris* a herdsman thus describes the place on the Euxine shore where Orestes and Pylades landed, a haunt of purple-fishers:

ἐπεὶ τὸν εἰσρέοντα διὰ Συμπληγάδων
βοῦς ὑλοφορβοὺς πόντον εἰσεβάλλομεν,
ἦν τις διαρρὼξ κυμάτων πολλῷ σάλῳ
κοιλωπὸς ἀγμός, πορφυρευτικαὶ στέγαι.

(260-63.)

The chorus in the *Oedipus Coloneus* imagine the fight between the guards of Creon and the Athenian pursuers as taking place 'either by the shores dear to Apollo, or by the torch-lit strand where the august goddesses cherish dread rites for mortals' (1047-51). The Pythian shores are part of the bay of Eleusis, beyond the pass of Daphnè, six miles from Colonus. A temple of Apollo stood in the pass. The torch-lit strand is the neighbourhood of Eleusis and the allusion is to the torch-light processions along the

c   33

Sacred Way. Perhaps, the chorus think, the captors took another road, 'or perhaps they will draw near to the pastures west of Oea's snowy rock.' That is, 'they went round the north end of Mount Aegaleos, and will soon be emerging on the Thriasian plain, to the west of Aegaleos, near the deme of Oea.'

In this play a mournful interest attaches to the vivid relation of the incidents connected with the last moments of the aged hero. He leaves the stage, followed by Theseus and attendants, no longer guided but leading the way. In the quiet words of one awe-struck at the sight of a strange thing, the messenger particularises the exact spot and the manner of his passing. Oedipus sits down midway between the bowl-like cleft in the rock, where is the memorial of the covenant between Theseus and Peirithous, the Thorician Stone, the hollow pear-tree, and the stone-built tomb. At his bidding, his daughters go to the hill of Demeter Euchlous and from a fountain bring water wherewith to wash him in preparation for the end (1590-97). Here the poet is partly following, partly making, tradition.[1]

The *Bacchae* and *Prometheus Bound* will figure in a subsequent chapter. In the *Persae* the chorus enumerate the cities and islands conquered by Darius, after the manner of a Homeric catalogue (853-96). An inheritance from Homer too is the indication of a district by naming the river that fertilises it:

μίμνουσι δ' ἔνθα πεδίον Ἀσωπὸς ῥοαῖς
ἄρδει, φίλον πίασμα Βοιωτῶν χθονί.

(805-6.)

Remarkable for grim realism are parts of the messenger's tale of the disaster that has overtaken

[1] For variety see also *Oedipus Coloneus*, 1044-64; *Antigone*, 407-21; *Hercules Furens*, 348-450; *Hippolytus*, 1104-1152.

the Persian armaments. One great commander, he says, now haunts sea-lashed Salamis; the bodies of others are bumping on an iron shore, round the island where doves abound:

> Τενάγων τ', ἄριστος Βακτρίων ἰθαγενὴς,
> θαλασσόπληκτον νῆσον Αἴαντος πολεῖ.
> Λίλαιος, Ἀρσάμης τε, κἀργήστης τρίτος,
> οἵδ' ἀμφὶ νῆσον τὴν πελειοθρέμμονα
> νικώμενοι κύρισσον ἰσχυρὰν χθόνα.[1]

(306-10.)

The epithet πελειοθρέμμονα recalls the Homeric πολυτρήρων, and its use here heightens the horror by contrast, doves being emblems of timidity. In keeping with this scene is that presented by the summary words of the chorus:

> αἱμαχθεῖσα δ' ἄρουραν
> Αἴαντος περικλύστα
> νᾶσος ἔχει τὰ Περσῶν.

(595-97.)

The island of Psyttaleia is shown in a more gracious light:

> νῆσός τις ἐστὶ πρόσθε Σαλαμῖνος τόπων,
> βαιά, δύσορμος ναυσίν, ἣν ὁ φιλόχορος
> Πὰν ἐμβατεύει, ποντίας ἀκτῆς ἔπι.

(447-49.)

The mention of 'dance-loving Pan' in the last quotation is an example of what we have already found in Sophocles, the mythological treatment of nature. By a kind of plastic symbolism a scene is associated with, and suggested by, the figure of a deity. A stereotyped romantic personality is placed in the foreground; the romantic background is either

---

[1] Probably some islet in the Saronic gulf rather than Salamis itself.

slightly sketched, or, as here, left entirely to the imagination. A divine actor, named and localised,
acts as an index and prompts the imagination to
fill out the scene. The poet thus keeps in touch with
popular and communal religious sentiment, and it is
significant that these words of Aeschylus are placed
in the mouth of the messenger. An instance of the
brief and pregnant use of mythology and legend is
found in a stasimon of the *Philoctetes*. The chorus
sing how Neoptolemus will conduct the hero to his
ancestral home, 'haunt of the Malian nymphs,' and
to the banks of Spercheus, where Heracles drew near
to the gods, on Oeta (719-29). The reference to the
nymphs—Oreads, Dryads, Naiads—at once 'suggests
the hills, woods, and streams of Malis.'

Greek tragedy moves within a narrower circle
and shows less variety than the Elizabethan. Its
fables were not exotic, but national, and, with few
exceptions, drawn from the storehouse of heroic legend.
Poets might vary the particulars and innovate on epic
and lyric tradition, but the staple was fixed. It is as
if Shakespeare and his contemporary dramatists had
restricted their *répertoire* to subjects taken from
Teutonic saga or Celtic and Early English chronicle,
and had worked on stories similar to those of *King
Lear* and *Macbeth*. Incidents and situations, the same
or similar, recurred, and interest was again and again
focussed on the same legendary sites and scenes.
Owing to this cyclic movement the poet was induced
to change the angle of vision, so to speak, from time
to time, and the modern reader perusing the extant
plays enjoys a kaleidoscopic view. The Trojan
expedition plays a large part in Greek tragedy, and
one might say that in the land of Greek saga all
roads wind to Troy. The Judgment of Paris finds

place in five of Euripides' dramas. It presents opportunities for landscape reference and description. Let us see how far the poet has availed himself of them. In *Hecuba* we find:

> ἐκρίθη δ' ἔρις, ἂν ἐν ᾽Ι-
> δα κρίνει τρισσὰς μακάρων
> παῖδας ἀνὴρ βούτας.
>
> (643-45.)

Later in the play the chorus curse Paris, the shepherd of Ida (943-46). In the *Troades* Helen defends herself by blaming Cypris, and she reports the bribes of the three goddesses (924-57). In the Prologue of the *Helena*, Helen recounts her history and says the goddesses came

> ᾽Ιδαῖον ἐς κευθμῶν' ᾽Αλέξανδρον πάρα.
>
> (24.)

She speaks of Paris playing on the pipe among the ox-steads (358-59). She curses the springs where the goddesses bathed:

> ὤμοι ἐμῶν δεινῶν, λουτρῶν καὶ κρηνῶν,
> ἵνα θεαὶ μορφὰν
> ἐφαίδρυναν, ἔνθεν ἔμολεν κρίσις.
>
> (676-78.)

A whole choral ode in the *Andromache* is devoted to this theme. Hermes leads the three to Ida, to the steadings of the oxen and the lonely lodge of the herdsman. When they come to the tree-clad glen they bathe their shining bodies in the waters of the mountain springs (274-86).

In *Iphigeneia at Aulis* the fountains are again referred to (182), and Paris is pictured piping among the snow-white heifers and full-uddered kine (573-81).[1] In a

---

[1] Both passages are suspected. But they are Greek at any rate.

monody Iphigeneia apostrophises the snow-smitten glen in Ida where the infant Paris was exposed, and she wishes his home had never been by the fountains of the nymphs and the meadow blooming with roses and hyacinths (1291-98). Here we have the bare rudiments of one stanza of Tennyson's elegiac monologue, *Oenone*, in which he rivals in words the colours of Titian.

It is a commonplace of criticism that in the plays of Euripides the chorus often has less vital connection with the action than in those of his predecessors. Some choral odes treat of subjects quite apart from the action, others are relevant to the theme as a whole but not specially appropriate at the juncture where they are sung, in others the thread of relevancy is slight. But it is in these independent odes that Euripides indulges in fuller treatment of myth and legend and in more detailed descriptions of various kinds than are found in the plays of Aeschylus and Sophocles. In the *Phoenissae* (638-61), the feckless and bewildered band of Phoenicians who form the chorus celebrate the coming of Cadmus to Thebes, and in lyric rapture picture the loveliness of Dirce spreading luxuriance around, the ivy that encircled the infant Dionysus and screened him from jealous eyes,[1] and the deadly dragon keeping restless watch on the waters that mirror the greenness of the banks :

νάματ' ἔνυδρα καὶ ῥέεθρα
χλοερὰ δεργμάτων κόραισι
πολυπλάνοις ἐπισκοπῶν.

[1] Cf. Wordsworth, *The Brownie's Cell* :

'Where bud, and bloom, and fruitage glowed,
Close-crowding round the infant god ;
All colours,—and the liveliest streak
A foil to his celestial cheek.'

38

A stasimon of the *Alcestis* (568-605) eulogises the hospitality of Admetus, whose flocks Apollo had tended, piping the while on the hill-slopes—δοχμιᾶν διὰ κλιτύων—so that the sweet strains brought together lions from Othrys' glen and the fawn from the shelter of the pine-woods. Therefore the king's wide domains are blessed. Then in a few sweeping lines the poet makes the eye travel from fair Lake Boebeis over the tilth and level pastures of Thessaly to the Molossian mountains on the west ('the Stalls of the Steeds of Day'), and to Pelion and the harbour-less coast of the Aegean on the east:

> τοιγὰρ πολυμηλοτάταν
> ἑστίαν οἰκεῖ παρὰ καλλίναον
> Βοιβίαν λίμναν· ἀρότοις δὲ γυᾶν
> καὶ πεδίων δαπέδοις ὅρον ἀμφὶ μὲν ἀελίου κνεφαίαν
> ἱππόστασιν αἰθέρα τὰν Μολοσσῶν τίθεται,
> πόντιόν τ᾽ Αἰγαιῶν᾽ ἐπ᾽ ἀκτὰν
> ἀλίμενον Πηλίου κρατύνει.

In strong contrast with this substantial landscape the *Iphigeneia in Tauris* (392-438) wafts us over perilous seas to romantic shores. The chorus ask who are the strangers (Orestes and Pylades)? Have they come from the banks of Dirce or Eurotas? How did they pass the Symplegades, the sleepless shores of Phineus, and the place where the fifty Nereids dance and sing? Did the West Wind bring them past the White Strand, the home of many birds, where is the race-course of Achilles?

> τὰν πολυόρνιθον ἐπ᾽ αἶαν,
> λευκὰν ἀκτάν, ᾽Αχιλῆος
> δρόμους καλλισταδίους,
> ἄξεινον κατὰ πόντον.

39

Λευκὴ 'Ακτὴ was an island somewhere in the Euxine, where Achilles was supposed to dwell with Helen after death. The epithet πολυόρνιθος is not used at random. Philostratus, in his *Heroica*, tells how white sea-birds keep fresh and clean a shrine of Achilles on the island by sprinkling it with water shaken off from their wings as they fly low (34). He also says that those who anchored near the island declared that they heard trampling of horses, the din of arms, and shouting as of warriors (38).[1]

Take another type of ode. Consider the following lines from the *Troades*. The chorus of captive Trojan women speculate on their future home in Greece. Is it to be Corinth, Athens, Thessaly, Sicily, or Thurii? Any place but Sparta, the home of Helen!

Πειρήνας ὑδρευσομένα
πρόπολος σεμνῶν ὑδάτων ἔσομαι.
τὰν κλεινὰν εἴθ' ἔλθοιμεν
Θησέως εὐδαίμονα χώραν.
μὴ γὰρ δὴ δίναν γ' Εὐρώτα,
τὰν ἐχθίσταν θεράπναν 'Ελένας,
ἔνθ' ἀντάσω Μενέλᾳ δούλα,
τῷ τᾶς Τροίας πορθητᾷ.

τὰν Πηνειοῦ σεμνὰν χώραν,
κρηπῖδ' Οὐλύμπου καλλίσταν,
ὄλβῳ βρίθειν φάμαν ἤκουσ'
εὐθαλεῖ τ' εὐκαρπείᾳ·
τάδε δεύτερά μοι μετὰ τὰν ἱερὰν
Θησέως ζαθέαν ἐλθεῖν χώραν.
καὶ τὰν Αἰτναίαν 'Ηφαίστου
Φοινίκας ἀντήρη χώραν,

---

[1] See also Euripides' *Andromache*, 1231-72, Pindar, *Nem.*, iv. 49, and Pausanias' *Description of Greece*, iii. 19, 11, with Sir J. Frazer's notes. The tradition forms the subject of a poem by Robert Bridges, *The Isle of Achilles*.

Σικελῶν ὀρέων ματέρ', ἀκούω
καρύσσεσθαι στεφάνοις ἀρετᾶς.
τάν τ' ἀγχιστεύουσαν γᾶν
'Ιονίῳ ναίοιν πόντῳ,
ἂν ὑγραίνει καλλιστεύων
ὁ ξανθὰν χαίταν πυρσαίνων
Κρᾶθις ζαθέαις παγαῖσι τρέφων
εὔανδρόν τ' ὀλβίζων γᾶν.

(205-229.)[1]

And add these lines from a later ode in the same play:

μελισσοτρόφου Σαλαμῖνος, ὦ βασιλεῦ Τελαμών,
νάσου περικύμονος οἰκήσας ἕδραν
τᾶς ἐπικεκλιμένας ὄχθοις ἱεροῖς, ἵν' ἐλαίας
πρῶτον ἔδειξε κλάδον γλαυκᾶς 'Αθάνα,
οὐράνιον στέφανον λιπαραῖσί τε κόσμον 'Αθήναις.

(799-803.)

Here we have studied eulogies of blessed plots of
Grecian earth. Note the epithets σεμνός, ζάθεος, ἱερός
applied to land and water, and the words ὄλβος, ὀλ-
βίζω, εὐθαλής, εὐκαρπεία denoting wealth and fertility.
Sicily stands for prowess in war and success in the
games. The river Crathis dyes hair, enriches the
soil, and rears sturdy men. Athens receives special
glorification as the propagator of the olive. River
and river-basin are awarded a meed of beauty. The
epithet μελισσοτρόφος prefixed to Salamis is more a
reminder of the part played by honey in the domestic
economy of the Greeks than a stray memory of the
poet's boyhood in the cave. Religion and patriotism
are the mainsprings of the verses. Euripides puts into
the mouth of the chorus sentiments involving
anachronisms and alien to Trojans, the sentiments
of his own time and of himself; not of Euripides the

---

[1] See also *Hecuba*, 444-483; *Bacchae*, 402-411.

41

sceptic or the man apart airing irresponsible fancies, but of Euripides the Athenian, member of a Greek city-state and its spokesman in an assembly of compatriots.

Scott's *Marmion*, Canto IV. 30, contains the well-known description of Edinburgh, the poet's 'own romantic town,' and the further landscape, as seen from the top of Blackford Hill at early morning. The smoke-wreaths round the sable turrets are tinged 'with a lustre proud,' the Castle rock and all the heights are clothed in 'dusky grandeur'; far to the north each heathy peak of the Ochils, kissed by the sun, gleams 'a purple amethyst,' and the islands in the Firth float 'like emeralds chased in gold.' Ruskin chose the passage as an illustration of Scott's love of colour. Contrast with it lines 275-313 of Aristophanes' *Clouds*. The cloud-goddesses prepare to raise their dewy mobile forms from Ocean to the wooded mountain-tops, whence they may view a panorama of distant peaks, fruitful plains, and rivers that run murmuring to the loud-sounding sea. As in *Marmion*, the sun is up:

$$\text{ὄμμα γὰρ αἰθέρος ἀκάματον σελαγεῖται}$$
$$\text{μαρμαρέαις ἐν αὐγαῖς.}$$

But the landscape lies in the pure sunlight as if independent of it, sound takes the place of colour, the scene is not localised, the land is sacred (ἱερός), and the rivers are divine (ζάθεος). In the antistrophe the Clouds propose to visit Attica and Athens:

$$\text{λιπαρὰν χθόνα Παλλάδος, εὔανδρον γᾶν}$$
$$\text{Κέκροπος ὀψόμεναι πολυήρατον.}$$

There the Mysteries are held in reverence, there are temples and statues of the gods, there are sacred processions and festivals at all seasons, and in the beginning of spring, at the celebration of the Dionysia, the music of choirs is heard. Admittedly, there is no common measure between dissimilar situations in romance and drama, but the contrast may serve as a reminder of Greek devotion to the type and the permanent, Greek centrality and sociality, and the pervasiveness of Greek religion.

CHAPTER III

MOUNTAINS

WITH reference to the lack of feeling for the picturesque shown in the Homeric poems, Ruskin has the following remark:—'It is sufficiently notable that Homer, living in mountainous and rocky countries, dwells thus delightedly on all the flat bits; and so, I think, invariably the inhabitants of mountain countries do, but the inhabitants of the plains do not, in any similar way, dwell delightedly on mountains.' He goes on to say: 'If one talk to the mountaineer, he will usually characterise his own country to us as a "pays affreux," or in some equivalent, perhaps even more violent German term; but the lowland peasant does not think his country frightful; he either will have no ideas beyond it, or about it; or he will think it a very perfect country.' This would seem to mean that both mountaineer and lowlander regard their respective countries from a utilitarian point of view. Another authority, Archdeacon Hare, in *Guesses at Truth*, narrates a conversation he had with a boatman on the lake of Zug. After telling some stories of the Russian Suwarrow's march through the neighbourhood, this mountaineer asked, 'Is it true that he came from a country where there is not a mountain to be seen?' On being told that he might go hundreds of miles without coming to one, 'That must be beauti-

44

ful,' he exclaimed—*das muss schön sein!* Evidently, as
Hare remarks, the man was thinking of the difficulties
which mountains oppose to traffic and agriculture.
But had you transported him to those plains, he would
'probably have been seized with the homesickness
which is so common among his countrymen, as it is
also among the Swedes and Norwegians.' Certainly
it is easy to underestimate the strange unconscious
influence of natural surroundings on the silent sons
of the soil. In his Introduction to Canto III. of
Marmion, Sir Walter Scott speaks of this passion of
sympathy between man and his surroundings as
being from birth 'rather part of us than ours,' or
due to the sway of habit, which resists all the appeals
of reason and taste; and he gives the following
illustrations of its power:—

'Look east, and ask the Belgian why,
  Beneath Batavia's sultry sky,
  He seeks not eager to inhale
  The freshness of the mountain gale,
  Content to rear his whiten'd wall
  Beside the dank and dull canal?
  He'll say, from youth he loved to see
  The white sail gliding by the tree.
  Or see yon weather-beaten hind,
  Whose sluggish herds before him wind,
  Whose tatter'd plaid and rugged cheek
  His northern clime and kindred speak;
  Through England's laughing meads he goes,
  And England's wealth around him flows;
  Ask, if it would content him well,
  At ease in those gay plains to dwell,
  Where hedgerows spread a verdant screen,
  And spires and forests intervene,

And the neat cottage peeps between?
No! not for these will he exchange
His dark Lochaber's boundless range;
Not for fair Devon's meads forsake
Bennevis grey, and Garry's lake.'

As supplement to the foregoing I set down two quotations, one from Shakespeare and another from Scott. They need no comment; the inferences to be drawn are obvious. The following are the words of Northumberland to his companion Bolingbroke, in *Richard II.*, ii. 3:—

'Believe me, noble lord,
I am a stranger here in Gloucestershire:
These high wild hills and rough uneven ways
Draws out our miles, and makes them wearisome;
And yet your fair discourse hath been as sugar,
Making the hard way sweet and delectable.'

The following is the report of a conversation between Jeanie Deans and the landlord of an inn at Newark, in *The Heart of Midlothian*:—'It was all plain road, she was assured, except a high mountain called Gunnerby Hill, about three miles from Grantham, which was her stage for the night. "I'm glad to hear there's a hill," said Jeanie, "for baith my sight and my very feet are weary o' sic tracts o' level grund—it looks a' the way between this and York as if a' the land had been trenched and levelled, whilk is very wearisome to my Scotch een. When I lost sight of a muckle blue hill they ca' Ingleboro', I thought I hadna a friend left in this strange land."

'"As for the matter of that, young woman," said mine host, "an you be so fond o' hill, I carena an

46

thou couldst carry Gunnerby away with thee in thy lap, for it's a murder to post-horses."'

Homer's most characteristic attitude to mountains is purely objective. He speaks of them as great, or high, or steep. He does not indulge in mountain description or in mountain sentiment. A truthful pictorial epithet now and again is all he cares to give. Ida is 'many-fountained' and 'mother of wild beasts.' It is 'wooded,' and its valleys lie like fold on fold. Olympus is 'steep,' 'many-ridged,' 'glittering,' 'snow-capt.'

Mountains in general are 'shadowy' ($\sigma\kappa\iota\acute{o}\epsilon\iota\varsigma$) and 'lonely' ($o\grave{\iota}o\pi\acute{o}\lambda os$). The mountain of Phthires is called $\grave{a}\kappa\rho\iota\tau\acute{o}\phi\upsilon\lambda\lambda o\nu$, with reference to its mass of foliage, so thick that the separate trees are indistinguishable (*Il.*, ii. 868). Neriton in Ithaca is 'clothed with wood' ($\kappa\alpha\tau\alpha\epsilon\iota\mu\acute{\epsilon}\nu o\nu$ $\H{\upsilon}\lambda\eta$), and it has 'quivering leafage' ($\epsilon\grave{\iota}\nu o\sigma\acute{\iota}\phi\upsilon\lambda\lambda o\nu$). Chapman styles it 'shake-leaf hill.'

Homer compares huge Polyphemus to a wooded peak (ix. 191), and the wife of Antiphates is of the same ample proportions (x. 113), with the consequence that the followers of Odysseus 'loathed her.' Both passages have been adduced in proof of Homer's feeling about mountains. Yet one might have considerable respect for mountain peaks without caring to associate with specimens of humanity built on so liberal a scale. Perhaps the least appropriate of all Homer's similes is that in which he compares Hector, rushing against the enemy and shouting loud, to a snowy mountain (*Il.*, xiii. 754-5). We do not get rid of the incongruity by supposing that the main point of reference is to the white helmet-crest, for that would be nodding as the warrior ran. Virgil copies Homer and compares Aeneas in a similar

47

situation to Athos or Eryx or father Apennine, but
he softens the violence of the figure by deft personification:

> Quantus Athos, aut quantus Eryx, aut ipse, coruscis
> Cum fremit ilicibus, quantus, gaudetque nivali
> Vertice se attollens pater Apenninus ad auras.

(xii. 701-3.)

In Milton's imitation the hero is standing at bay:

> 'On th' other side Satan alarm'd
> Collecting all his might dilated stood,
> Like Teneriff or Atlas unremov'd:
> His stature reach'd the sky, and on his crest
> Sat Horror plum'd.'

(P.L., iv. 985-89.)

Fine discrimination is shown by Hebrew writers
in their figurative use of the mountains Lebanon and
Carmel. 'Lebanon is used by a very bold figure for
the whole people of the Jews, or for the state of the
church; for Jerusalem; for the temple of Jerusalem;
for the king of Assyria even, and for his army; for
whatever, in a word, is remarkable, august, and
sublime; and in the same manner, whatever possesses
much fertility, wealth, or beauty is called Carmel.' [1]

It is significant of much that Homer can regard
Parnassus with as little reverence or holy fear as
inspired the rash modern who spoke ill of the equator.
In *Odyssey*, xix. (412-66), the poet tells of the visit
which Odysseus paid, when a lad, to his rascally
maternal grandfather, Autolycus, and of a boar-hunt
in which he took part. The band of men and dogs
ascend Parnassus in the early morning:

> αἰπὺ δ' ὄρος προσέβαν καταειμένον ὕλῃ
> Παρνησοῦ, τάχα δ' ἵκανον πτύχας ἠνεμοέσσας.

[1] A. Lowth, *De Sacra Poesi Hebraeorum*, translated by G. Gregory.

48

ʹΗέλιος μὲν ἔπειτα νέον προσέβαλλεν ἀρούρας
ἐξ ἀκαλαρρείταο βαθυρρόου ʹΩκεανοῖο,
οἱ δʹ ἐς βῆσσαν ἵκανον ἐπακτῆρες.

The feeling implied is that of the true huntsman, exhilaration, as he brushes the dew and sniffs the morning air; excitement, as he thinks of the coming sport. So far it is similar to the mountain scene in Shakespeare's *Cymbeline*. But Homer's interest is centred on the lair of the boar, the brute's attack, and the wounding of the young hero. Compare Scott's narrative of the chase in *The Lady of the Lake* with its more romantic particularity, or Arnold's account of the hunt on Cyllene in *Merope*, a laboured imitation of Greek art, yet betraying the modern hand in its attention to scenery. With true instinct Scott does not set Fitz-James contemplating and moralising the scene until he is alone and unhorsed. And if we turn to the version of this passage given by Pope, or rather by his henchmen Fenton, we get a glimpse of the mountain-feeling prevalent in the English Augustan age, which is without Homeric authority:

'Parnassus, *thick perplex'd with horrid shades*,
With deep-mouth'd hounds the hunter troop invades;
What time the sun from ocean's peaceful stream,
Darts o'er the lawn his horizontal beam.
The pack impatient snuff the tainted gale;
The thorny wilds the woodmen fierce assail.'

Homer's successors work on much the same lines, but with greater variety. They note the mountains' wooded sides, the grassy lower slopes, and the snow-clad topmost peaks. Such epithets as νιφόεις, νιφό-βολος, χιονόκτυπος, χιονοτρόφος, χιονοθρέμμων are

frequent. Pindar calls the hill at Olympia 'far-seen'
or 'sunny'—εὐδείελον Κρόνιον (*Oly.*, i. 111). He also
speaks of the 'shady, immemorial mountains of Phlius':

$$\delta\alpha\sigma\kappa\acute{\iota}o\iota\varsigma^{1}$$
$$\Phi\lambda\iota o\hat{\upsilon}\nu\tau o\varsigma\ \acute{\upsilon}\pi'\ \mathring{\omega}\gamma\upsilon\gamma\acute{\iota}o\iota\varsigma\ \mathring{o}\rho\epsilon\sigma\iota\nu.$$

(*Nem.*, vi. 45, 46.)

Ὑφιμέδων used of Parnassus might be understood
both objectively and subjectively. He calls Aetna
'nurse the whole year long of biting snow':

$$A\mathring{\iota}\tau\nu\alpha,\ \pi\acute{\alpha}\nu\epsilon\tau\epsilon\varsigma\ \chi\iota\acute{o}\nu o\varsigma\ \mathring{o}\xi\epsilon\acute{\iota}\alpha\varsigma\ \tau\iota\theta\acute{\eta}\nu\alpha.$$

The last quotation is from the description of Aetna
in eruption, a picture full of grandeur and awe (*Pyth.*,
i. 13-28). It is also an instance of the Greeks' preference for movement to still life in nature and of
their fondness for mythological personification. In
his description of a lofty rocky height in his *Suppliants*
Aeschylus has massed together a series of striking
epithets:

$$\lambda\iota\sigma\sigma\grave{\alpha}\varsigma\ \alpha\mathring{\iota}\gamma\acute{\iota}\lambda\iota\psi\ \mathring{\alpha}\pi\rho\acute{o}\sigma\delta\epsilon\iota\kappa\tau o\varsigma\ o\mathring{\iota}\acute{o}\phi\rho\omega\nu\ \kappa\rho\epsilon\mu\grave{\alpha}\varsigma$$
$$\gamma\upsilon\pi\iota\grave{\alpha}\varsigma\ \pi\acute{\epsilon}\tau\rho\alpha\text{—} \qquad\qquad (794\text{-}96.)$$

'beetling, smooth, unvisited by goats, the haunt of
vultures, not to be pointed at, haughty in its isolation.'
The words are appropriately put into the mouth of
the chorus, who prefer suicide in such a spot to
compulsory wedlock.

The scene of Aeschylus' *Prometheus Vinctus* is laid
among the Scythian mountains. But it is in accordance with the principles of Greek dramatic art that
there should be no mountain sentimentality in the
piece. To admit any excuse for such is to cut at the
root of the tragic significance of the play. The scene

---

[1] Some editors read ἀσκίοις. Cp. Aristophanes, *Thesm.*, 997;
Euripides, *Bacchae*, 218; Simonides Amorginus (*Bergk*, 14).

is essential to the action. The motive is the punishment, by a god of superior might, of a defiant benefactor of mankind. The place of punishment forms part of the punishment. Prometheus is there to suffer, not to dream. The sentiments of Childe Harold or of Manfred are inadmissible in this situation. To hear any of the actors exclaiming, 'Beautiful! This is not solitude!' would be as incongruous as to imagine the immortals saying, 'Now stirs the feeling Infinite!' At the same time, to utilise the scene so as to allow it to compete with the sufferer for a place in our minds would have seemed to a Greek an unpardonable enormity. All references to the immediate scene call up a picture of lofty, rugged, storm-beaten peaks, and pathless wilds, a region lying outside of nature's amenities. It is joyless—ἀτερπής, a word seldom used of nature—as are the rocky shore of Scheria and the realm of Persephone to Odysseus. The spirit of Prometheus himself may be called sublime and likewise his address to the elements and his last words of defiance. But the silent scene is not rendered sublime. The whole stress is laid on the anti-social aspects so that the sense of repulsion or of the terrible never gives place to that feeling of self-expansion or of union with the object which is generally considered necessary for experiencing the sublime. And our fear for Prometheus has its source elsewhere. The passage that describes the future wanderings of Io is a sort of versified geography of regions little known, for which reason the play is said to have been a favourite with ancient schoolmasters. Such speeches would fall flat in a modern theatre, but the forceful boulder-language in which mountain travels are sketched interests the student, who remembers Shakespearian phrases like ἀστρογείτονας κορυφάς, 'star-neighbouring peaks.' The prophecy of the eruption of Aetna in this play contrasts curiously with the picture of that phenomenon given by Pindar. In the words of Jebb, 'Aeschylus—thoroughly Greek in this—fixes our thoughts on the scathe done to man's labour.' He is thinking of the ruin wrought on the fields of fertile Sicily (374-77).[1]

The *Bacchae*, if not the greatest, is the most fascinating of the extant plays of Euripides. By the influence of the god Dionysus, the women of Thebes are driven out to Mount Cithaeron to practise his ritual. But the mountain is not the cause of the ecstasy. The thoughts of the Maenads are centred on the young effeminate deity. The joy is in Bromius, and it is the enthusiasm of a throng. The play is a religious romance, a mixture of sensuousness and mysticism; and one would require to be a Pater to find in it all that Pater found. The place counts for more than in any other Greek drama, *Prometheus Vinctus* perhaps excepted, so local colour is not wanting. The Messenger announces that he has come from Cithaeron, 'where the glistening snow-flakes never cease to lie' (661, 62). Dionysus describes the women as sitting on roofless rocks beneath the green firs:

$$\chi\lambda\omega\rho\alpha\hat{\iota}\varsigma\ \dot{\upsilon}\pi'\ \dot{\epsilon}\lambda\acute{\alpha}\tau\alpha\iota\varsigma\ \dot{\alpha}\nu\rho\rho\acute{o}\phi\iota\iota\varsigma\ \hat{\eta}\nu\tau\alpha\iota\ \pi\acute{\epsilon}\tau\rho\alpha\iota\varsigma$$

(38.)

The Messenger sees them in the morning light, asleep, resting on leaves of fir and oak:

$$\eta\hat{\upsilon}\delta o\nu\ \delta\grave{\epsilon}\ \pi\hat{\alpha}\sigma\alpha\iota\ \sigma\acute{\omega}\mu\alpha\sigma\iota\nu\ \pi\alpha\rho\epsilon\iota\mu\acute{\epsilon}\nu\alpha\iota,$$
$$\alpha\grave{\iota}\ \mu\grave{\epsilon}\nu\ \pi\rho\grave{o}\varsigma\ \dot{\epsilon}\lambda\acute{\alpha}\tau\eta\varsigma\ \nu\hat{\omega}\tau'\ \dot{\epsilon}\rho\epsilon\acute{\iota}\sigma\alpha\sigma\alpha\iota\ \phi\acute{o}\beta\eta\nu,$$
$$\alpha\grave{\iota}\ \delta'\ \dot{\epsilon}\nu\ \delta\rho\upsilon\grave{o}\varsigma\ \phi\acute{\upsilon}\lambda\lambda o\iota\sigma\iota\ \pi\rho\grave{o}\varsigma\ \pi\acute{\epsilon}\delta\dot{\omega}\ \kappa\acute{\alpha}\rho\alpha$$
$$\epsilon\dot{\iota}\kappa\hat{\eta}\ \beta\alpha\lambda o\hat{\upsilon}\sigma\alpha\iota\ \sigma\omega\phi\rho\acute{o}\nu\omega\varsigma.$$

(683-86.)

[1] Cp. Virgil, *Aeneid*, iii. 570-82; Lucretius, *D.R.N.*, vi. 680 ff.

The speech of the Second Messenger shows accurate topographical knowledge, but once only is any portion of the mountain-side selected for brief, direct description. It is a dell, cliff-surrounded, watered by a stream and made shady by stone-pines:

$$\mathring{\eta}\nu \; \delta' \; \mathring{a}\gamma\kappa\circ\varsigma \; \mathring{a}\mu\phi\acute{\iota}\kappa\rho\eta\mu\nu\circ\nu, \; \mathring{\upsilon}\delta a\sigma\iota \; \delta\iota\acute{a}\beta\rho\circ\chi\circ\nu,$$
$$\pi\epsilon\acute{\upsilon}\kappa a\sigma\iota \; \sigma\upsilon\sigma\kappa\iota\acute{a}\zeta\circ\nu.$$
(1051-52.)

Humboldt, in his *Kosmos*, ranks this among 'descriptions disclosing a deep feeling for nature.' It is a pleasant spot enough for the Maenads to sit in while busied ἐν τερπνοῖς πόνοις. But it is only a step in the crisp narration of one of the best Messengers' speeches in Greek tragedy. More romantic in quality are the words of the First Messenger:

$$\pi\mathring{a}\nu \; \delta\grave{\epsilon} \; \sigma\upsilon\nu\epsilon\beta\acute{a}\kappa\chi\epsilon\upsilon\sigma' \; \mathring{o}\rho\circ\varsigma$$
$$\kappa a\grave{\iota} \; \theta\mathring{\eta}\rho\epsilon\varsigma, \; \circ\mathring{\upsilon}\delta\grave{\epsilon}\nu \; \delta' \; \mathring{\eta}\nu \; \mathring{a}\kappa\acute{\iota}\nu\eta\tau\circ\nu \; \delta\rho\acute{o}\mu\dot{\omega}.$$
(726-27.)

The shouts of the Maenads echoed among the heights, all the wild things were startled, they scurried and added their confused cries to the uproar, till the whole mountain seemed to join in the revelry. This smacks of the supernatural, but it is not altogether an unexpected flight of fancy on the part of the herdsman-messenger. It is founded on mountain experience, and a modern poacher (νυκτερευτής) could corroborate. Perhaps the lines in which the Chorus liken themselves to a timid fawn which has cleared the hunters' nets and bounds along the river-side, delighting in haunts free from human foot, in the shady foliage of the greenwood (866-76), show a finer feeling for nature than can be found elsewhere in this play.

53

Let us revert to Homer for a little. There is one passage in the *Odyssey* which shows to what small compass this mountain question is narrowed, and how much may depend on the interpretation of a single word. When Telemachus announces to Menelaus his intention of departing for home, he refuses a gift of three horses and a car, with these words: 'Whatever gift thou wouldst give me, let it be something to treasure; but I will not lead horses to Ithaca, but rather leave them here as a glory for thyself, for thou rulest over a wide plain in which is abundance of lotus, and galingale, and wheat, and spelt, and white broad-eared barley. But in Ithaca there are no broad courses, nor is there any meadow land. It is good for feeding goats, and *more pleasant than a land that pastures horses*; for none of the islands that slope to the sea are fit for the driving of horses or possessed of fine meadows, and Ithaca least of all' (iv. 600-608). The crux lies in the words μᾶλλον ἐπήρατος ἱπποβότοιο. It is a question quite as much of rocks as of mountains, but it comes to the same thing. There is at least one mountain in Ithaca, Neriton. Telemachus is comparing low land with high land, a plain with a rocky and hilly country, and he gives the preference to the former on the score of utility, to the latter on the score of picturesqueness. But can the word ἐπήρατος bear this absolute meaning? While it is used elsewhere of places, it need not be associated with scenery. The same is true of a whole class of epithets—πολυήρατος, ἐρατός, ἐρατεινός, ἐραννός, καλός. Gladstone has remarked that 'ἐρατεινή is applied to Emathia (*Il.*, xiv. 226), and to Scheria (*Ody.*, vii. 79), and both these are mountainous.' But the answer is easy. These places may be pleasant, desirable, charming, beautiful—translate

54

as you please—not by reason of their mountains but
in spite of them. There is nothing to prove that the
poet is thinking of mountains at the time. If Homer
calls Calydon 'rocky' (*Il.*, ii. 640) and 'steep' (*Il.*,
xiii. 217; xiv. 116), and again 'pleasant' (*Il.*, ix.
531, 577), we need not conclude that the two points
of view are associated in the poet's mind. Nor need
we vex our souls about Homer's inconsistency. Again
and again he uses epithets in a breezy heroic way to
cast a halo round spots he has never seen. When he
calls now one river and then another the finest that
flows over the face of the earth, we do not stop to test
his statements by the dry facts of geography, any more
than we inquire too closely into the possible truth of
the breathless narrative of a boy whose enthusiasm
for things seen and admired has outrun his sense of
comparison. In his Commentary, Nitzsch supposes
that ἐπήρατος may not mean 'pleasant' or 'lovely,'
in this instance, but 'steep,' deriving it from αἴρω.
Unfortunately the examples quoted in support of this
supposition do not prove it. But no more do they
prove that ἐπήρατος must mean intrinsically 'lovely,'
and refer exclusively to the configuration of the land.
Certainly, it would be less surprising to hear
Telemachus say,—'Ithaca is a land fit for feeding
goats, and steeper than a horse-pasturing country.'
Others prefer to water down the sentiment so as to
make the word mean 'lovely in my sight'; as if
Telemachus meant to say,—'Ithaca is a rocky country,
and I don't think much of rocky countries in general,
in comparison with plains, but I make an exception
of Ithaca because it is my home.' There is reason in
that; it is patriotic. So, when Helen in Troy remembers Lacedaemon she calls it ἐρατεινή (*Il.*, iii.
239). Virgil makes Diomede, the Aetolian, speak of

55

pulchram Calydona (*Aen.*, xi. 270); and he says of the dying Antores,—

> Caelumque
> Aspicit, et dulces moriens reminiscitur Argos.
>
> (*Aen.*, x. 781-82.)

And if we wish to find an instance of this feeling attached to a specific mountain, Aristophanes furnishes one. In the *Lysistrata*, the chorus of Spartans sing of Taygetus, which they have left behind:

> Ταΰγετον αὖτ᾽ ἐραννὸν ἐκλιπῶα.
>
> (1297.)

This home-feeling is a different thing from an independent, reasoned love of nature. It has no aesthetic basis. But it is felt by the dullest clown.

If we may judge from one instance, the iambic poet Archilochus preferred low land to high land. Speaking of the island of Thasos, he says it is like the back of an ass, crowned with wild wood, not at all a beautiful or delightful or desirable place like the region about the streams of Siris:

> Ἥδε δ᾽ ὥστ᾽ ὄνου ῥάχις
> ἕστηκεν ὕλης ἀγρίης ἐπιστεφής·
> οὐ γάρ τι καλὸς χῶρος οὐδ᾽ ἐφίμερος
> οὐδ᾽ ἐρατός, οἷος ἀμφὶ Σίριος ῥοάς.
>
> (*Bergk*, 20.)

What does this prove? It shows that, if Archilochus is thinking of scenery at all, he counts it as nothing in the balance against the lack of fertility. The comparison is between a productive and an unproductive land. The first two lines were preserved by Plutarch (*De Exil.*, 12), the second two by Athenaeus (xii. 523, D). Plutarch says that Archilochus overlooked the fruit-bearing parts and the vineyards and

56

slandered Thasos. Athenaeus remarks: ὁ ποιητὴς ὑπερτεθαύμακε τὴν χώραν τῶν Σιριτῶν διὰ τὴν εὐδαιμονίαν· περὶ γοῦν τῆς Θάσου λέγων ὡς ἥσσονός φησιν· Οὐ γὰρ κ.τ.λ. It is another reminder that καλός and similar epithets require cautious handling. The sole passage in Greek poetry where I have found καλός expressly applied to a mountain occurs in the Homeric Hymn *To Aphrodite*. When the goddess appears to Anchises on Ida, he wonders whether she is one of the Graces,

> ἤ τις Νυμφάων, αἵτ᾽ ἄλσεα καλὰ νέμονται,
> ἢ Νυμφῶν, αἳ καλὸν ὄρος τόδε ναιετάουσι
> καὶ πηγὰς ποταμῶν καὶ πίσεα ποιήεντα.

(97-99.)

Even this leaves room for argument. Anchises' foot was on his native hill, and he was a keeper of cattle. A Scottish poet praises God for giving us 'the fructuall mountains for our bestiall.' But there is at least one passage in Greek prose which speaks of mountains as possessing beauty. It is in Plato's *Critias*, 118, B.— 'He celebrated the surrounding mountains for their number and size and beauty (κάλλος), in which they exceeded all that are now to be seen anywhere.' To the modern nature-lover κάλλος seems a helpless word, totally inadequate to express the feelings he is accustomed to experience in the face of nature's sublimities, but it bears evidence to Greek contentment with the finite and with the sensuous pleasure imparted by the contemplation of form and outline.

In the medley called the Homeric Hymns, mountains are often the playgrounds of gods and goddesses, the scene of their adventures and escapades. The Delian Apollo takes delight in high mountains,

in forelands, and in rivers running seaward. Apollo
Pythius traverses mountain and plain and forest, till
he comes to 'Crisa beneath snowy Parnassus. . . .
Above it hangs a cliff and under it runs a hollow
rugged glen,' which is said to be a correct description.
Dionysus speeds through the woodlands, garlanded
with ivy and laurel and round him the nymphs fill
the forest with wondrous din. Hermes, lord of Cyllene
and pastoral Arcadia, hurries to the misty heights of
Pieria, where he finds the divine cattle of the blessed
gods grazing on the pleasant unmown meadows—
λειμῶνας ἀκηρασίους ἐρατεινούς. In the Hymn *To
Aphrodite*, the goddess is pictured coming to Ida.
Wolves and lions, bears and leopards fawn upon her,
and in virtue of her presence and power they mate
in pairs in the shady vales. In the Hymn *To Pan*,
that rural god, with attendant nymphs, is the chief
figure in a series of scenes which bring before us with
Theocritean freshness and charm the various aspects
of wild nature in mountain solitudes of which he is
the impersonation. Nowhere else in Greek poetry
are the sights and sounds of nature so exquisitely
suggested by means of successive actions. 'Tell me,
O Muse, of the dear son of Hermes, the goat-footed,
the two-horned, the music-lover, who haunts the
wooded glades with dancing nymphs who tread the
tops of steep rocks, calling on Pan, the god of pastures,
long-haired and rough. He is lord of every snowy
ridge, of mountain peaks and rocky heights. Here
and there he wanders through the thick brushwood,
now lured on by soft-flowing streams, and now he
fares among steep crags and mounts the highest peak
that looks down upon the flocks. Often he runs over
the clear high mountains, and often on the shoulders
of the hills, keen of eye, he charges and slays wild

beasts. Only at evening, when he has returned from the chase, he pipes a sweet strain on his reeds. Not even could that bird surpass him in melody which among the leaves in flowery spring pours forth her gushing lament of honey-sweet song. At that time the clear-voiced mountain-nymphs are in his company and move with swift feet, singing by some spring of dark water; and Echo sighs round the mountain-top. Now to this side, now to that, and again moving into their midst, the god dances with quick steps. On his back he wears the tawny skin of a lynx, and he delights his heart with clear strains in a soft meadow where crocus and hyacinth, fragrant and flourishing, are blended everywhere with the grass (1-26).'

In the Hymns, owing to association with deity, temples, altars, halls and caves are ' fragrant '— θυόεις, εὐώδης, θυώδης. When Apollo came to Cyllene,

$$\text{ὀδμὴ δ' ἱμερόεσσα δι' οὔρεος ἠγαθέοιο κίδνατο.}$$

(*To Hermes*, 231-32.)

Olympus is θυώδης (*To Demeter*, 331). For the same reason hills are 'holy.' Pythian Apollo went up 'a green and holy hill'—ὄρος ζάθεον, χλωρόν (223)— probably Mount Messapius. Ida is ὄρος μέγα τε ζάθεόν τε (*To Aphrodite*, 258); in the Hesiodic *Theogomy* (2) Helicon is spoken of in identical terms. In drama and lyric the epithets ἱερός, ζάθεος, ἠγάθεος applied to mountains abound. Mountain κορυφαί are ἄβατοι and the πλάκες are σεμναί. Parnassus has two peaks (or rather cliffs several thousand feet from the summit) one of which was sacred to Apollo and the other to Dionysus. 'For the greater part of the day those resplendent rocks (the Phaedriades), facing nearly south, reflected the full rays of the sun on the temple

59

of Apollo; but at sunset, when the light had left the lower portions, those brilliant cloud-effects were seen which poetic fancy called the torches held aloft by Dionysus as he leaped along the ridges of Parnassus; while the sunbeams, darting athwart the two peaks, to the east and to the west of the Castalian forest, were described as the shooting and brandishing of the wand of Dionysus.'[1] Hence the declaration of Teiresias regarding the certain spread of the religion of Dionysus:

ἔτ' αὐτὸν ὄψει κἀπὶ Δελφίσιν πέτραις
πηδῶντα σὺν πεύκαισι δικόρυφον πλάκα,
πάλλοντα καὶ σείοντα βακχεῖον κλάδον.

(Bacchae, 306-308.)[2]

On Parnassus there were rocks called Corycian, and caverns of the same name, sacred to Dionysus and his attendant nymphs. In *Eumenides* (23) Aeschylus describes the Corycian rocks as δαιμόνων ἀναστροφή. In a stasimon of the *Oedipus Tyrannus* Artemis is invoked along with Apollo, and referred to as carrying torches while she darts over the Lycian hills (204-208). In the *Trachiniae* (212) she is called ἀμφίπυρος. Probably volcanic phenomena inspired the fancy. Oeta is sacred to Zeus (*Trachiniae*, 436 and 1191). Hermes and his son Pan are associated with Cyllene (*Ajax*, 695; *Oed. Tyr.*, 1104).

No doubt local cults attached their own fancies to the neighbouring heights, and these may never have become articulate in poetry. But, so far as classical Greek poetry is concerned, it is not too bold a generalisation to say that to the Greeks 'the power of hills'

[1] Dr. Sandys in his edition of the *Bacchae*.
[2] *Loci classici* in this matter are *Antigone*, 1126; *Ion*, 716; *Phoenissae*, 226; Aristophanes' *Clouds*, 603, etc.

was a religious power and that their mountain sentiment rested on a basis of sacred associations.

'The silent spectacle—the gleam—
The shadow—and the peace supreme'

did not move in them the sublime transports of Wordsworth but compelled thoughts of deity. 'Far-distant images' did indeed 'draw nigh,'

'Tempting Fancy to ascend,
And with immortal Spirits blend.'

Why do the Bacchants of Euripides desire to be in beautiful Pieria, on hallowed Olympus? Is it to commune with nature? They wish Dionysus to lead them there that they may pursue their orgies in peace:

οὗ θ' ἁ καλλιστευομένα
Πιερία μούσειος ἕδρα,
σεμνὰ κλιτὺς Ὀλύμπου,
ἐκεῖσ' ἄγε μ', ὦ Βρόμιε, Βρόμιε,
προβακχήιε δαῖμον.
ἐκεῖ Χάριτες, ἐκεῖ δὲ Πόθος·
ἐκεῖ δὲ βάκχαισι θέμις ὀργιάζειν.

(*Bacchae*, 409-15.)

'O blest Pieria!' they cry, 'Dionysus honours thee' (565, 6). In an ode of the *Helena* Euripides takes us to the mountains, but we are following the footsteps of Demeter, who throws herself down in grief among the rocky thickets deep with snow (1319-26). In the *Iphigeneia in Tauris* (1234-83) the Chorus celebrate the coming of Apollo to Parnassus, the slaying of the dragon,

ποικιλόνωτος οἰνωπὸς δράκων
σκιερᾷ κατάχαλκος εὐφύλλῳ δάφνᾳ,

and the establishing of his oracle. The Chorus in the *Phoenissae*, Tyrian maidens detained at Thebes on

61

their way to Delphi, hail in anticipation the mysterious flame on the Parnassian peaks, the miraculous vine,

$$\zeta\acute{a}\theta\epsilon\acute{a}\ \tau'\ \mathring{a}\nu\tau\rho\alpha\ \delta\rho\acute{a}\kappa o\nu\tau o\varsigma\ o\mathring{\upsilon}\text{-}$$
$$\rho\epsilon\iota\alpha\acute{\iota}\ \tau\epsilon\ \sigma\kappa o\pi\iota\alpha\grave{\iota}\ \theta\epsilon\hat{\omega}\nu$$
$$\nu\iota\phi\acute{o}\beta o\lambda\acute{o}\nu\ \tau'\ \mathring{o}\rho o\varsigma\ \iota\epsilon\rho\acute{o}\nu.$$
(226-38.)

Later they address the dell in Cithaeron, 'dear to Artemis, the nurse of snow, haunt of many a wild beast, full of sacred foliage' (801, 2).

In this respect Homer occupies a peculiar position. No epithet implying sacredness or connection with the gods is attached to any mountain, with the exception of Νυσήϊον, that is, Nysa, in Thrace, which is called ἠγάθεον (Il., vi. 133). This would seem to imply that Homer had heard something about Dionysus and his worship. His immortals congregate on 'snowy' Olympus. Tmolus is 'snowy' (Il., xx. 385). Ida is not sacred, though Zeus has a fragrant altar on Gargarus (Il., viii. 48). Crisa is ζάθεος (ii. 520), Pytho is πετρήεσσα (ii. 519); Delphi is not in the Catalogue; in the *Odyssey* Parnassus is merely καταειμένον ὕλη (ii. 519); it is not mentioned in the *Iliad*. The great days of Apollo and Dionysus are yet to come.

CHAPTER IV

RIVER AND SEA

UNLIKE the steadfast mountains, even in Homer the moving rivers are sacred and divine. At the beginning of Book xx. of the *Iliad*, Zeus bids Themis summon all the gods to council, and no River was absent except Oceanus. In *Iliad*, iii. (276-78), Agamemnon calls on Rivers, along with Zeus, Sun, Earth, Hades, and Persephone to bear witness to his oath. On one occasion Odysseus prays to a river as to a god (*Ody.*, v. 445-50). Bulls and horses are sacrificed to rivers (*Il.*, xxi. 131). Scamander has a priest, Dolopion (*Il.*, v. 77). Generally in Homer and later, the river divinity varies between a personality with no fixed plastic shape and a vague power immanent in the water, there being few traces of pure animism. In virtue of their strength and fertilising power rivers are figured as bulls (Euripides, *Ion*, 1261; *Iph. at A.*, 275). Because of their fluidity they have the power of assuming various transformations as in the *Trachiniae* (13 ff.), where, in the contest with Heracles, Acheloüs becomes a bull, a snake, and a bull-headed man. In the Hesiodic *Theogony* rivers are children of Oceanus and Tethys. Of them all Acheloüs is chief, worshipped over all Greece, the name being a synonym for water in general. According to Hesiod also, Tethys bore to Oceanus 'a holy company of daughters, who with the lord Apollo and rivers have youths in their keepings (κουρίζουσι)'; and to rivers as sustainers of

life, κουροτρόφοι, young men offered nurture-locks
(*Il.*, xxiii. 141; Aeschylus, *Choeph.*, 6, etc.). These
nymphs are catalogued by Hesiod, who assigns them
names appropriate to the various characteristics
of rivers (*Theog.*, 346-61). Homeric heroes have river-
gods as putative fathers or river-nymphs as mothers
(*Il.*, xxi. 141; vi. 21, etc.). Springs and smaller
waters, personified as nymphs, are called the daughters
of the greater rivers—Acheloüs, Alpheus, Asopus—
and these became brides of heroes and guardian-
deities of cities.[1]

Homer says that the four maidens who waited on
Circe were 'born of the wells and the groves and the
holy rivers that flow seawards' (*Ody.*, x. 350-51).
Again he speaks of nymphs haunting 'the steep
mountain-tops, river-springs, and grassy water-
meadows' (*Ody.*, vi. 123-24). But nymphs of rivers,
as distinct from those of river-springs (Naiads)—if
we except Hesiod's rather ambiguous Ὠκεανῖναι—
have no generic name, any more than those of groves
and fen-land. 'There were no river-nymphs in
Greece,' a recent writer has said.[2] In truth, most
Greek rivers are raging torrents in winter and little
more than dry beds in summer, so that they could
not have afforded happy habitations. The nymphs
preferred springs and rivcr-heads,[3] and lived mostly
in caves.[4] But they dwelt in lakes too. Pindar
addresses Kamarina as Ὠκεανοῦ θύγατερ, with reference
to the lake after which the city was named (*Oly.*, v. 2).[5]

[1] For 'the gracious daughter of loud-sounding Aropus' see Bacchylides'
fine ode, viii. in Jebb's numeration.
[2] Mr A. E. Zimmern in *The Greek Commonwealth*.
[3] Tennyson's 'old well-heads of haunted rills.'
[4] Cp. Virgil's *Nymphae, Laurentes Nymphae, genus amnibus unde est* (*Aen.*,
viii. 71).
[5] Cp. Homer, *Iliad*, ii. 865, etc. In Milton's *Comus*, Sabrina is addressed as 'Goddess of the silver lake.'

Greek towns, however, generally grew up round a
κρήνη, about which local legends gathered, such as
Dirce—εὐπάρθενος Δίρκα—at Thebes, and Peirene—
σεμνὸν Πειρήνης ὕδωρ—at Corinth. Herodotus says
the Corinthians 'dwell round fair Peirene' (v. 92),
and Pindar calls Corinth 'the city of Peirene'
(*Oly.*, xiii. 61). Cyrene, in Libya, was named
after the fountain Cyre dedicated to Apollo
(Pindar, *Pyth.*, iv. 294). Wells were as precious in
Greece as in Palestine. Euripides shows a special
affection for κρῆναι. When the Messenger in the
Iphigeneia at Aulis announces the arrival of the maid
and her mother, he describes them as cooling their
feet at a fair-flowing spring—perhaps a reminiscence
of Homer's Aulis passage. And when Agamemnon
is dispatching the Old Man from Aulis to Argos, with
a letter for Clytemnestra, he warns him not to linger
by the wells in the woodlands:

> μή νυν μήτ᾽ ἀλσώδεις ἵζου
> κρήνας, μήθ᾽ ὕπνῳ θελχθῇς.   (141-42.)

The Messenger in the *Persae* says pathetically that
some of the retreating Persians died of thirst ἀμφὶ
κρηναῖον γάνος (483). To Clytemnestra the return of
Agamemnon is as delightful as spring-water to the
thirsty wayfarer (*Agam.*, 901).

Utilitarian interest in rivers is therefore marked.
The water of the Nile is praised because it fattens
cattle and makes the blood of men fruitful:

> ἀλφεσίβοιον ὕδωρ,
> ἔνθεν ἀεξόμενον
> ζώφυτον αἷμα βροτοῖσι θάλλει.
> (Aeschylus, *Supp.*, 827-29.)[1]

[1] Cp. Spenser, *F.Q.*, i. 1-21.

It cannot be polluted by disease—νόσοις ἄθικτον (540).
In the *Persae* (33) it is πολυθρέμμων; in the *Prometheus
Vinctus* (812) it is εὔποτον ῥέος. The daughters of
Danaus are no longer to pay homage to the Nile but
to the rivers of their new home, Argos, which 'pour
their mild draught and make the children many'
(*Supp.*, 1025-6). The Asopus is φίλον πίασμα Βοιωτῶν
χθονί (*Persae*, 806).

Homer is realistic when he places elms, tamarisks,
lotus, rushes, and galingale on the banks of the
Scamander, and so is Euripides when he decks the
Eurotas with reeds and puts these words into the
mouth of Menelaus:

> Σπάρτη δὲ ποῦ γῆς ἐστι πλὴν ἵνα ῥοαὶ
> τοῦ καλλιδόνακός εἰσιν Εὐρώτα μόνον;
>
> (*Helena*, 492-93.[1])

'Ces bords de l'Eurotas,' says Patin, 'tant de fois
maudits par sa muse, il les couronne ici avec com-
plaisance, dans l'harmonieuses épithètes, des beaux
roseaux qu'y a retrouvées de nos jours Chateaubriand.'[2]
But the same poet descends to conventional flattery,
when he extols the muddy Apidanus for its beauty as
well as for its fertilising power:

> πατέρα τε τὸν ἔκλυον
> εὔιππον χώραν ὕδασιν
> καλλίστοισι λιπαίνειν.
>
> (*Bacchae*, 573-75.[3])

Κάλλιστος, however, like the English 'finest,' is not
single-edged. For colour's sake, Bacchylides calls
the Nile 'flowery,' ἀνθεμώδης (xviii. 39); the Hebrus,

---

[1] Cp. *Helena*, 209, 348; *Iph. at A.*, 179; Theognis, 784.
[2] 'L'Eurotas mérite certainement l'épithète de καλλιδόναξ, aux
beaux roseaux, que lui a donnée Euripide.' (Chateaubriand: *Itinéraire
de Paris à Jerusalem*.)
[3] Cp. *Hecuba*, 451.

usually associated with wintry rigours, is ἀνθεμόεις
(xv. 5); and the banks of the Lycormas or Evenus,
'one of the fiercest and most treacherous torrents in
Greece,' are 'rose-clad,' ῥοδόεις (xv. 34).[1]

Other characteristics of rivers that appeal to Greek
poets are their full volume, strong current, deep bed,
silvery swirls, and water-breaks. Hence a series of
conventional haphazard epithets—ἀκάμας, εὐρυδίνης,
εὔροος, εὐρρείτης, ὠκύροος, καλλιδίνης, καλλιρέεθρος,
καλλίροος, καλλίναος, ἀργυροδίνης, ἀργυρορρύτης.[2]
Similarly English poetry is full of 'silver' streams,
'glassy' waves, and 'crystal' floods. Spenser's
enumeration of the rivers present at the marriage
of Thames and Medway is in the Greek manner,
with greater variety and more realism.

To Greek rivers one praise is lacking. Greek heroes
were not Izaak Waltons; they would have scorned
the gentle Piscator's motto, 'Study to be quiet.' In
classical Greek literature anglers patronise the sea,
not fresh water. Homer calls only one river ἰχθυόεις,
the Hyllus (Il., xx. 392). The companions of
Odysseus take to fishing only when hard pressed by
hunger. In Iliad, xxi., when Hephaestus turns his
fire on the river Scamander, the poet tells how the
eels and fishes tumbled this way and that in agony, and
in an earlier passage he draws a gruesome picture
of the same fry busy with the dead body of Astero-
paeus. But it was Oppian, not Homer, that wrote:

πολλὴ γάρ βλεφάροισι καὶ ἐν φρεσὶ τέρψις ἰδέσθαι
παλλόμενον καὶ ἑλισσόμενον πεπεδημένον ἰχθύν.
(Halieutica, i. 71-72.)

Book xxi. of the Iliad contains the account of

---

[1] Cp. Milton's 'Sandy Ladon's lilied banks.' (Arcades.)
[2] ἀκαμαντορόας and πορφυροδίνας are found only in Bacchylides.

Achilles' fight with the River Scamander, one of the
most powerful parts of the poem in reach of imagination and energy of movement. In the general
prologue the river-bed is loud with the splash of
falling bodies, the cries of men whirled round in the
eddies, the groans of the dying:

πλῆτο ῥόος κελάδων ἐπιμὶξ ἵππων τε καὶ ἀνδρῶν.

Achilles is dealing death on every side, and the water
runs red. Angered by the slaughter and piqued at
Achilles' insulting words, the River is moved to speech
and action. Assuming personality, the new combatant
plays the part of a human hero, gabbing, boasting,
and praying. The water-body works like a tidal bore.
It foams and bellows; it rears its dark-towering
crest; it arches and curls; with a roar it sweeps on
over the plain after Achilles; from above it falls in
deluge on his shoulders, and devours the earth from
beneath. The climax is reached in the lines:

ἦ, καὶ ἐπῶρτ' Ἀχιλῆϊ κυκώμενος, ὕψοσε θύων,
μορμύρων ἀφρῷ τε καὶ αἵματι καὶ νεκύεσσι.

Hera fears for Achilles and summons Hephaestus,
whose fierce flame soon prevails. A feature of the
narrative is the recurrence of water-figures, illustrating the grand and heroic by the little and homely—
locusts huddling in a stream to escape from a raging
fire, fishes swarming into a sheltering haven from the
attack of a dolphin, a man irrigating a field, a swine-
herd boy swept away by a torrent. In the midst of
the hurly-burly the words ἐρατεινὰ ῥέεθρα, and ἀγλαὸν
ὕδωρ, and καλὰ ῥέεθρα several times repeated, catch
the eye of the reader. Are they chance expressions?
Or is this Homer's way of saying that the Scamander
was 'looking so beautiful all the time,' like Stevenson's

Oise in flood? It is on this note that he closes the scene:

$$ἄψορρον \ δ᾽ \ ἄρα \ κῦμα \ κατέσσυτο \ καλὰ \ ῥέεθρα.^1$$

Homer has several notable similes, in which he illustrates the sound and movement of hosts or of single combatants by the violent action of rivers. He seems to speak from personal observation, not of minute details, but of striking characteristics of rivers made raging torrents by the force of autumn rains. 'The numerous torrents are the natural result of the configuration of the country, for the steep limestone mountains have but little of a spongy surface to act as a reservoir for the rain. It is especially at the time of the autumn rains that the greatest floods take place, and the sudden swelling and violent rush of the stream has furnished Homer with some of his finest similes' (Tozer). The first river simile in the *Iliad* illustrates the mighty clash and din of the first encounter between the Greek and Trojan hosts:

ὡς δ᾽ ὅτε χείμαρροι ποταμοὶ κατ᾽ ὄρεσφι ῥέοντες
ἐς μισγάγκειαν συμβάλλετον ὄβριμον ὕδωρ
κρουνῶν ἐκ μεγάλων κοίλης ἔντοσθε χαράδρης,
τῶν δέ τε τηλόσε δοῦπον ἐν οὔρεσιν ἔκλυε ποιμήν·
ὡς τῶν μισγομένων γένετο ἰαχή τε πόνος τε.

(iv. 452-56.)

Flooded streams coming from great springs in the mountains flow down ravines and pour their combined waters into a chasm where the ravines meet. Ὄβριμος is not used elsewhere of a great weight of water. The sound implied by δοῦπος is perhaps expressed by Tennyson's 'drumming thunder of the Lugar fall' in *Geraint and Enid*. The arrangement of line 453 gives

---

[1] Anyone inclined to undervalue Homer here should read the story of Hippomedon and the Ismenus in Statius' *Thebaid.*, ix. 315-539.

69

a very happy onomatopoetic effect. Chapman makes the shepherd 'frighted,' and Pope, who is conspicuously unsuccessful in his translation of the simile as a whole, makes him 'tremble.' So Virgil:

Stupet inscius alto
Accipiens sonitum saxi de vertice pastor.
(*Aeneid*, ii. 307.)

The Διομήδους ἀριστεία contains some fine figures. In one, Diomedes rushing over the plain and charging the close battalions of the Trojans, is likened to a torrent that breaks the dykes and the fences of fruitful orchards, and lays low far and wide 'the fair works of active men' (v. 87-94).[1] Homer's implied concern for the husbandman's blighted hopes is thus voiced by Spenser in a simile otherwise nearer to the Greek than other imitations:

'The wofull husbandman doth loud complaine,
  To see his whole yeares labour lost so soone,
  For which to God he made so many an idle boone.'
(*F.Q.*, iii. 7, 34.)

Lucretius, i. 280 ff. and Virgil, *Aeneid*, ii. 496 ff., differ from Homer in details. Burns's flooded Ayr

'Sweeps dams, an' mills, an' brigs a' to the gate.'

At one point in the ἀριστεία of Patroclus the poet wishes to impress us with the tremendous rearing and snorting of Hector's horses and the rattling of his car in the rapid flight from the attack of the Greek hero. He is in a religious mood, and he pictures a day in autumn when the whole earth is darkened with tempest and Zeus pours down rain furiously, being angry with men who give crooked judgments, re-

---

[1] Cp. Ariosto, *Orlando Fur.*, xxxvii. 110; xl. 31.

gardless of the vengeance of the gods. So their rivers run full, and the torrents plough the slopes as they rush headlong from the mountains to the dark sea— μινύθει δέ τε ἔργ' ἀνθρώπων (xvi. 384-393). There is a remarkable and unusually close parallelism in these lines:

ἐς δ' ἅλα πορφυρέην μεγάλα στενάχουσι ῥέουσαι
ὡς ἵπποι Τρωαὶ μεγάλα στενάχοντο θέουσαι.

Virgil imitates the former in the line:

In mare purpureum violentior effluit amnis.

(*Georg.*, iv. 373.)

Ajax too has his river counterpart. As he rushes over the field routing horse and man he is like a river that sweeps along with it many oaks and pines and forces much mud into the sea (xi. 492-97). In xvii. (746-53), Menelaus and Meriones are carrying off the body of Patroclus, and the two Ajaces in the rear keeping off the Trojan attack are compared to a wooded spur of land that juts out over a plain and turns aside a flooded river. In xiii. (136-146), Hector's onset and check are compared to a boulder which a torrent has loosened from a crag. The course of the huge stone, as it bounds along till it reaches the plain, where it rolls no more, must be followed in the original:

ὕψι τ' ἀναθρώσκων πέτεται, κτυπέει δέ θ' ὑπ' αὐτοῦ
ὕλη· ὁ δ' ἀσφαλέως θέει ἔμπεδον, ὄφρ' ἂν ἵκηται
ἰσόπεδον, τότε δ' οὔτι κυλίνδεται, ἐσσύμενός περ.

As Pope says, 'There is a beauty in the numbers: the verses themselves make us see; the sound of them makes us hear what they represent.'

When Odysseus tells to Penelope many false tales

71

to seem like truth, she weeps as she listens, and the poet compares her cheeks melting beneath her tears to the melting of snow on the high hills, which makes the rivers run full (*Ody.*, xix. 203-9). The extended figure fills a pause and marks a point of tension, though it seems to us somewhat grotesque. When the Greeks are in panic, and Agamemnon stands up in the assembly and counsels flight, he is said to weep, 'even as a fountain of black water that from a steep cliff pours its dark stream' (*Il.*, ix. 14, 15). The same words are used of the weeping Patroclus (xvi. 3-4). Some critics take exception to the epithet δνοφερόν applied to running water seen against a rock. Defence of Homer is neither easy nor worth while.[1] In a picturesque simile in which he compares tears that bring relief to a brook which bursts forth from a mountain top, rushes down a rocky slope, thence to a plain, past a highway, where it may refresh the thirsty traveller, Catullus lays stress on the clear whiteness of the water:

> *Qualis in aerei perlucens vertice montis*
> *Rivus muscoso prosilit e lapide*, etc.
>
> (lxviii. 57-62.)

Two more river similes are worth notice, if only for lines that illustrate the correspondence of sound and sense. Diomedes, shrinking in fear at the sight of Ares helping Hector, is likened to a man travelling over a great plain. He is suddenly brought to a stand

---

[1] In a similar figure Euripides calls the water *sunless*—ὡς πέτρας λιβὰς ἀνήλιος (*Andromache*, 534, 5). Commenting on Lucan's *Pharsalia*, iii. 411, 12—

> *Tum plurima nigris*
> *Fontibus unda cadit*—

Weise illustrates by Homer's simile. But Lucan is describing a scene of stagnation and desolation. Why is the water in the cistern mentioned in *Odyssey*, vi. 85-92 called first καλόν and then μέλαν?

by a foaming river which crosses his path. He gazes helplessly and then springs back:

στῆῃ ἐπ' ὠκυρόῳ ποταμῷ ἅλαδε προρέοντι,
ἀφρῷ μορμύροντα ἰδών, ἀνὰ τ' ἔδραμ' ὀπίσσω.

(v. 598-99.)

The noise made by the charging Trojans is like the bellowing sound heard when the waves of the sea and the current of a river meet:

βέβρυχεν μέγα κῦμα ποτὶ ῥόον, ἀμφὶ δέ τ' ἄκραι
ἠϊόνες βοόωσιν ἐρευγομένης ἁλὸς ἔξω.

(vii. 264-65.[1])

And this brings us to the sea:

'I'm on the sea! I'm on the sea!
I am where I would ever be!'

So wrote Barry Cornwall, who feared a furlong voyage. There is no such insincere sentimental twaddle in Greek poetry. The Greeks knew the sea too well to pose as 'light-hearted masters of the waves.' They could observe and admire it from the shore:

ὡς ἡδὺ τὴν θαλάτταν ἀπὸ τῆς γῆς ὁρᾶν [2]

says Archippus, anticipating Lucretius and Horace. 'It is a fearful thing to die among the waves,' thinks Hesiod, an inlander with a single cross-channel passage to his credit. But it is Laodamas, one of the Phaeacians, a nation of sailors, who declares that 'there is nothing worse than the sea to break down a man, however hardy he be.' The Greeks did not tempt the sea at its worst, for they made their voyages in summer only, when they could trust to steady

[1] Cp. Byron's *Giaour*, 620-31; and Swinburne's *Erechtheus*.
[2] Meineke: *Incert. Fab.*, Frag. 1.

73

winds. In the time of Homer commercial enterprise by sea was in its infancy. On the Shield of Achilles the sea is represented along with earth, the heavens, sun, moon, and stars; but there are no seafaring scenes. Trade was mainly in the hands of the Phoenicians, whose seamanship and sharp practice are spoken of with something like envy in the *Odyssey* (xiv., xv., etc.). Odysseus pays them the flattery of imitation, when as a pretended Cretan he makes ten imaginary expeditions; and Menelaus, in his leisurely return from Troy, visits many lands, snapping up sundry 'unconsidered trifles,' which he calls 'gathering much livelihood.' The wonder and curiosity roused by stories of distant voyages is seen in Nestor's description of the vast sea traversed by Menelaus— 'A sea, Oh, so big! ($\pi \acute{\epsilon}\lambda\alpha\gamma o \varsigma \ \mu \acute{\epsilon}\gamma\alpha \ \tau o \hat{\iota}o\nu$). From there not even birds can wing their way in the space of a year, for it is great and terrible' (*Ody.*, iii. 321-22).

Homer has stock epithets and phrases for the sea as well as for the land. Seen in the far distance it is $\mathring{\eta}\epsilon\rho o\epsilon\iota\delta\mathring{\eta}\varsigma$, misty. As a highway for ships it is $\epsilon\mathring{\upsilon}\rho\acute{\upsilon}\pi o\rho o\varsigma$, with wide ways. Its paths are $\mathring{\upsilon}\gamma\rho\grave{\alpha} \ \kappa\acute{\epsilon}\lambda\epsilon\upsilon\theta\alpha$, wet ways, and $\mathring{\upsilon}\gamma\rho\mathring{\eta}$ alone stands for the watery waste in the phrase $\mathring{\epsilon}\pi\grave{\iota} \ \tau\rho\alpha\phi\epsilon\rho\mathring{\eta}\nu \ \tau\epsilon \ \kappa\alpha\grave{\iota} \ \mathring{\upsilon}\gamma\rho\mathring{\eta}\nu$. Its back is broad and its bosom wide ($\epsilon\mathring{\upsilon}\rho\acute{\epsilon}\alpha \ \nu\hat{\omega}\tau\alpha$, $\epsilon\mathring{\upsilon}\rho\acute{\epsilon}\alpha \ \kappa\acute{o}\lambda\pi o\nu$). As opposed to the earth, the grain giver, it is $\mathring{\alpha}\tau\rho\acute{\upsilon}\gamma\epsilon\tau o\varsigma$, barren.[1] The sounding sea is $\pi o\lambda\acute{\upsilon}\phi\lambda o\iota\sigma\beta o\varsigma$, $\mathring{\eta}\chi\mathring{\eta}\epsilon\sigma\sigma\alpha$. When troubled it is $\pi o\rho\phi\acute{\upsilon}\rho\epsilon o\varsigma$, dark; in storm and calm alike it is $\mathring{\iota}o\epsilon\iota\delta\mathring{\eta}\varsigma$, violet-dark, and $o\mathring{\iota}\nu o\psi$, wine-dark. In surge and stress it is $\pi o\lambda\iota\mathring{\eta}$, gray. It is often $\delta\hat{\iota}\alpha$ ($\epsilon\mathring{\iota}\varsigma \ \mathring{\alpha}\lambda\alpha \ \delta\hat{\iota}\alpha\nu$), awful.

The various aspects of the sea supplied the Greek plastic imagination with ample material and produced

---

[1] Some authorities prefer to translate $\mathring{\alpha}\tau\rho\acute{\upsilon}\gamma\epsilon\tau o\varsigma$ *restless*, others *unconquered*, others *inexhaustible*. But *barren* is not out of date.

a rich mythology. The lord of the sea (and of rivers as well) is Poseidon, a dark-haired (κυανοχαίτης) divinity, but not a personification of any one aspect. He is the Earth-supporter (γαιήοχος) and Earth-shaker (ἐννοσίγαιος, ἐνοσίχθων, σεισίχθων)—

γαίης κινητῆρα καὶ ἀτρυγέτοιο θαλάσσης.
(Hymn *To Poseidon*, 2.)

The roaring of the sea is heard in his epithets βαρύκτυπος, ἐρίκτυπος, ἐρισφάραγος. As wielder of the trident he is ὀρσοτρίαινα. In Homer he is worshipped at Helice and has a palace at Aegae (*Ody.*, v. 381; *Il.*, viii. 203; xiii. 17-38, the last a splendid piece of stately narration). He has a wife, Amphitrite,[1] dark-eyed (κυανῶπις) and deep-voiced (ἀγάστονος). Among minor deities there is Phorcys, son of Pontus, of some account in Ithaca (*Ody.*, xiii.). Atlas 'knows the depths of the whole sea.' Proteus, servant of Poseidon, symbolises the ever-changing element. He watches and numbers the seals and tends the flocks of Amphitrite. He can assume any shape at will, and, like other sea-gods, he has the power of divination. Nereus is a venerable and beneficent god, husband of Doris and father of the fifty Nereides. Of these Hesiod gives a catalogue in the *Theogony* (240-64). They have beautiful and expressive names—Galene, 'the peaceful'; Cymothoe, 'swift wave'; Pherousa, 'the speeder of ships'; Eupompe, 'she who gives the good escort'; Cymodoce, 'wave-receiver' (the wave breaking on the rocks); Cymatolege, 'she who stills the waves.' Homer has a similar list in *Iliad*, xviii. (35-51), when they flock round their sister Thetis, and join in her lament for

[1] Amphitrite, 'the Sea that "*moans* (τρίζω, τρύζω) around the shores of earth."' (Jebb in note to Bacchylides, xvi. 111.)

75

the trouble of Achilles. Then all go up upon the shore of Troyland, one after another in long procession (ἐπισχερώ). Once again in Homer the immortal maidens stream up from the sea. Achilles is lying on his bier, and they stand round him wailing and clothe him in the garments of gods (*Ody.*, xxiv. 47-59).

The Greek epic of seafaring, of man on the sea, fills a great part of the first half of the *Odyssey*. It is a romantic story, but it is a romance of adventure, not of sentiment. Nor is it all of a piece. The voyage of Telemachus is, literally, all plain sailing, and we see only its beginning and end. The description of the secret preparations for the start, from the chartering of the vessel to the hauling up of the sail, shows how poetically Homer can handle matters which we moderns consider prosaic and negligible. As we read we are like boys standing on a quay for the first time, lost in wonder at the doings of sailormen. A fresh west wind is whistling, and as the ship glides from her berth, the water hisses round the stem. 'So all night long and through the dawn she bored her way':

παννυχίη μέν ῥ' ἥ γε καὶ ἠῶ πεῖρε κέλευθον.
(*Ody.*, ii. 434.)

The Third and Fourth Books contain narratives of the return from Troy of various heroes, which give a foretaste of the power of Poseidon. In the Fifth, Odysseus sets sail from Calypso's island, and on the eighteenth day he sees in the distance the land of the Phaeacians. Then begins a three days' drama, a struggle between a man and his god, between Odysseus and Poseidon; the god at a far distance shaking his head and muttering, now grasping his trident and troubling the waters, now lashing his steeds of the flowing manes as they race on to Aegae; the man sorrowfully communing with his own brave heart. Our interest is centred on this speck of humanity tossed on a tempestuous sea whose force is individualised as a great wave, μέγα κῦμα. The rising of the storm, the novel ball-play of the winds with the raft, the breakers thundering on the reefs and shrouding the shore in foam, proclaim the poet of the sea-similes in the *Iliad*. The air of realism with which Homer describes the resourcefulness of the hero from the scattering of the raft till the river-mouth is reached, and his picture of the battered sailor lying only not dead, recall Defoe and the landing of Crusoe on his island.

In Books ix. and x. the hero tells of his adventures during the first two years after the fall of Troy. Attempting to double Malea he and his company are driven from their course and find themselves in unknown waters. All is at haphazard. 'Some god' sends a wind, or lulls the waves, or guides them into harbour in the darkness. For many days on end they drift before the wind or with spent spirit row through leagues of calm. They light on this land and on that. Hungering for the sight of 'the labours of men and of oxen,' they encounter strange creatures. Now they feast all day till sunset on flesh galore and drink sweet wine; now for two nights and two days they lie on board, with muffled heads, heart-broken. The tale of them shrinks at each remove; again and again the burden rises:

ἔνθεν δὲ προτέρω πλέομεν ἀκαχήμενοι ἦτορ,
ἄσμενοι ἐκ θανάτοιο, φίλους ὀλέσαντες ἑταίρους.

The interlude of the visit to the underworld fills Book xi. In Book xii. the perils encountered all

77

come from the sea. Nowhere is the narration more vivid. Drawing near to the island of the Sirens they are becalmed, and the crew, aware of the danger, *whiten* the water with their polished pine-blades, the verb λευκαίνω being used for this occasion only instead of the usual τύπτειν ἅλα.[1] As they approach the Planctae, they see 'smoke and a great wave and hear a thundering sound.' The oars fly out of their hands and fall into the water with a splash (203-4). The episode of Scylla and Charybdis is one on which an inferior poet, Statius or Lucan, for instance, would have run wild. Homer, however, is at home in describing a commotion, and in the treatment of Charybdis he knows at what point to stop:

ἀλλ' ὅτ' ἀναβρόξειε θαλάσσης ἁλμυρὸν ὕδωρ,
πᾶσ' ἔντοσθε φάνεσκε κυκωμένη, ἀμφὶ δὲ πέτρῃ
δεινὸν βεβρύχει, ὑπένερθε δὲ γαῖα φάνεσκε
ψάμμῳ κυανέη· τοὺς δὲ χλωρὸν δέος ᾕρει.

(240-43.)

He does not intrude a repetition of Circe's description of Scylla's monstrous form. Pathos swallows up horror in the lines which tell of the fate of six of his men, who stretch out their hands to him in their agony, and call upon him by name for the last time—τότε γ' ὕστατον. The destruction of the vessel with the loss of all the crew, as retribution for the slaughter of the oxen of the Sun, is graphically told. Virgil has imitated the opening lines (*Aen.*, iii. 192 ff.). Homer makes most of the passage do duty again in recounting the disaster which overtook the Phoenicians and their ship (xiv. 301-13). But the words θεὸς δ' ἀποαίνυτο νόστον, 'a god took from them their day of return,' lose most of their pathos when applied to the make-

[1] The vigorous ἀναῤῥίπτω is used when they row for their lives from Laestrygonia and when the expert Phaeacians are the rowers.

shift Phoenicians. The account of the hero's second visit to Scylla and Charybdis is fairly tall, but clever.

Odysseus gained but half of the object of his striving :

ἀρνύμενος ἥν τε ψυχὴν καὶ νόστον ἑταίρων.

He himself reached Ithaca 'on a ship of strangers,' according to the prophecy. The description of the Phaeacian bark carrying home Odysseus sunk in sleep, a sleep 'sound, most sweet, nearest in seeming to death,' speeding more swift than wheeling falcon,[1] and lifting her stern at each bound after the manner of a team of galloping stallions, is a sample of Homer in his altitudes, a joy for ever.

When reading Homer we must put out of our minds our own modern conditions of seafaring. The Homeric ship had but one sail, its rudder was a hand-paddle, and it was decked only in part. Sailors had no means of 'dodging breezes and circumventing the winds of heaven.' The Northmen of the *Beowulf* were probably more at home on the sea than the Greeks of Homer's time. They sailed on less inviting waters; the waves are always 'wan,' 'brown,' 'murky,' 'fallow.' Homer does not dwell on the *coldness* of the sea. In Old English poetry the sea is 'ice-cold' and 'rime-cold,' and we meet with the epithet *sǣ-ceald*. The poets of *The Seafarer* and *The Wanderer* bemoan the comfortless night-watches, the rime, the snow, the hail showers, the feet imprisoned in ice-shackles. Sailors fear the rise of the water-terror (*waeter-egesa*). Compared with that of Old English poetry the sea-vocabulary of Homer is

---

[1] Cp. Byron's *Childe Harold*:

> 'Our fleetest falcon scarce can fly
> More merrily along.'

One of the few similes in *Beowulf* compares a ship to a bird—*fugle gelīcost* (218).

simple and limited. In a community that has been long in touch with the sea a stock of highly specialised terms grows up. But much of the Old English nautical vocabulary is purely literary and rhetorical. There are long lists of periphrastic terms to denote various aspects of the waters, compounds of *sǣ* and *ȳð* and *sund* and *brim*. *Sund-geblond*, *ȳð-geblond*, *ȳð-geweale*, *sǣ-wylm*, *brim-wylm*, etc., denote the surge and welter of the waves. Homer uses the expression ἰχθυόεντα κέλευθα: in Old English the sea is 'the fishes'-bath,' 'the gannets'-bath,' 'the whale-road,' 'the whales'-home,' etc. In Old English, kennings for *ship* can be counted by the score. Homer calls ships ἁλὸς ἵπποι: in Old English the sea-horse notion is expressed by *sǣ-hengest*, *brim-hengest*, *ȳð-hengest*, *sǣ-mearh*, etc.

In drama the finest description of a destructive storm at sea is in *Agamemnon*, 650-80, when fire and water, 'old wranglers, took a truce.' It is in the poet's most weighty, pregnant style, to which no translation can do justice. It is night. The ships dash against one another, 'butting and butted with violence beneath the force of the hurricane and the beating rain of the surge, on, on, out of sight, like cattle made spin before the whirlwind blows of an evil herdsman':

αἱ δὲ κεροτυπούμεναι βίᾳ
χειμῶνι τυφῶ σὺν ζάλῃ τ' ὀμβροκτύπῳ
ᾤχοντ' ἄφαντοι, ποιμένος κακοῦ στρόβῳ.

Day dawns:

ὁρῶμεν ἀνθοῦν πέλαγος Αἰγαῖον νεκροῖς
ἀνδρῶν Ἀχαιῶν ναυτικοῖς τ' ἐρειπίοις.[1]

---

[1] 'The sea is the plain or field which in the morning is seen to have broken out in flowers after the rain' (Verrall). But it is possible to drive even Aeschylean metaphors too hard, and prove a ποιμὴν κακός.

Agamemnon's ship and crew are saved, for 'Saviour Fortune with good-will took her seat aboard':

$$Τύχη \ δὲ \ σωτὴρ \ ναῦν \ θέλουσ' \ ἐφέζετο.$$

No doubt Τύχη is chosen to play the part of a kindly Ariel, because she was a Nereid (Homeric Hymn, *To Demeter*, 420), and, according to Pindar, she piloted swift ships over the deep (*Oly.*, xii. 3).

In the *Persae* Aeschylus gave to the Greeks what Shakespeare did not give to Englishmen, a play dealing with a recent naval victory. Such a play it would have been impossible for Shakespeare to produce on his ordinary methods. Owing to the individualising character of his romantic drama, many separate scenes and a large body of actors, some of them representing persons still living, would have been necessary. Shakespeare wisely preferred to go to his grave with his head on his shoulders. But by means of Chorus and Messenger Aeschylus could give epic and lyric treatment to his theme without invidious mention of Greek names; while, by laying the scene at Susa, he could portray the successive changes in the spirit of the Persians, and bring home to his countrymen the magnitude of the menace and the completeness of the victory. Hearts would beat hard while the actor declaimed the thrilling passage beginning

$$ἐπεί \ γε \ μέντοι \ λευκόπωλος \ ἡμέρα.$$

In the theatre there would be many who, as combatants or spectators from the shore of Salamis, would have vivid recollections of the scene of slaughter and the subsequent gruesome sights in the narrow sea. Even the most serious faces would relax at the account of the fate of Persian commanders—Dadaces' nimble

F   81

leap from his ship, $\pi\lambda\eta\gamma\hat{\eta}$ $\delta o\rho\acute{o}\varsigma$, and the bushy black beard of Matallus dyed purple—'something rich and strange.' The audience would be familiar with stories of Persian sufferings in the retreat and the crossing of the Strymon. Athenian salts would smile at the grave boast of their enemies having '*learned* to look upon the sacred expanse ($\mathring{a}\lambda\sigma o\varsigma$) of the broad sea whitened by the violent blast, trusting to fine-spun cables, contrivances for transporting hosts' (110-12). We think of Shelley's *Ode to the West Wind*, where he takes advantage of the original meaning of $\mathring{a}\lambda\sigma o\varsigma$:

'Thou
For whose path the Atlantic's level powers
Cleave themselves into chasms, while far below
The sea-blooms and the oozy woods which wear
The sapless foliage of the ocean know
Thy voice, and suddenly grow grey with fear,
And tremble and despoil themselves: Oh hear!'

and of Swinburne's *Erechtheus*:

'And the depths of the sea were aghast, and whitened,
And the crowns of their waves were as flame that lightened.'

Both poets knew their Aeschylus well.

Euripides sometimes writes of the sea in a manner which might be called mythologico-sentimental, and he is the Greek poet who comes nearest to modern feeling for a piping wind and music in the shrouds:

'A wet sheet and a flowing sea,
A wind that follows fast
And fills the white and rustling sail
And bends the gallant mast.'

In *Iphigeneia in Tauris* the Chorus imagine the ship of Orestes and Pylades running before a south wind, the sail bellying and the steady steering-oar hissing at the stern (430-33). Again, they picture the fifty-oared Argive vessel carrying Iphigeneia to splendid Athens, the rowers keeping time to the music of Pan's pipe and the seven-stringed lyre of Apollo, while the taut sheet-lines spread out sails to the breeze past the forestays and over the bow of the good ship scudding along (1123-36). The ship of Helen is apostrophised as 'Mother of foam, dear to rowers, leader of the dolphins beautiful in the dance, when the sea is windless, and Galaneia, azure daughter of Pontus, cries, "Shake out the sails! To the pine-blades, ye mariners! Speed Helen to the sheltering shores of Perseus' ancient home!"' (*Helena*, 1451-64.) In a similar apostrophe, the ships that went to Troy with Achilles are said to be escorted by dancing Nereids,[1] while the music-loving dolphin gambols round the dark prows (*Electra*, 432-41). At the marriage of Peleus and Thetis the Nereids dance in mazy circles on the white sand (*Iph. at A.*, 1055-58).

Though dolphins still play round ships in the Mediterranean, they are now most poetical in their picturesque dying hours:

> 'The dolphin, whom each pang imbues
> With a new colour as it gasps away—
> The last still loveliest.'

But the Greeks looked upon dolphins as 'the horses of the sea,' miraculous carriers, and famous for speed (Pindar, *Pyth.*, ii. 51; *Nem.*, vi. 66). They were supposed to like music, and Pindar calls them ταμίαι σοφοὶ Μοισᾶν (*Isth.*, Frag., i.). In the above instance

---

[1] Cp. Sophocles, *Oed. Col.*, 719.

they would be attracted by the τριηραύλης on board, just as one of their kind had been charmed by the Orthian strain of Arion.[1]

The Nereids, graceful and gracious beings, represent the more peaceful and inviting aspects of the sea, the manifold changes on its face as seen beneath an Eastern sky. 'The sheen on the waves' is in ἀργυρόπεζα, the epithet of Thetis—Milton's not altogether admirable 'Thetis' tinsel-slipper'd feet.' Instead of Galaneia (Galene) Milton selects Panope:

'On the level brine
Sleek Panope with all her sisters play'd.'

His 'Leucothea's lovely hands' is represented in Homer by καλλίσφυρος Ἰνώ, Λευκοθέη, daughter of Cadmus, to whom Zeus gave endless life and joy of life in the sea (Pindar, *Pyth.*, xi. 4). Thetis is καλλι-πλόκαμος, but Milton's

'Fair Ligea's golden comb'

is a product of Northern mythology. Nereids have golden distaffs (χρυσηλάκατοι), a mark of sex rather than of industry, though Naiads at least are diligent weavers. In fact, Milton's Ligea is the Greek Λίγεια, who, after Homer's time, figures as one of the Sirens; and the water-spirits of the Baltic and the North Sea have more in common with the Sirens than with the Nereids. The Nereids are well-disposed to mortals, but their Northern sisters are malicious and use their personal attractions as allurements to ill-starred unions with men.[2] The marriage of Thetis with Peleus was exceptional—a *mariage de convenance* and against her will, hence her transformations, which have parallels in our own fairy lore.

[1] For *Apollo Delphinius* see Homeric Hymn *To Pythian Apollo*, 474-501.
[2] Mermaids play a part in the *Nibelungenlied*, xxv.

84

Homer has his horrible Scylla—the product of sailors' fears and tall talk about dangerous rocks. Odysseus fears the many monsters fed by Amphitrite (*Ody.*, v. 422). Few such, however—κήτεα or κνώδαλα —are specially named in Greek poetry. Homer knew the polypus (*Ody.*, v. 432). In Aeschylus' *Choephoroe*, 994, a sort of sea-serpent, μύραινα, is mentioned and intended to be terrifying. But it is not of the kind sometimes seen and described nowadays by 'credulous sailors, imaginative landsmen, and common liars'; for in Aristophanes' *Frogs*, 475, commentators shrivel it to a lamprey. Homer refers to the sea-beast sent by Poseidon against Troy (*Il.*, xx. 147). In the magnificent Messenger's speech which recounts the circumstances of the death of Hippolytus the effect is all the greater from the fact that Euripides does not attempt precise description of the sea-monster. First it is ταῦρος, ἄγριον τέρας (1214), then ταῦρος (1229), then τὸ δύστηνον τέρας ταύρου (1247). In *Phèdre*, on the other hand, Racine is tempted to particularise:

'Son front large est armé de cornes menaçantes;
Tout son corps est couvert d'écailles jaunissantes;
Indomptable taureau, dragon impetueux,
Sa croupe se recourbe en replis tortueux.' [1]

In Greek poetry there is at least one notable picture of 'the world below the brine.' It is in Bacchylides, Ode XVI., one of the most beautiful of his extant poems. The theme turns on the legend of the double paternity of Theseus. A ship is sailing from Athens on the way to Crete with the destined victims of the Minotaur. Minos and Theseus are on board. Minos throws a ring into the sea and challenges Theseus to

[1] Racine follows Seneca rather than Euripides.

85

bring it back to him, if he be, as he asserts, the son of Poseidon. Theseus leaps from the stern, and the ship speeds on. 'Meanwhile, dolphins, dwellers in the sea, were swiftly bearing mighty Theseus to the abode of his sire, lord of steeds; and he came unto the hall of the gods. There beheld he the glorious daughters of blest Nereus, and was awe-struck; for a splendour as of fire shone from their radiant forms; fillets inwoven with gold encircled their hair; and they were delighting their hearts by dancing with lissom feet. And in that beautiful abode he saw his father's well-loved wife, the stately, ox-eyed Amphitrite; who clad him in gleaming purple, and set on his thick hair a choice wreath, dark with roses, given to her of yore at her marriage by wily Aphrodite.' [1]

. This is a picture of something *on* rather than *of* the ocean-floor. Not a word of the sunken treasures, mortal relics, sea-blooms, pearled thrones, crystalline columns, gleaming diamonds, glowing amber, and blushing coral of Shakespeare, Shelley, and Keats. It is a 'beautiful abode'—ἐρατοῖσι δόμοις—Homer's ἀργύφεον σπέος. The splendour is that of the bright forms of goddesses and glorious attire. The lines treat a situation in a myth, and the poem is a paean to Apollo, to be sung at a Delian festival. The quotation is a cameo, suggested by vase paintings, in Bacchylides' characteristic manner, elegant, picturesque, full of colour, and serene.

For the present, let us pass over Pindar lightly. He has occasional sculpturesque phrases, such as βαθυκρήμνου πολιᾶς ἀλὸς θέναρ (*Isth.*, iv. 56). Most arresting is the invocation of Jason at the start of *Argo*: 'The leader took a golden goblet in his

---

[1] Jebb's translation.

hands, and stood on the stern, and called on Zeus, father of the Heavenly One, whose spear is the thunderbolt, and the swift blasts of winds and rush of waves, and the nights and paths of the deep, and days of gladness, and a kind fate in the return' (*Pyth.*, iv. 193-96).

Quieter than these rolling rhythms, but of an indefinable charm, are the words in the same ode that tell of the disappearance of the fateful clod of earth: 'Now I hear that it was washed overboard, and went into the sea with the spray, following the flowing waters of the main, at eventide' (38-40).

The pathos of human helplessness on the sea is found in the Threnos of Simonides (*Bergk*, 37), where the outcast Danae in the drifting ark talks to her babe lying cosy in the darkness, unconscious of wind and wave:

> ἅλμαν δ' ὕπερθε τεᾶν κομᾶν βαθεῖαν
> περιόντος κύματος οὐκ ἀλέγεις,
> οὐδ' ἀνέμου φθόγγον πορφυρέᾳ
> κείμενος ἐν χλανίδι. . . .
> . . . εὗδε βρέφος, εὑδέτω δὲ πόντος,
> εὑδέτω δ' ἄμετρον κακόν.

Here too we may put the lines of Alcman, perhaps part of a Parthenion (*Bergk*, 21): 'No longer, ye maidens, sweet-voiced singers of lovely songs, no longer will my limbs bear me. Would I were a ceryl-bird,[1] that flies over the flower of the wave with the halcyons, no care at his heart, sea-blue bird of the spring.' But read the original, which drops honey and distils as the dew:

> Οὔ μ' ἔτι, παρθενικαὶ μελιγάρυες ἱμερόφωνοι,
> γυῖα φέρειν δύναται· βάλε δὴ βάλε κηρύλος εἴην,

---

[1] Male halcyon; when feeble with age it is carried on the wings of the females.

NATURE IN GREEK POETRY

ὅς τ᾽ ἐπὶ κύματος ἄνθος ἅμ᾽ ἀλκυόνεσσι ποτῆται
νηλεγὲς ἦτορ ἔχων, ἀλιπόρφυρος εἴαρος ὄρνις.[1]

We do not see much of the calm sea. This line
is supposed to be Alcman's—χερσόνδε κωφὸν ἐν φύ-
κεσσι πιτνεῖ (*Bergk*, 6): '(The wave) falls hushed on
the beach among the sea-weed.' Once read never
to be forgotten are the words that fall unexpectedly
from the lips of the Herald in the *Agamemnon*, when
he is describing the climatic conditions in Troyland.
'O the heat!' says the fellow. Like Balak we look
for a curse from this Balaam; but lo, a blessing!

εὖτε πόντος ἐν μεσημβριναῖς
κοίταις ἀκύμων νηνέμοις εὗδοι πεσών.

(565-66.)

Conington's translation runs—'When on his mid-day
couch windless and waveless ocean sank to sleep.'
Compare Tennyson's

'Calm on the seas, and silver sleep,
And waves that sway themselves in rest.'

Aristophanes has his

κύματά τ᾽ ἔσβεσε νήνεμος αἴθρη.

(*Birds*, 778.)

And Aeschylus again—

ποντίων τε κυμάτων
ἀνήριθμον γέλασμα,

(*Prom. B.*, 89-90.)[2]

which, who can translate, may. Shelley, more

---

[1] Suggested Tennyson's 'sea-blue bird of March.' For the fable of
the halcyon days see Simonides, *Bergk*, 12.
[2] With these is associated the Helen figure φρόνημα νηνέμου γαλάνας
(*Agam.*, 740).

expansively, gives the sense of the two snatches from Aeschylus:

> 'The lightest wind was in its nest,
>   The tempest in its home,
> The whispering waves were half asleep,
>   The clouds were gone to play,
> And on the bosom of the deep
>   The smile of heaven lay.'

Euripides includes a calm sea among the fair sights possible to man, fair yet not so fair as the light of children in the home:

γύναι, φίλον μὲν φέγγος ἡλίου τόδε,
καλὸν δὲ πόντου χεῦμ' ἰδεῖν εὐήνεμον,
γῆ τ' ἠρινὸν θάλλουσα πλούσιόν θ' ὕδωρ,
πολλῶν τ' ἔπαινόν ἔστί μοι λέξαι καλῶν·
ἀλλ' οὐδὲν οὕτω λαμπρὸν οὐδ' ἰδεῖν καλὸν
ὡς τοῖς ἄπαισι καὶ πόθῳ δεδηγμένοις
παίδων νεογνῶν ἐν δόμοις ἰδεῖν φάος.

(Nauck, Danae, Frag.)

No poetry is richer than the Greek in analogies between the sea and the world of man. In the *Iliad* Homer draws many of his similes from the movement of the sea. Owing to the nature of his subject these figures generally illustrate action, illustrate it and aggrandise it. Seldom do the illustration and the thing illustrated fit each other like hand and glove. 'Secure of the main likeness,' says Pope, 'Homer makes no scruple to play with the circumstances.' *Fervet opus*: 'It is joy to see his business.'

The assembly of the Greeks sways like the long waves on the Icarian sea (ii. 144-46). As the Greeks hasten back to the assembly the noise is like the roaring of waves on the beach: σμαραγεῖ δέ τε πόντος

(ii. 207-10).[1] The Greeks moving to the first encounter, rank upon rank, are likened to wave after wave driven on by the west wind, rising to a head out at sea, breaking with a roar on the beach, curling and arching round the promontories, and spitting far the foam (iv. 422-28).[2] The sound, and much else besides, is not necessary for the comparison:

> 'Save heavy tread, and armour's clang,
> The sullen march was dumb.'

Catullus uses a similar figure in describing the departure of guests streaming out from palace gates. It is an early morning scene and the waves reflect the light of dawn:

> *Purpureaque procul nantes ab luce refulgent.*
>
> (lxiv. 269-75.)

Scott is Homeric in the following:

> 'Now onward, and in open view,
> The countless ranks of England drew,
> Dark-rolling like the ocean-tide,
> When the rough west hath chafed his pride,
> And his deep roar sends challenge wide
> To all that bars his way.'
>
> (*Lord of the Isles*, vi.)

In *Iliad*, vii. (61-66) the close ranks of the hosts, bristling with shields and helmets and spears, are compared to the ripple caused by the west wind, which spreads over the sea—μελάνει δέ τε πόντος ὑπ' αὐτῆς. Homer's φρὶξ Ζεφύροιο is Catullus's *horrificans Zephyrus*, Virgil's *inhorruit unda tenebris*, and Lucan's *niger inficit horror Terga maris* (*Phars.*, v. 564-65).

Sudden squalls coming from the mountains off the

---

[1] See also ii. 394-97.
[2] Cp. Virgil, *Aeneid*, vii. 528; and Silius Italicus, *Punica*, 1, 468.

coast suggested other similes. Hector bursts upon the fight:

$$\text{ὑπεραέϊ ἶσος ἀέλλῃ}$$
$$\text{ἥτε καθαλλομένη ἰοειδέα πόντον ὀρίνει.}$$

(xi. 297-98.)

The same hero smiting the enemy is likened to the west wind in a hurricane sweeping before it the clouds gathered by the south wind. But Homer brings his κῦμα into action in the memorable lines:

$$\text{πολλὸν δέ τρόφι κῦμα κυλίνδεται, ὑψόσε δ' ἄχνη}$$
$$\text{σκίδναται ἐξ ἀνέμοιο πολυπλάγκτοιο ἰωῆς.}$$

(xi. 305-9.)

What is, in some respects, the finest simile of the series opens with another squall, which falls upon the sea with terrific roar. Then follows a grand picture of multitudinous waves, some before, some behind, all churning and seething, curling and cresting and foaming:

$$\text{θεσπεσίῳ δ' ὁμάδῳ ἀλὶ μίσγεται, ἐν δέ τε πολλὰ}$$
$$\text{κύματα παφλάζοντα πολυφλοίσβοιο θαλάσσης,}$$
$$\text{κυρτά, φαληριόωντα, πρὸ μέν τ' ἄλλ', αὐτὰρ ἐπ' ἄλλα.}$$

(xiii. 797-99.)

When these and similar lines face him, the boldest and craftiest English verse-translator must feel how weak is his uninflected language compared with Greek —Homer's Greek.

The fight at the ships is illustrated by a rich variety of figures. The Greeks stand firm against Hector's attack, like a rock that abides the coming of shrill winds and the swelling waves that soar against it (xv. 618-21). Virgil's imitation ends with an original touch—*laterique illisa refunditur alga* (*Aeneid*,

vii. 590). The following lines are an instance of
Swinburne's rapid, tangential, and telescopic manner:

> 'As the arched wave's weight against the reef
> Hurls, and is hurled back like a leaf
> Storm-shrivelled, and its rage of grief
> Speaks all the loud broad sea in brief,
> And quells the hearkening hearts of men.'
>
> *(Tale of Balen.)*

Then Hector leaps into the throng as a wave falls on
a swift ship. The vessel is buried in foam, the blast
roars in the sail, and the sailors tremble in their
hearts, for death is very near. The figure has a
double application, the fear of the sailors being
paralleled by the vexed hearts of the Greeks.
Longinus has high praise for Homer here (x.).
Besides other felicities, note the protracted recurrence
of dentals in the following:

> ἀνέμοιο δὲ δεινὸς ἀήτης
> ἱστίῳ ἐμβρέμεται· τρομέουσι δέ τε φρένα ναῦται
> δειδιότες, τυτθὸν γὰρ ὑπ' ἐκ θανάτοιο φέρονται·
> ὣς ἐδαΐζετο θυμὸς ἐνὶ στήθεσσιν Ἀχαιῶν.
>
> (xv. 626-29.)

A few other similes illustrate a state of mind. The
Greeks are in panic, and their souls are troubled like
the sea by the action of two winds meeting (ix. 1-8).[1]
Chapman's translation is worth quoting for its quaint-
ness and for his use of the word *blore*, now lost to
the language:

> 'And as two lateral-sited winds, the West wind and
> the North,
> Meet at the Thracian sea's black breast, join in a
> sudden blore,

[1] Cp. Lucan, *Phars.*, ii. 454-60.

Tumble together the dark waves, and pour upon the
shore
A mighty deal of froth and weed, with which men
manure ground;
So Jove and Troy did drive the Greeks, and all their
minds confound.'

Nestor in doubt is like the deep troubled with a
dumb wave, which idly waits for a sure wind (xiv.
16-21).[1] Chapman says the sea

'Pants and swells confusedly, here goes, and there
will stay.'

Compare Lucan's line:

Et dubium pendet vento cui pareat aequor.
                                    (*Phars.*, v. 602.)

Hector and Paris issuing from the gates are as welcome
to the Trojans as a wind to sailors weary with rowing
(vii. 1-7). The brightness of Achilles' shield is like
to a fire in a lonely steading on the hills, seen from
the sea by sailors whom winds bear all unwilling over
the waters, far from their friends (xix. 375-80). The
fire, whatever its exact nature, makes them think of
home. This is Chapman's alarming interpretation:

'And as from sea sailors discern a harmful fire let run
By herdsmen's faults, till all their stall flies up in
wrastling flame,
Which being on hills is seen far off, but being alone,
none came
To give it quench, at shore no neighbours, and at sea
their friends.'

One instinctively thinks of the plight of Odysseus
when the winds bear him far from Ithaca,

[1] Cp. Thomson, *Winter*, 148; Tennyson, *Merlin and Vivien*.

after he has been so near it as to see men tending the watch-fires (*Ody.*, x. 29, 30).[1] The *Odyssey* furnishes one simile. The sight of Odysseus is as welcome to Penelope as land to ship-wrecked sailors (xxiii. 235-39).[2]

Outside of Homer there are few Homeric similes. We find one in Bacchylides (xii. 134-140) in the midst of a Homeric episode. The thankfulness of the Trojans, when they hear that Achilles tarries in his tent on account of Briseis, is like that of sailors who, in the morning, find a calm sea and reach the haven, after having been buffeted all night by Boreas on the Thracian sea. Sophocles provides three. In *Oedipus Coloneus*, 1239-48, the Chorus liken the aged Oedipus to a cape lashed on all sides by wintry waves; troubles break upon him like billows from all quarters— west, east, south, and north:

$$αἱ μὲν ἀπ' ἀελίου δυσμᾶν,$$
$$αἱ δ' ἀνατέλλοντος,$$
$$αἱ δ' ἀνὰ μέσσαν ἀκτῖν',$$
$$αἱ δὲ νυχιᾶν ἀπὸ 'Ριπᾶν.$$

The curse passing from generation to generation is like the surf driven over the dark sea by Thracian winds, and rolling the black sand from the depths, while the headlands roar beneath the blows of the storm (*Antigone*, 583-91). The toils of Heracles are thick as waves on the Cretan sea; as one goes another comes (*Trachiniae*, 112-20).

Euripides has very few detailed sea-similes, *Heracleidae*, 427-32, and *Troades*, 681-91, being conspicuous exceptions. These, however, are not Homeric in form, and as the point of comparison is found in the

[1] Imitated by Matthew Arnold in *Balder Dead*, iii.
[2] Cp. Spenser, *F.Q.*, i. 3, 31.

plight of the ship and the crew, they might be called nautical figures. Nautical metaphors abound in the tragedians. Λιμήν in a metaphorical sense is of as frequent occurrence as κακῶν πέλαγος and its many variants. When Aeschylus can term Parthenopaeus a βλάστημα καλλίπρῳρον (S.C.T., 533) and can speak of the στόματος καλλιπρῴρου of Iphigeneia (Agam., 235), we see how easily such figures came to Athenian poets. The metaphor or allegory of the Ship of State had a long run in Greek poetry. It is found first in Archilochus (Bergk, 54), if, as is possible, the lines are to be understood metaphorically. It appears in Theognis, 667-82. Better known is the fragment of Alcaeus (Bergk, 18), which refers figuratively to the political troubles under the tyrant Myrsilus. Horace imitated Alcaeus in Odes, i. 14, but without catching the realistic spirit of the Greek. The Septem Contra Thebas of Aeschylus opens with a similar figure, and it reappears at intervals throughout the play. Eteocles is a helmsman on the poop (1-3). The Messenger bids him make firm the bulwarks of the vessel, before the blasts of Ares sweep over them, for a land-wave is roaring—βοᾷ γὰρ κῦμα χερσαῖον στρατοῦ (62-64). See also 114-15; 208-10; 602-4; 758-61. The end matches the beginning: the helmsman is no more, but he, after the gods, has saved the city from being overwhelmed by a wave of aliens. Sophocles makes use of the figure in Antigone, 162 and 189, and in Oedipus Tyrannus, 22; Euripides in Andromache, 479-84, and in Orestes, 698-709, etc.[1]

No moral metaphor of the nautical kind is finer than one in Aeschylus' Eumenides (558-65). The froward transgressor shall soon find his vessel of injustice labouring in a tempestuous sea, with broken yard-

[1] This figure is often used to good purpose by Swinburne in Erechtheus.

arm. From the midst of the whirlpool he calls, but no one hears. An angry god laughs at the rash fool. His fortunes founder on the reef of avenging justice, and no eye pities him. Another metaphor characteristic of Aeschylus is that in which Cassandra tersely blends wind and wave and sun. 'And now my oracular word shall no longer look out from a veil like a newly-wedded bride; but it shall come as a clear fresh wind blowing toward the sunrise, to dash in a wave to the light a woe far greater than this' (*Agam.*, 1178-1183). It is morning on the sea; a strong wind is blowing and the sunlight is playing on the rolling waves.

Sometimes poets speak of themselves as sailors or ships and their poems as ships or cargoes. But there is nothing in Greek poetry to be compared with the voyage of the bark of the spirit on mystic deeps in Shelley's *Adonais* and Tennyson's *Crossing the Bar*.

Bacchylides opens an ode with the words, 'I will go towards the temple of Apollo at Pytho, since fair-throned Urania has sent me from Pieria a golden galley laden with glorious songs' (xv. 1-4). Pindar, however, has a place all his own in nautical metaphor. Such figures are most frequent in his celebrations of Aeginetan victors, but few of his odes are without an occasional whiff of the sea, whether he is speaking of his own art and the difficulties of his task, or flattering a patron, or vending maxims of worldly wisdom, or giving utterance to some deeper moral reflection. His poems, he tells us, are not statues that stand idly on their pedestals: 'O sweet song, fare from Aegina on board of every merchantman and skiff to carry the tidings' (*Nem.*, v. 1-4). Some of his songs did so literally. His odes are ships. 'My soul, to what promontory of a strange land dost thou turn aside the course of my ship?' (*Nem.*, iii. 26, 27). Lest the ship be dashed on the rocks of a long story he gives orders to anchor fast (*Pyth.*, x. 51). He sails as a privateer 'in the fleet of common joy' (*Oly.*, xiii. 49). His song is a wave that sweeps away the shingle of debt (*Oly.*, x. 9, 10). He is up to the waist in the sea of myth (*Nem.*, iv. 36). He hopes to swim out of a sea of victories (*Oly.*, xiii. 114). Two homes are as two anchors in a storm (*Oly.*, vi. 100, 101). To speak out loud is to hoist the sail to the topyard (*Nem.*, v. 50, 51). To stint hospitality is to take in sail (*Isth.*, ii. 39-42). To have attained to the highest excellence is to have reached the Pillars of Heracles: 'Beyond Gadeira to the darkness of the west one may not pass' (*Nem.*, iii. 20, 21; cp. iv. 69, 70; *Oly.*, iii. 44). The Bassidae, an ancient clan, 'carry in their vessels the burden of their own renown' (*Nem.*, vi. 32, 33). Tranquillity (ἡσυχία) can sometimes be angry and sink the vessel of Insolence (ὕβρις) (*Pyth.*, viii. 11). 'Up and down men's hopes are often tossed, as they plough a sea of airy illusions' (*Oly.*, xii. 5, 6). 'To all men alike comes the wave of Death; yea, it falls on one expecting it and on another at unawares' (*Nem.*, vii. 30, 31).

CHAPTER V

SOME NATURAL PHENOMENA (I)

IN its widest sense the subject of this chapter would include an inquiry into the origin and meaning of a whole section of mythology and an examination of the physical theories of the ancient Greeks. It would be necessary to try to gather into a reasoned whole those notions and hypotheses which served in place of astronomical records and reports of Weather Bureaus. We are dealing, however, with a time when science was largely indistinguishable from popular fancy. Science had not yet a go-cart of her own but rode on the splendid car of Poetry. This renders it impossible to examine the one entirely apart from the other. But it is possible to pay chief regard to the poetry of the science rather than to the science in the poetry, to endeavour to show how the poet's 'commercing with the skies' is reflected in his use of natural phenomena for the purposes of description and illustration.

Homer's map of the heavens is given in his account of the Shield of Achilles. 'On it he fashioned the earth, and the heavens, and the sea, and the untiring sun, and the full moon, and all the signs wherewith the heavens are crowned, Pleiades and Hyades and the might of Orion, and the Bear that men call also the Wain, and that turns in her place and watches Orion, and alone has no part in the baths of Ocean'

(*Il.*, xviii. 483-89). From a passage in the Odyssey (v. 272-5) we learn that Homer knows 'Boötes that sets late.' In Hesiod we find the same stars mentioned, with the addition of Sirius, which Homer calls 'Orion's dog' (*Il.*, xxii. 29). Hesiod knows Boötes and the name Arcturus as well. Homer does not know the Little Bear, the name of which is said to have been introduced from the East by Thales; and Ἑλίκη is not found in poetry before Alexandrian times. Homer knows the Evening Star, Ἕσπερος (*Il.*, xxii. 318), and the Morning Star, Ἑωσφόρος (*Il.*, xxiii. 226); but neither he nor Hesiod is aware that these are names for one and the same star under different aspects. There is a reference to the solstice in *Odyssey*, xv. 403-4: 'There is an island called Syria, if perchance thou hast heard, beyond Ortygia, where are the turnings of the sun.' The Sun is a god, who hears and sees all things, and he brings light and joy to men (φαεσίμβροτος, τερψίμβροτος). Dawn is a goddess, but Homer has no Moon-goddess. Night is personified in Hesiod, but in Homer only in *Iliad*, xiv. 259-62, with any distinctness. It is rather remarkable that in Homer the Sun has no car and horses, and that horses are assigned to Dawn in *Odyssey*, xxiii. 246 only. In the Homeric Hymns Ἥλιος, Ἠώς, and Σελήνη[1] have their teams. In his description of the tapestry in *Ion*, 1122-65, Euripides gives Ἥλιος and Νύξ their steeds, and here for the first time we find φωσφόρος used in conjunction with Ἕως. In *Orestes*, 1004, Dawn is called μονόπωλος,

---

[1] In the Hymn *To Selene*, the epithet τανυσίπτερος, 'long-winged,' is used of the Moon. In their edition of the Hymns, Sikes and Allen consider this a sign of late composition—'There appears to be no other example of a winged Selene in literature, and the type is very uncertain in art.' The Moon has wings in Manilius' *Astronomica*, i. 218—

Ultima ad Hesperios infectis volveris alis.

perhaps in contrast with the stronger Sun. On vase-paintings Selene is often represented riding on a single steed.

Homer's dawns and sunrises are brief formulae, but as such they show ingenious variety. The following are types:

Ἠὼς μὲν κροκόπεπλος ἐκίδνατο πᾶσαν ἐπ' αἶαν.

Ἠὼς δ' ἐκ λεχέων παρ' ἀγαυοῦ Τιθωνοῖο
ὤρνυθ' ἵν' ἀθανάτοισι φόως φέροι ἠδὲ βροτοῖσι.

ἦμος δ' ἠριγένεια φάνη ῥοδοδάκτυλος Ἠώς.

This is his most lengthy form:

Ἠέλιος δ' ἀνόρουσε λιπὼν περικαλλέα λίμνην,
οὐρανὸν ἐς πολύχαλκον ἵν' ἀθανάτοισι φαείνοι
καὶ θνητοῖσι βροτοῖσιν ἐπὶ ζείδωρον ἄρουραν.

He often synchronises the end of a speech or an action with the phenomenon:

ὣς ἔφατ', αὐτίκα δὲ χρυσόθρονος ἤλυθεν Ἠώς.

His sunsets are sudden and sharp, like the oncoming of night in the East:

ἐν δ' ἔπεσ' Ὠκεανῷ λαμπρὸν φάος ἠελίοιο.

δύσετό τ' ἠέλιος σκιόωντό τε πᾶσαι ἀγυιαί.

ὣς ἔφατ', ἠέλιος δ' ἄρ' ἔδυ καὶ ἐπὶ κνέφας ἦλθε.

In these and similar instances the beautiful compounds κροκόπεπλος, ῥοδοδάκτυλος, χρυσόθρονος are the only words of colour. But the artistry is perfect. Contrast the following lines of simpler and ruder art from *La Chanson de Roland*:

'Bels fut li jurz, si prist a decliner.'

'Bels est li jurz, e li soleilz est clers.'

'Tresvait li jurz, la noit est aserie.'

'Tresvait la noit, e apert la clere albe.'[1]

In Homer there is no system of *Kennings* or periphrastic synonyms, so characteristic of Old English— *rodores candel*, 'the candle of the sky'; *woruld-candel*, 'the candle of the world'; *heofones gim*, 'the jewel of heaven,' all standing for 'the sun'; *scadu-helm*, 'shadow-covering'; *niht-helm*, 'night-cover' for 'the darkness of night.' The following are typical expressions in *Beowulf* for the coming or the departure of light:

Woruld-candel scān
Sigel sūðan fūs.

'The world-candle shone, the sun, hastening from the south.'

Syððan heofones gim
glād ofer grundas.

'When the jewel of heaven had glided away over the lands.'

Niht-helm geswearc
deorc ofer dryht-gumum.

'The cover of night grew dim and dark over the warriors.'

Homer's light of morning is almost static. It strikes upon the fields and spreads over the land or

---

[1] In Modern French:—

Le jour fut beau, et commençait à decliner.
Le jour est beau, le soleil clair.
Le jour s'en va, la nuit se fait noire.
La nuit s'en va, et l'aube apparaît claire.

the sea; but we do not see its effects. The morning does not 'gild pale streams with heavenly alchemy,' nor does the sun turn 'the meagre cloddy earth to glittering gold.' In this respect, as well as in a more frequent use of colour, Virgil makes an advance on Homer and other classical Greek poets:

> *Postera vix summos spargebat lumine montes*
> *Orta dies; quum primum alto se gurgite tollunt*
> *Solis equi, lucemque elatis naribus efflant.*
> > (*Aeneid*, xii. 113-15.)

> *Jamque rubescebat radiis mare, et aethere ab alto*
> *Aurora in roseis fulgebat lutea bigis.*
> > (*Aeneid*, vii. 25, 26.)

There is a similar difference in their sunsets:

> *Ni roseus fessos iam gurgite Phoebus Hibero*
> *Tingat equos, noctemque die labente reducat.*
> > (*Aeneid*, xi. 913, 914.)

> *Et iam summa procul villarum culmina fumant,*
> *Maioresque cadunt altis de montibus umbrae.*
> > (*Ecl.*, i. 83, 84.)

> *Et sol crescentes decedens duplicat umbras.*
> > (*Ecl.*, ii. 67.)

Roman poets of the Silver Age copy Virgil's method and even intensify it, and so do Renaissance writers, as in the following lines of Tasso:

> Così pregava; e gli sorgeva a fronte,
> Fatta già d'auro, la vermiglia Aurora,
> Che l'elmo e l'armi, e intorno a lui del monte
> Le verdi cime illuminando indora.
> > (*G.L.*, xviii. 15.)

After Homer the best sunrise is in Euripides' *Ion*. The sun with its first rays gilds the peaks of Parnassus:

ἅρματα μὲν τάδε λαμπρὰ τεθρίππων
ἥλιος ἤδη κάμπτει κατὰ γῆν,
ἄστρα δὲ φεύγει πῦρ τόδ' ἀπ' αἰθέρος
ἐς νύχθ' ἱεράν,
Παρνησιάδες δ' ἄβατοι κορυφαὶ
καταλαμπόμεναι τὴν ἡμερίαν
ἀψῖδα βροτοῖσι δέχονται.

(82-88.)

The sunrise in Aristophanes' *Clouds* has been noted in a previous chapter. In a fragment of Euripides' *Phaethon* (Nauck, 775), it is the reawakening of animate creation to activity in the early morning that is portrayed. In Sophocles' *Electra* (17-19) the bright light of the sun wakens loud the matins of the birds. The best sunset is in Sophocles' *Trachiniae*, when the Chorus call upon the sun whom starry night, despoiled of her glories, brings forth and again lulls to rest in fire:

ὃν αἰόλα νὺξ ἐναριζομένα
τίκτει κατευνάζει τε φλογιζόμενον,
Ἅλιον, Ἅλιον αἰτῶ.

(94-96.)

It is Byron's sun:

'Slow sinks, more lovely ere his race be run,
Along Morea's hills the setting Sun;
Not, as in northern climes, obscurely bright,
But one unclouded blaze of living light.'

(*Corsair*, iii.)

The myth of the Sun's journey back from West to East, over Ocean, in a golden cup, is found in three poets. It appears first in Mimnermus (*Bergk*, 12), who pities the Sun, because he knows no respite from labour:

τὸν μὲν γὰρ διὰ κῦμα φέρει πολυήρατος εὐνὴ
κοίλη, Ἡφαίστου χερσὶν ἐληλαμένη
χρυσοῦ τιμήεντος, ὑπόπτερος, ἄκρον ἐφ᾽ ὕδωρ
εὕδονθ᾽ ἁρπαλέως, κ.τ.λ.

In a fragment of a poem by Stesichorus (*Bergk*, 8), Heracles has borrowed the cup from Helios. Dr. Farnell says, 'The story of Hercules borrowing the cup of Helios to sail over the ocean probably arises from a confusion in mythological tradition. The cup seems to have been the attribute originally, not of Helios, but of Hercules, in his character as a sun-god, corresponding to Melcart. As this aspect of Hercules was lost sight of, the myth was transferred to Helios, the sun-god proper.'[1] The few lines preserved from Aeschylus' *Heliades* (Nauck, 67) are of no help in the interpretation of the myth.

From sunrise to sunset and from sunset to sunrise Homer marks the passage of time without much reference to the phenomena of the heavens. He says that the 'sacred' day was growing, that the sun had reached the highest point of heaven, or that it was passing on to the time of the loosing of oxen.[2] Now it is the time when a woodman makes ready his mid-day meal in a mountain dell (*Il.*, xi. 86 ff.); now it is the hour when a man rises from the assembly and goes to supper (*Ody.*, xii. 439 ff.). The Odysseus of Homer does not, like the Odysseus of Tennyson, mark the lights beginning to twinkle from the rocks, the long day waning, and the slow moon climbing;

---

[1] *Greek Lyric Poetry.*
[2] Milton makes more of a picture at this point:—

> 'What time the labour'd ox
> In his loose traces from the furrow came.' (*Comus.*)

nor does he note the coming out of the stars one by one, or their fading, even to the loveliest—*in fino alla pui bella*—as Dante does. Homer's night is divided into three parts (*Il.*, x. 253; *Ody.*, xii. 312). The rising of the Morning Star marks the time when the pyre of Patroclus burns low (*Il.*, xxiii. 226-28), and the hour when Odysseus lands in Ithaca (*Ody.*, xiii. 93-95). In this respect Dante forms a great contrast to Homer. At almost all hours Dante registers the aspects of the sky and associates them with human feeling and his own sensations. The Morning Star makes all the Orient laugh (*Purg.* i.).[1] He notes how:

'Aurora's white and vermeil-tinctured cheek
  To orange turned, as she in age increased.'
                                        (*Purg.*, ii.)

The sea-beach is seen quivering in the early light—*il tremolar della marina* (*Purg.*, i.). The sun itself is hidden in excess of light (*Parad.*, v.). Three hours before sunset the level beams are blinding (*Purg.*, xv.). The moon makes the stars wink and fade, and her disk is like a crag on fire (*Purg.*, xviii.). When we read the opening of *Purgatorio*, viii., with its vesper bell and the conceit which Gray adopted for the first line of his *Elegy*, we recognise the greatness of the gulf between ancient Greece and mediaeval Italy. Dante dwells on the phenomena of light at once with the curious mind of a scientist and the soul of a poet touched by the glorious spectacles of the heavens. It has been said that Homer's is the epic of the body, Dante's of the soul. The antithesis is much too sharp, as it ignores the tremendous hold on reality possessed by Dante. He had been a traveller, his mind was stored with recollections of scenes of travel, and these

---

[1] Imitated by Chaucer in *The Knight's Tale*.

he turns to account in his poem, which is the record of a journey. For a full parallel between Homer and Dante the *Iliad* is valuable on account of its similes, but, as the story of a voyage told by the voyager, part of the first half of the *Odyssey* would have to be considered for the purpose of personal contrast. Dante's interests were almost encyclopaedic and they crowd his poem; the narrative of Odysseus is limited to the impressions of a simple seaman, as interpreted by a poet whose sole object is to tell a good story to an unsophisticated audience. Similarly, Hesiod in his *Works and Days*, rather than Homer, gives us the proper contrast to Virgil in his *Georgics*, figures again excluded.

The moon does not play much of a part in Homer's narratives. She does not look down upon the night escapade of Odysseus and Diomedes in the Tenth Book of the *Iliad*. She would have been an unwelcome intruder and would have spoiled the grim sport. The taking of Troy is not in Homer's programme. But a difference in choice of subject brings different opportunities, as we see from the Second Book of the *Aeneid*. It is night, and the ships of the Greeks are sailing from Tenedos *per amica silentia lunae* (254-56). Rhipeus and Epytus, Hypanis and Dymas and Coroebus and Aeneas, all meet in the moonlight and make their way through the burning city (339-42). When the images of the gods and the Phrygian Penates seem to stand before the sleeping Aeneas, a full moon pours a flood of light through the lattice (iii. 147-52). In the opening of the Seventh Book Aeneas sets sail from Caieta. The white moon is shining and the deep glitters in the quivering light. They skirt the shore of the land of Circe. A fire of fragrant cedar-wood lights up the witch's halls. They can hear the roaring of wild beasts and the rattling of chains. The ghostly effect is carefully prepared for and worked up by Virgil. Aeneas knows well whither he goes; he is on the track of Odysseus. But the Greek hero followed no trail. Escaped from the Laestrygons, he and his crew row on, sick at heart, thinking neither of sun nor of moon; and they happen on the island of Aeaea.[1]

After Homer there are some moonlight scenes. The season of the full moon was the time for festivals. The Chorus in *Alcestis* declare that the heroine, best of spouses, shall be celebrated in song and recital at Sparta as often as the month of the Carneia comes round and the moon shines all night long. It was also a lucky time for marriages (Pindar, *Isth.*, viii. 44; Euripides, *Iph. at A.*, 717). The Olympian games were held at the time of the first full moon after the summer solstice.[2] To stand among the modern excavations beneath a Grecian sky may do much to make one realise the scene of Panhellenic contests, but the words of Pindar are of power too. His Third Olympian is in honour of Theron of Acragas, who had been victorious in the chariot-race. The poet recalls the institution of the games, and tells how Heracles brought from the springs of Ister a plant of gray-green olive to rear shade for all comers and furnish crowns for conquerors. Till then the place by the Alpheus had been treeless, though the altars had been sanctified to his father Zeus; 'and in his face the mid-month moon on her golden car lit up the full orb of the Eye of Evening' (19, 20). In another ode (*Oly.*, x.) he celebrates the victory of a boy boxer, Agesidamus of Thebes, and gives details

[1] For the effect of moonshine at a critical moment, see the encounter of Grettir and Glam in the saga of *Grettir the Strong*, and *Burnt Njal*, lxxiv.
[2] Some say the second.

of the origin of the games and the first meeting. At the close of the day 'the lovely light of the fair-faced moon lit up the evening scene, and all the sacred precinct rang to sounds of festal glee':

ἐν δ' ἕσπερον
ἔφλεξεν εὐώπιδος
σελάνας ἐρατὸν φάος.

(73-75.)

One can imagine how grateful to the throng was the change from the broiling sun and dust of the day to the evening cool and the softer radiance of the moon. Pindar knew the scene well. His picture is objective, but do we require to ask whether he really *felt* the spectacle? Tennyson could be objective too. But would anyone have dared to ask him whether his thoughts were on the business of land-surveying when he wrote the lines which George Meredith called the finest in English poetry?

'On one side lay the ocean, and on one
Lay a great water, and the moon was full.'

Among writers of lyric Sappho, μία καὶ μόνη Σαπφώ, holds a unique place as a lover of all beautiful things: 'Sun, moon, and stars, brother, all sweet things.' The following fragment may have formed part of a simile:

ἄστερες μὲν ἀμφὶ κάλαν σελάνναν
αἶψ' ἀποκρύπτοισι φάεννον εἶδος,
ὅπποτα πλήθοισα μάλιστα λάμπῃ
. . . γᾶν . . .
. . . ἀργυρία.

(*Bergk*, 3.)

'The stars about the beautiful moon quickly hide their bright form when she is near the full and lights up the earth. . . .' It is full moon in another fragment:

> πλήρης μὲν ἐφαίνετ' ἀ σελάννα,
> αἰ δ' ὡς περὶ βῶμον ἐστάθησαν.
>
> (*Bergk*, 53.)

'The moon was rising full, and they stood as round an altar.' The following words of passion breathed into the night are a triumph in simplicity, reserve, and calm strength:

> δέδυκε μὲν ἀ σελάννα
> καὶ Πληΐαδες, μέσαι δὲ
> νύκτες, παρὰ δ' ἔρχετ' ὦρα,
> ἔγω δὲ μόνα κατεύδω.
>
> (*Bergk*, 52.)

'The moon is set and the Pleiades; it is midnight; the hour is passing; but I sleep alone.'

Similar in its simplicity yet different in spirit, yearning but mystical, which Sappho never is, is the little piece by Matthias Claudius, beginning:

> 'Ich sehe oft um Mitternacht
>   Wenn ich mein Werk getan,
> Und niemand mehr im Hause wacht,
>   Die Stern' am Himmel an.'

Sometimes, in a phrase merely, Homer compares bright things to the sun, or the moon, or to a star. The most charming example is found in the account of the meeting of Hector and Andromache. The nurse is present, bearing on her bosom 'the tender child, an infant yet, the beloved son of Hector, like to a beautiful star—ἀλίγκιον ἀστέρι καλῷ,' (*Il.*, vi. 399-401). The phrase made even Hobbes deviate into poetry:

> 'And like a star upon her bosom lay
>   His beautiful and shining golden head.'

The image fascinated Tennyson. In *The Princess* the babe is 'headed like a star,' and again it

'Lay like a new-fall'n meteor on the grass.'

But particular stars furnish more lengthy comparisons. The fire from Diomedes' helmet and shield is like Sirius, 'the star of late summer, that shines in bright pre-eminence after being bathed in Ocean' (*Il.*, v. 4-8). When Achilles is compared to the same star, it is called 'Orion's Dog; for an evil sign is he set, and he brings much burning sickness on wretched mortals' (*Il.*, xxii. 25-31). The baleful star, now bursting from the clouds, now hidden among them, to which Hector is compared, is probably Sirius (*Il.*, xi. 62-64). There is not much trace, either in Homer or in later classical Greek poetry, of astrological superstition. Sirius is said to bring heat and fever, but it is not called a portent. Virgil's Sirius is more malignant:

Ille sitim morbosque ferens mortalibus aegris
Nascitur, et laevo contristat lumine caelum.

(*Aen.*, x. 274-75.)

The comet of Milton

'from his horrid hair
Shakes pestilence and war.' [1]

Homer's rainbow, however, is a sign of storm or of war (*Il.*, xvii. 547). Athena darts down from Olympus like a bright star, 'a portent for sailors or a great host of men, and many sparks come from it'—a meteor seemingly (*Il.*, iv. 74-78). The light from Achilles' lance is like that of Hesperus, 'fairest of all stars set in heaven' (*Il.*, xxii. 317-19).

[1] Cp. Shakespeare, 1 *Henry VI.*, i. 1 ; *Julius Caesar*, ii. 2 ; Tasso, *G.L.*, vii. 52.

One figure of this kind in Homer has received special notice from commentators. It is the one that illustrates the number of the blazing Trojan watch-fires:

ὡς δ' ὅτ' ἐν οὐρανῷ ἄστρα φαεινὴν ἀμφὶ σελήνην
φαίνετ' ἀριπρεπέα, ὅτε τ' ἔπλετο νήνεμος αἰθήρ·
ἐκ τ' ἔφανεν πᾶσαι σκοπιαὶ καὶ πρώονες ἄκροι
καὶ νάπαι· οὐρανόθεν δ' ἄρ' ὑπερράγη ἄσπετος αἰθήρ,
πάντα δέ τ' εἴδεται ἄστρα, γέγηθε δέ τε φρένα ποιμήν·
τόσσα μεσηγὺ νεῶν ἠδὲ Ξάνθοιο ῥοάων
Τρώων καιόντων πυρὰ φαίνετο Ἰλιόθι πρό.

(*Il.*, viii. 555-61.)

The third and fourth lines occur again in xvi. 299, 300. They are suitable there, after a clearing away of clouds. But they do not suit their context here. Moreover, brilliant moonlight and a clear display of stars are inconsistent. But a dark night would not have pleased the shepherd. 'Just in proportion, as rocks, and peaks, and wooded glens appeared distinct, the lesser lights of heaven, and with them the fundamental idea of the comparison, must have become effaced; and the poet, accordingly, as if with a misgiving that the forms of his fancy had led him to stray from the rigid line of his purpose, volunteered the assurance that "all the stars were visible"—as, to his mind's eye, they doubtless were.' [1] The piece is best known in Tennyson's translation, not to mention Pope's notorious hash, with its 'vivid planets,' 'glowing pole,' 'refulgent lamp of night,' etc. But let us be just even to Pope. He says:

'The conscious swains, rejoicing in the sight,
Eye the blue vault, and bless the *useful* light.'

[1] Miss A. M. Clerke in *Familiar Studies in Homer*.

'Useful' has given great offence is some quarters. Christopher North sarcastically spoke of Pope's 'second-sight of utilitarianism.' Second-sight or not, it was at least second or third thought. His manuscript shows that he tried 'vivid' and 'glorious' before fixing on 'useful.' His mistake lay in suggesting any reason for the shepherd's delight. He might have given himself away badly; but he hasn't. Nor has he traduced Homer. Pope's interpretation is beautifully Homeric. The shepherd is on the mountains, and his first thought is of his sheep, as a good shepherd's ought to be. So in *Iliad*, iii. 10-14, we are told that a mist is 'in no wise dear to the shepherd, but for the thief it is better than night.' Similarly, Dante (*Inferno*, xxiv.) makes a countryman (*villanello*) rejoice at the disappearance of hoar frost, and Arnold's peasant in *Balder Dead* is glad when a thaw comes, the signs of it being such as would appeal also to an artist who, unlike the peasant, would not think first of field-work. Homer caters for an audience, and his first intention is decided by certain of the interests of his audience. It has been gravely asked, 'Had Homer no pleasure in the sight?' Well, Homer, or someone whom it has been agreed to call Homer, composed the simile and drew the picture. What more would you have? Homer's reticence has paid him well. He pleased the pastoral-minded of his own time, and he pleases modern view-hunters. Pope's expansiveness has got him into trouble with such of the latter as never experienced the fearful joy of sheep-stealing and think it beneath the dignity of genius to exhibit utilitarian interest and intimacy with the things of the work-a-day world.

It is remarkable that the Greeks made so little of the rainbow. It is a sign to men, but not of comfort, as we have seen. There is but faint appreciation of its colours either in Homer or later. The goddess Ἶρις is noted for speed mainly—ποδήνεμος, ὠκέα, ἀελλόπος, χρυσόπτερος. Virgil calls her *decus coeli* (*Aen.*, ix. 18) and arrays her in a thousand changing hues:

> *Ergo Iris croceis per coelum roscida pennis,*
> *Mille trahens varios adverso sole colores.*
>
> > (*Aen.*, iv. 700, 701.)

Ovid says that Iris

> *induit velamina mille colorum.*
>
> > (*Met.*, xi. 589.)

In *Iliad*, xi. 27, dark-blue snakes figured on a breast-plate are said to be like rainbows. But Virgil compares the lustrous scales of a snake to the changing colours of the bow in the clouds seen athwart the sun, much as before—

> *ceu nubibus arcus*
> *Mille jacit varios adverso sole colores.*
>
> > (*Aen.*, v. 88, 89.) [1]

Athena coming down from heaven and entering the Greek host clad in a dark cloud (πορφυρέῃ νεφέλῃ) is compared to a dark rainbow (πορφυρέην ἶριν) which Zeus stretches from heaven to be a sign to mortals (*Il.*, xvii. 547-52). The meaning would seem to be that Athena in her cloud is as much of a portent as the rainbow is. The interpretation, that Athena in the cloud is like the rainbow projected on a cloud, is inadmissible; no cloud is mentioned in connection with the rainbow. Among the Hebrews the bow in the cloud met with greater appreciation. It is a

---

[1] For the most beautiful snake in all English literature see Keats's *Lamia*.

sign of hope, a token of a covenant, and also a symbol of glory (*Ezekiel*, i. 28). Best of all are the words of Sirach in *Ecclesiasticus*:

'Look upon the rainbow, and praise Him that made it;
Exceeding beautiful in the brightness thereof.
It compasseth the heaven round about with a circle
    of glory;
The hands of the Most High have stretched it.'

(xliii. 11, 12.)

In this department few analogies, physical or moral, are found in later classical Greek. In Bacchylides, viii. 27-29, Automedes is said to have shone above his competitors in the pentathlon as the beautiful mid-month moon, which makes the stars pale. In a Parthenion (*Bergk*, 23), badly preserved, Alcman extols the beauty of Agido, which makes one think that the sun has risen in the night. And the doves Agesichora and Agido 'rising before us like Sirius, as we bear the garment to Artemis through the ambrosial night, contend in beauty.' [1] The glory of the house of Cleonymus had fallen on sleep, but in virtue of Pindar's hymn of victory 'she rises again and shines pre-eminent, as among stars the Morning Star' (*Isth.*, iv. 23, 42). In human life sorrow succeeds to joy and joy to sorrow, in endless round, like the circling paths of the Bear (Sophocles, *Trach.*, 129-30). Man's fortunes are never in one stay. They resemble the moon, which does not preserve the same form for long; no sooner has she grown to full beauty than she begins to wane and come to nothing (Sophocles, *Fab. Incert.*, Nauck, 786).

[1] Farnell's interpretation. I can only refer to one of the new fragments of Sappho (*Pap. Berol.*, 9722) in which Mnasidica is compared to the moon. See J. M. Edmonds' *New Fragments of Alcaeus, Sappho and Erinna.*

One of the best passages in the Hesiodic *Theogony*, imitated by Milton at the beginning of Book VI. of *Paradise Lost*, is the picture of the interchange of day and night: 'There stands the dread habitation of murky Night shrouded in dark clouds. In front of it stands the son of Iapetus, holding immovably the wide heaven, with head and hands unwearying. There Night and Day draw near and greet each other as they pass the great threshold of bronze. The one is about to go down into the house and the other comes forth. The house never holds both within, but evermore the one is outside wandering over the earth, while the other bides inside and awaits the time of her going; the one holding in her hands all-seeing light for dwellers on the earth; the other, baneful Night wrapped in a misty cloud, holds Sleep, the brother of Death' (744-57). In Hesiod Night is a goddess, daughter of Chaos and mother of Aether and Day (*Theog.*, 123-24). In Homer she can subdue both gods and men (*Il.*, xiv. 259). Night with its darkness is θοή; owing to its thwarting power it is κακή and ὀλοή. The darkness closing up the day suggests death that seals up all, and Homer's heroes speak of covering an enemy with black night. Apollo in his wrath comes down like the night (*Il.*, i. 47); Hector leaps into the midst 'with face like the sudden night' (*Il.*, xii. 462). Heracles in Hades is like black night (*Ody.*, xi. 606). Its divine connection is seen in the epithets ἄμβροτος (ἄβροτος) and ἀμβροσίη, the latter suggestive of fragrance.[1] In later poetry attributes which testify to its sacredness, majesty, and personality become frequent. It is ἁγνή, ἱερά, πότνια. As opposed to λευκόπεπλος ἡμέρα Night is μελάνιππος.

[1] In the Hymn *To Hermes* (97) we find δαιμονίη. Milton has 'ambrosial night' and Tennyson 'Immantled in ambrosial dark.'

Her garments are black (μελάμπεπλος—Milton's 'sable-vested Night') or spangled (ποικιλείμων).

The sack of Troy was not part of Homer's theme, so he had no opportunity of providing a model for Virgil in the Second Book of the *Aeneid*, the finest thing of its kind in ancient poetry. In post-Homeric poetry references to the actual work of destruction are scanty. In the opening of the *Troades* Troy is a smoke-shrouded desolation. Later the Chorus sing of the entry of the Wooden Horse and the merriment of song and dance, while lamps shed a gloomy light on sleeping men. Murderous shouts are heard, and scared infants cling to their mothers' skirts. Altar and bed become scenes of butchery (511-76). The Chorus-leader of the *Hecuba* sings of the midnight hour of doom, when, the dance being done, her lord lay asleep, his spear on its peg. She was ranging her tresses in the light of the mirror's interminable rays, when a clamour arose and war-cries filled the street (914-32). The only extended scene of nocturnal action in the *Iliad* is the adventure of Diomedes and Ulysses in the Tenth Book. It is full of indications of the dark. Sleepless Agamemnon wonders at the many fires blazing in front of Ilium, at the sound of flutes and pipes and the noise of men. Reference is made to the devious paths through the camp, puzzling in the darkness. Nestor is found abed, and his girdle and accoutrements lying beside him are gleaming. Diomedes and his comrades are sleeping, head on shield, and their spears driven into the ground shine afar like the lightning. Dead men lie where they had fallen in the fierce fight of the day. It is the third watch of the night, and dawn is near. The shrill cry of a heron, sent as an omen by Athena, is heard by the pair. The spoils stript from Dolon are set on a tamarisk bush, and the place is marked with reeds and tamarisk shoots. A shining whip is part of the equipment of Rhesus' splendid chariot. Quick-eared Nestor is the first to hear the sound of horses approaching the ships. In addition the narrative is starred with such phrases as 'the ambrosial night,' 'the dark night,' 'the black night,' 'the swift black night,' 'the wicked night.' In fact this phraseology is overdone, though in keeping with the grotesqueries which mark off this book from the rest of the *Iliad*.[1]

There are a few short passages in which mention of night is made impressive by the power of style. When Odysseus describes his pretended murder of Orsilochus in Crete, he says: 'Night the murkiest held the heavens, and no man marked us, but all unseen I took his life away' (*Ody.*, xiii. 269, 270). Pindar gives a picture of Pelops standing 'by the hoary sea, alone in the darkness (οἶος ἐν ὄρφνᾳ), and calling on loud-thundering Poseidon of the goodly trident: and he appeared close at his foot' (*Oly.*, i. 71-74). And there is a companion picture of young Iamus going down into the middle of the Alpheus and praying to his grandsire Poseidon, 'in the night, beneath the open sky'—νυκτὸς ὑπαίθριος (*Oly.*, vi. 58-61)[2]. In the *Choephoroe* an awful shriek from the inner chamber, begotten of hair-raising dream-terror, is heard shrilling through the palace at dead of night (29-33). In the loveless home of Menelaus dream-forms seem to offer delight, but in vain. The vision slips from his arms, gone that moment, 'on wings that

---

[1] The proper Virgilian parallel to this is the episode of Nisus and Euryalus (*Aen.*, ix. 168-445). See also the *Nibelungenlied*, xxvi.
[2] Like Jacob

'In the field of Luz
Dreaming by night under the open sky.'
(Milton, *P.L.*, iii. 513-14).

follow the ways of sleep'—πτεροῖς ὀπαδοῖς ὕπνου κελεύθοις (*Agam.*, 426).

Owing to Greek dramatic form and method, which need not again be particularised, there are few marks of time in Greek tragedy.

'Stir with the lark to-morrow, gentle Norfolk,' Shakespeare makes his King Richard III. say on the night before a battle. Though in few instances is the action of a Greek play restricted to the ideal time-unity of the theorists, yet it might be said without much exaggeration that there are no to-morrows in Greek tragedy. In the majority of the extant plays the action takes place in the full sunlight of a single day. In some cases advantage is taken of the latter end of night; the play begins at the approach of dawn and ends in clear day. At the opening of the *Agamemnon* it is night. At line 254 the Chorus look forward to the coming dawn (σύνορθρον αὐγαῖς). Troy is said to have fallen 'in the same night that now brings forth the day' (279). 'To-day the Achaeans are in possession of Troy' (320). A herald is seen coming from the shore (493), and he thinks it right to boast 'before this beam of the sun' (575). The *Antigone* opens at early morning and the Chorus address the sun, 'the eye of golden day.' The first watch of the day is mentioned at line 253. The sun is in mid-heaven when Antigone does the deed (416). In the *Electra* of Euripides the heroine addresses Night, 'nurse of the golden stars' (54). The peasant is to take his team to the field at dawn (79). Soon after (102) Orestes says that Dawn 'is raising her white face.' At 867 Electra speaks of night as lately gone. When the *Electra* of Sophocles opens the night has just vanished. On the other hand, in the *Choephoroe*, it is the fall of evening when Orestes knocks at the gate:

τάχυνε δ᾽, ὡς καὶ νυκτὸς ἄρμ᾽ ἐπείγεται
σκοτεινόν, ὥρα δ᾽ ἐμπόρους μεθιέναι
ἄγκυραν ἐν δόμοισι πανδόκοις ξένων.

(660-63.)[1]

We start at the coincidence—it is nothing more—when
we recall the words of the First Murderer in *Macbeth*:

'The west yet glimmers with some streaks of day;
Now spurs the lated traveller apace
To gain the timely inn.'

(iii. 3.)

The opening (or pseudo-opening) of the *Iphigeneia at
Aulis* is almost Shakespearian. It is night; a lamp
is burning in the tent of Agamemnon, who has been
writing a letter. He calls an Old Servant and asks
what star is that which is passing, just as one of
Shakespeare's characters might ask, 'What is't
o'clock?' It is Sirius that moves through mid-
heaven near the Pleiads. Perfect stillness reigns.
Wind and wave are hushed, and no birds sing. At
line 157 Agamemnon bids the Old Man be off on his
mission, for the sky is flushing with dawn. Similarly,
the Duke in *Measure for Measure*, when giving in-
structions to the Provost, exclaims, 'Look, the un-
folding star calls up the shepherd.' At line 1509
Iphigeneia can bid farewell to the light of the sun,
without illusion.

There are some resemblances between the *Rhesus* and
the opening of Act IV. of Shakespeare's *King Henry V.*:

'From camp to camp, through the foul womb of night,
The hum of either army stilly sounds,
That the fix'd sentinels almost receive
The secret whispers of each other's watch:
Fire answers fire, and through their paly flames
Each battle sees the other's umber'd face.'

[1] This is probably the first mention of the car of Night.

The *Rhesus* opens in the course of the Fourth Watch; in *Henry V*. it is three o'clock. Hector might take the place of King Henry and Aeneas stand for Gloster, Bedford, and Erpingham. The nearness of the two hosts is referred to in the *Rhesus* (20-22) as well as in Shakespeare. French Chanticleer must do his best to represent the Trojan nightingale. There is a moon in the *Rhesus* (534), but the moonlight in *King Henry V.* is introduced more romantically:

> 'Their gesture sad,
> Investing lank-lean cheeks, and war-worn coats,
> Presenteth them unto the gazing moon
> So many horrid ghosts.'

To go further and make the valiant Fluellen do duty for a mere Thracian or a Trojan shepherd might be finding 'salmons in both.' In Shakespeare day breaks before the battle begins, but in the *Rhesus* the action ends at dawn. All through the Greek play there is a sense of the presence of night. The members of the Chorus are sentinels and they call up Hector. They have seen the Grecian fires blazing and heard great commotion near Agamemnon's tent. Torches are burning on board the ships, and it would seem that preparations are being made for flight. Line 331 gives the first mention of the coming dawn. It is night—καὶ γὰρ εὐφρόνη—when Hector assigns a place of encampment to Rhesus (518). At 527 there is a change of watch. The earliest stars have set, the Pleiads have risen, and the Eagle shines in the midst of heaven. The dawn is near; see, the star which is its forerunner! Down by the Simois the nightingale is singing, the flocks are wending to pasture on Ida, and the sound of the shepherd's pipe comes through the dark. Sleep, sweetest towards the dawn, weighs on the eyes of the watchers. Searching for the quarters of Hector, Diomedes and Odysseus hear the noise made by the retiring guards and the clanking of horses' chains (565-69). The white Thracian steeds of Rhesus gleam in the darkness like the wing of a river-swan (617, 618). The light is yet dim (737). 'Yonder is the light of day' (985). Hector points to the rising sun (992).

CHAPTER VI

SOME NATURAL PHENOMENA (II)

PINDAR opens his Eleventh Olympian Ode with the words:

Ἔστιν ἀνθρώποις ἀνέμων ὅτε πλεῖστα
χρῆσις, ἔστιν δ' οὐρανίων ὑδάτων
ὀμβρίων, παίδων νεφέλας.

'Men have most need, sometimes of winds, sometimes of rainy waters from the heavens, children of the clouds.' The poet is thinking of ships and ploughs. Ruskin, an authority on cloudland, says, 'Precisely in the degree in which the Greek was agriculturally inclined, in that degree the sight of clouds would become to him more acceptable than to the mediaeval knight, who only looked for the fine afternoons in which he might gather the flowers in his garden, and in no wise shared or imagined the previous anxieties of his gardener.' And again, 'The love of mountains is closely connected with the love of clouds, the sublimity of both depending much on their association.' [1] The Athenian knight was a townsman and probably thought as seldom as his mediaeval counterpart about the perplexities of gardeners. But no matter. It must be granted, I think, that clouds are of considerable utilitarian interest in Greek poetry, and that Greek poets do not regard mountains and clouds with the feelings of a

1 *Modern Painters*, Part IV., chap. xv.

Shelley or a Wordsworth.[1] But between these extremes there is room for a certain amount of observation, with or without the expression of associated feelings; and it is in this region that we find the most characteristic treatment of clouds by Greek poets, Homer especially.

According to Ruskin, Aristophanes was the only Greek poet who studied clouds attentively. For proof he comments on those lines in the *Clouds* in which Socrates bids Strepsiades look towards Parnes, and points to the imaginary clouds in their multitudes trailing slantwise through the hollows and the thickets:

χωροῦσ᾽ αὗται πάνυ πολλαί,
διὰ τῶν κοίλων καὶ τῶν δασέων, αὗται πλαγίαι.

(324-25.)

The last line 'could have been written by none but an ardent lover of hill scenery, one who had watched, hour after hour, the peculiar, oblique, sidelong action of descending clouds, as they form along the hollows and ravines of the hills. There are no lumpish solidities, no pillowy protuberances here. All is melting, drifting, evanescent; full of air, and light, and dew.' [2] In other words, they are not storm-clouds, but gay deceivers fit for Aristophanes' purpose. Very beautiful are the lines which describe the quarters from which the clouds come:

εἴτ᾽ ἐπ᾽ Ὀλύμπου κορυφαῖς ἱεραῖς χιονοβλήτοισι κάθησθε,
εἴτ᾽ Ὠκεανοῦ πατρὸς ἐν κήποις ἱερὸν χορὸν ἵστατε
  Νύμφαις,
εἴτ᾽ ἄρα Νείλου προχοαῖς ὑδάτων χρυσέαις ἀρύεσθε
  προχοῖσιν,
ἢ Μαιῶτιν λίμνην ἔχετ᾽ ἢ σκόπελον νιφόεντα Μίμαντος.

(271-74.)

---

[1] Lucretius is the Latin poet of cloudland.
[2] *Modern Painters*, vol. i., Preface to Second Edition.

Socrates' fooling with Strepsiades has reminded commentators of Hamlet and Polonius, and of the serious use made of cloud-shapes by Shakespeare in *Antony and Cleopatra*, iv. 14.

Homer's screening clouds are 'shadowy' (σκιόεις). Ideally, against the sun, they are 'golden,' and this is the conventional epithet for clouds that envelop or canopy deities seen at a distance. Zeus and Hera lie on Gargarus on the flowery grass, 'clothed with a cloud, fair, golden; and from it glittering dewdrops fell' (*Il.*, xiv. 351-52). Ares sits on the peak of Olympus beneath golden clouds (*Il.*, xiii. 523-24). Athena covers the head of Achilles with a golden cloud (*Il.*, xviii. 205). Virgil employs the same convention:

> *Junonem interea Rex omnipotentis Olympi*
> *Alloquitur, fulva pugnas de nube tuentem.*
>
> (*Aen.*, xii. 791-92.)

Such a cloud may also be 'fragrant':

> εὗρον δ' εὑρύοπα Κρονίδην ἀνὰ Γαργάρῳ ἄκρῳ
> ἥμενον· ἀμφὶ δέ μιν θυόεν νέφος ἐστεφάνωτο.
>
> (*Il.*, xv. 152-53.)[1]

It is in his similes that Homer's cloud interests are best seen. The quick flight and din of the Trojans is compared to a cloud which comes out of the upper air and from Olympus spreads over the sky (*Il.*, xvi. 364-65). Diomedes sees Ares speeding heavenwards like a thunder-cloud standing out in a dark mass from the rest of the clouds (v. 864-67). The Greeks, standing steadfast against the Trojan attack, are like motionless

---

[1] Normally Zeus is κελαινεφής.

clouds on the mountains, in calm weather, when all
the winds are asleep. Commenting on this figure
Pope says, 'The whole compass of nature cannot
afford a nobler and more exact representation of a
numerous army, drawn up in line of battle and
expecting the charge. The long extended even
front, the closeness of the ranks, the firmness, order
and silence of the whole, are all drawn with great
resemblance in this one comparison.' The cloud-
figure in *Iliad*, xvi. 297-302, is of special interest, and
the original must be given:

ὡς δ' ὅτ' ἀφ' ὑψηλῆς κορυφῆς ὄρεος μεγάλοιο
κινήσῃ πυκινὴν νεφέλην στεροπηγερέτα Ζεύς,
ἔκ τ' ἔφανεν πᾶσαι σκοπιαὶ καὶ πρώονες ἄκροι
καὶ νάπαι, οὐρανόθεν δ' ἄρ' ὑπερράγη ἄσπετος αἰθήρ,
ὡς Δαναοὶ νηῶν μὲν ἀπωσάμενοι δήϊον πῦρ
τυτθὸν ἀνέπνευσαν, πολέμου δ' οὐ γίγνετ' ἐρωή.

'As when from the lofty crest of a great hill Zeus, the
Gatherer of the Lightning, stirs a dense cloud, and
out shine all the peaks and sharp spurs and dells, and
from heaven above the infinite upper air is burst
open, even so the Danaans having driven away the
raging fire from the ships breathed free for a little
while, but there was no rest from fighting.' Lines
299 and 300 are in place here, and they are certainly
not so in the passage in Book VIII. already commented on. Some critics understand the phenomenon
to be a cleaving with a flash of lightning. The use of
the epithet στεροπηγερέτα would seem to support this
view. This is the sole instance of the use of the word,
and the poet must have felt that the customary
νεφεληγερέτα would not be suitable in this connection.
Nevertheless, this lightning theory is far from satis-
factory. Could a flash of lightning produce all the

125

effect? Must not κινήσῃ imply, if not total dislodge-
ment, at least a setting in motion of the whole mass?
Dr. Mackail translates—'As when from the great crest
of a high hill Zeus the Light-gatherer pierces the
dense cloud, etc.' The action of lightning requires
κινήσῃ to mean *pierce*. But this it cannot mean in
conjunction with ἀφ᾽ ὑψηλῆς κορυφῆς. From Dr.
Mackail's translation it might be supposed that
Zeus was standing on the mountain top. Statius
seems to have had this simile in mind, and to have
supposed the action to be that of lightning flash,
when he wrote:

> *Sic ubi nocturnum tonitru malus aethera frangit*
> *Juppiter, absiliunt nubes, et fulgure claro*
> *Astra patent, subitusque oculis ostenditur orbis.*
>
> (*Theb.*, x. 373-75.)

Astra patent suggests the scene in Book VIII. also.

In *Iliad*, iv. 272-282, the two Ajaces are arming and
a cloud of men on foot follows them—ἅμα δὲ νέφος
εἵπετο πεζῶν. The dense and dark ranks of young men
bristling with shields and spears move to war. Such
an array, Homer implies, is likely to strike terror into
the hearts of the enemy and make them flee. 'So,
when a goatherd sees a cloud coming over the sea,
blacker than pitch, and bringing with it a great
whirlwind, he shudders and drives his flock into a
cave.' A first-rate simile certainly. Yet surprise has
been expressed at its utilitarian character. Cope says,
'There is not the least symptom in it of any feeling of
pleasure or interest derivable from the contemplation
of the gathering of the storm—all is unmixed terror.' [1]

---

[1] *Cambridge Essays*, 1856—a long time ago, but the echoes of the
comment are sometimes heard to this day.

However valid such criticism may be as regards
Homer's general reticence, it is quite out of place here.
Homer had to choose a phenomenon with elements
of terror in it, and a spectator likely to feel terror at
the sight. That a hurricane is an apt choice most
will admit, and Cope's criticism does not apply to
the selection. The goatherd has the flock of a master
and a skin of his own to save The poet's choice and
treatment of this natural force are proof of his interest
in it. To have given expression to pleasurable feeling
would have been to bungle the simile. There is room
for two opinions about the cause of the shepherd's
rejoicing in the moonlight passage of Book VIII. The
shepherd is not necessary to the simile, the point of
which turns on the number of fires and stars. But
the shuddering of the goatherd, if not indispensable,
balances the implied fear of the Trojans, and rounds
off the figure. A figure on similar lines but with new
features is found in *Aeneid*, xii. 451-57.[1] The simile
which Tennyson uses to illustrate the sadness that
fell on Ida's soul in *The Princess* might well have been
suggested by Homer and Virgil:

'And she, as one that climbs a peak to gaze
O'er land and main, and sees a great black cloud
Drag inward from the deeps, a wall of night,
Blot out the slope of sea from verge to shore,
And suck the blinding splendour from the sand,
And quenching lake by lake and tarn by tarn
Expunge the world: so fared she gazing there.'
(vii.)

In the *Iliad* there are examples of what might be
called the atmospheric supernatural. On three
occasions in Book VIII. Zeus marks a crisis with thunder

[1] See the comments by Dr. Fowler in the *Death of Turnus*, p. 93.

and lightning (75-77; 132-138; 170-171). In Book VII. both hosts feast all night long and all night long Zeus thunders, fear falls upon them, and they spill the wine from the cups (476-82). Dew dank with blood rains down (xi. 53-55), and bloody rain-drops fall (xvi. 458-60). 'The portent indicated is probably an actual shower of rain tinged red by a microscopic alga.' [1] In Book XXIII. Apollo brings a dark cloud from heaven and covers the place where the body of Hector lies, 'so that the sun's strength may not shrivel the flesh' (188-91). In Book XVII. Zeus sheds a thick mist on the bright helmets of the Greeks who guard the body of Patroclus (268-70). The same cloud, intensified, is described later (366 ff.) in a suspected passage: 'So they strove after the likeness of fire, nor wouldst thou have thought that there was sun or moon any more, for over that part of the field where the chief fighters stood round the slain son of Menoetius they were shrouded in dark mist, but the other Trojans and well-greaved Achaeans fought at ease beneath a clear sky, and the undimmed light of the sun was spread over them, and no cloud appeared on all the plain or the hills.' [2] Later in the book, when Hector in flashing bronze comes to the van, Zeus takes up his glittering tasselled aegis, covers Ida with clouds, and lightens and thunders terribly (591-95). Once more the poet returns to the great mist in the centre of the field, when Ajax prays for light:

$$\text{ἐν δὲ φάει καὶ ὄλεσσον, ἐπεί νύ τοι εὔαδεν οὕτως.}$$

(647.)

---

[1] Miss A. M. Clerke, *Familiar Studies in Homer*.
[2] Some refer this and the vision of Theoclymenus in the *Odyssey* to an actual eclipse of the sun; but Homer had some imagination.

The contrasted darkness and light in Arnold's account of the duel in *Sohrab and Rustum* is a direct imitation of Homer, and Tennyson had not forgotten Books IV. and XVII. of the *Iliad* when he wrote his description of that 'last, dim, weird battle of the west,' when

> 'On the waste sand by the waste sea they closed,'

and there were heard

> 'Cryings for the light,
> Moans of the dying, and voices of the dead.'
> *(Passing of Arthur.)*

Finally, there is the terrible thundering in Book XX. (θεομαχία)—'and all the spurs and crests of many-fountained Ida were shaken, and the city of the Trojans, and the ships of the Achaeans. And Aïdoneus, the king of the world below, was afraid, and he leapt from his throne and cried aloud in his terror, lest his dwelling-place might be revealed to mortals and immortals, a place dank and gruesome, which even the gods abhor' (59-65).[1]

In connection with the sea we have already seen something of the winds. Hesiod attempts a genealogy of the winds (*Theog.*, 377-80; 869-72). Four winds are named in Homer—Βορέης, Ζέφυρος, Νότος, Εὖρος; all four are mentioned together in *Odyssey*, v. 295-96. Boreas, the north wind, is the most violent, it seems to have lent itself most easily to personification, and it is of some importance in mythology. It is Pindar's βασιλεὺς ἀνέμων, and Homer's favourite epithet for it is αἰθρηγενής, αἰθρηγενέτης, 'born in

---

[1] See the comments of Longinus (ix). Some consider the passage an interpolation. Here might be classed the commotion at the end of the *Prometheus Vinctus* and the stormy sky, thunder, and voices in the *Oedipus Coloneus*.

the upper air.' Homer places the home of Boreas in Thrace:

> 'He speaks, and the leaves lie dead,
> When winter awakes as at warning
> To the sound of his foot from Thrace.'

Zephyrus is sometimes said to blow from the same quarter, being then, as often, a north-west wind. Zephyrus is rainy and gusty (ἔφυδρος, δυσαής), except in Scheria and the Elysian plain; in *Odyssey*, xix. 206, it brings snow; but in later poetry it is a welcome wind in the hot noonday. In *Odyssey*, xii. 286-90, Notus, the south wind, and Zephyrus are said to be the chief wreckers of ships. Notus brings rain and mist, and when it brings white clouds into the sky it is called ἀργεστής (*Il.*, xi. 306; xxi. 334). In this respect it differs from Horace's *Notus albus detergens nubila coeli.* In Bacchylides, xii. 130, it is a gentle wind in comparison with Boreas; in *Antigone*, 335, we find the expression χειμερίῳ νότῳ. In considering seeming inconsistencies in the characterisation of winds we have to make allowance for the point of view, the context, greater or less precision, and convention. Eurus, the east, or rather south-east wind, has less individuality than the others. It is stormy (*Il.*, ii. 145; xvi. 765); it brings a thaw (*Ody.*, xix. 206). Homer's λαῖλαψ and ἄρπυια, and sometimes θύελλα and ἄελλα, are of the nature of hurricanes or whirlwinds, and to them his heroes in their fierce attacks on the enemy are likened (*Il.*, xi. 747; xii. 40; 375).[1]

In a memorable passage of the Twenty-third Book of the *Iliad* two of the winds are represented as deities who can be propitiated with offerings. The pyre

[1] For the scope and complexity of the subject of winds see Sir D'Arcy W. Thompson's article, *The Greek Winds*, in the *Classical Review*, May-June, 1918.

of Patroclus refuses to burn, and Achilles prays to the winds Boreas and Zephyrus, pouring libations and promising goodly offerings if they come and cause the pile to blaze up. Iris carries his prayer to the Winds. She finds them feasting in the house of the gusty West Wind.

ἡ μὲν ἄρ' ὣς εἰποῦσ' ἀπεβήσετο, τοὶ δ' ὀρέοντο
ἠχῇ θεσπεσίῃ, νέφεα κλονέοντε πάροιθεν·
αἶψα δὲ πόντον ἵκανον ἀήμεναι, ὦρτο δὲ κῦμα
πνοιῇ ὕπο λιγυρῇ· Τροίην δ' ἐρίβωλον ἱκέσθην,
ἐν δὲ πυρῇ πεσέτην, μέγα δ' ἴαχε θεσπιδαὲς πῦρ.
παννύχιοι δ' ἄρα τοί γε πυρῆς ἄμυδις φλόγ' ἔβαλλον,
φυσῶντες λιγέως.

(212-18.)

'So saying, she departed; and they rose with marvellous din, driving the clouds before them. Speedily did they come blowing over the sea, and the wave lifted beneath the shrill blast; and they came to deep-soiled Troyland, and fell upon the pyre, and the mighty fire roared loud. Then all night long they smote upon the flame of the pyre together, blowing shrill' (212-18).

With the feeling of energy, speed, and ease conveyed by Homer's lines, contrast the sense of frustration and wearisome monotony produced by the wedge-like phrasing, the clogged rhythm, and the repetition of similar vowel-sounds, in the passage of Aeschylus' *Agamemnon* which describes the winds that detained the Greek fleet at Aulis:

πνοαὶ δ' ἀπὸ Στρυμόνος μολοῦσαι
κακόσχολοι, νήστιδες, δύσορμοι
βροτῶν ἄλαι, νεῶν τε καὶ πεισμάτων ἀφειδεῖς,
παλιμμήκη χρόνον τιθεῖσαι
τρίβῳ κατέξαινον ἄνθος Ἄργους.

(192-96.)

'Blasts blowing from Strymon, staying them in idleness, starving them, wearing men out in bad anchorage and preying on ships and tackling, doubling the lapse of time, and withering the flower of the Argives.'

In the *Antigone* a furious squall plays a dramatic part, and enables the heroine to visit the body of Polynices. The Watchman describes it as 'a trouble in the heavens,' filling the plain, rending the foliage of the trees, and choking the sky:

$$\kappa\alpha\grave{\iota} \ \tau\acute{o}\tau' \ \dot{\epsilon}\xi\alpha\acute{\iota}\phi\nu\eta\varsigma \ \chi\theta\text{ο}\nu\grave{o}\varsigma$$
$$\tau\upsilon\phi\grave{\omega}\varsigma \ \dot{\alpha}\epsilon\acute{\iota}\rho\alpha\varsigma \ \sigma\kappa\eta\pi\tau\acute{o}\nu, \ \text{ο}\dot{\upsilon}\rho\acute{\alpha}\nu\iota\text{ο}\nu \ \ddot{\alpha}\chi\text{ο}\varsigma,$$
$$\pi\acute{\iota}\mu\pi\lambda\eta\sigma\iota \ \pi\epsilon\delta\acute{\iota}\text{ο}\nu, \ \pi\hat{\alpha}\sigma\alpha\nu \ \alpha\dot{\iota}\kappa\acute{\iota}\zeta\omega\nu \ \phi\acute{o}\beta\eta\nu$$
$$\ddot{\upsilon}\lambda\eta\varsigma \ \pi\epsilon\delta\iota\acute{\alpha}\delta\text{ο}\varsigma, \ \dot{\epsilon}\nu \ \delta' \ \dot{\epsilon}\mu\epsilon\sigma\tau\acute{\omega}\theta\eta \ \mu\acute{\epsilon}\gamma\alpha\varsigma$$
$$\alpha\dot{\iota}\theta\acute{\eta}\rho.$$

(417-21.)

Homer makes use of the winds for illustration, but in few instances are such similes confined to land scenes. The Greek assembly heaves like a field of corn bending its ears before the blast of the west wind (*Il.*, ii. 144-49). Homer stops short at movement, but in a similar figure Silius Italicus notes the glistening of the waving crop:

Huc atque huc it summa seges, nutansque vicissim
Alterno lente motu incurvata nitescit.

(ix. 360 ff.)

Tennyson goes one step further:

'A light wind blew from the gates of the sun,
And waves of shadow went over the wheat.'
(*The Poet's Song.*)

The Greek ranks are white with dust as a threshing-floor at winnowing time becomes white with chaff (*Il.*, v. 499-505). The opposing hosts are like conflicting winds whirling on high a great cloud of dust

(*Il.*, xiii. 334-37). The shout of the meeting Trojans and Achaeans is like the roaring of the wind in the foliage of lofty oaks (*Il.*, xiv. 398). The forces meet and contend as when east and south winds strive in tossing about the trees in a thick wood, 'which clash together their tapering boughs with marvellous din, and there is a noise of snapping and crashing' (*Il.*, xvi. 768-69).

Compare the *silvifragis flabris* of Lucretius (*D.R.N.*, i. 275), and his

> *Scilicet, ut, crebram silvam cum flamina cauri*
> *Perflant, dant sonitum frondes ramique fragorem;*
> (vi. 135-36.)

and Tennyson's wood in winter

> 'which grides and clangs
> Its leafless ribs and iron horns.'
> (*In Mem.*, cvii.)

In a moral illustration Solon compares the judgments of Zeus which purify the world to a wind in spring: it stirs the sea to the bottom and destroys the fair works of man; but in the heavens it makes clear air, the sun shines out in beauty, and no cloud is to be seen (*Bergk*, 13). Eros shakes the soul of Sappho as 'a wind on the mountain falling on the oaks' (*Bergk*, 42). Pindar, however, has a way of his own with winds, as with most things. His song is an οὖρος. In honour of Arcesilas of Cyrene he will 'freshen the gale of song' (*Pyth.*, iv. 3). He is to send a gale of glorious verses straight upon the house of Alcimidas (*Nem.*, vi. 29). Men's fortunes are as variable as the winds (*Oly.*, vi. 97; *Pyth.*, iii. 104; *Isth.*, iii. 18). The Sixth Pythian Ode, in honour of Xenocrates of Acragas, winner in the chariot-race, was perhaps sung at Delphi soon after the victory, and it has traces of local colour. The poet is visiting 'the centre-stone of loud-roaring earth'—ὀμφαλὸν

ἐριβρόμου χθονός. Ἐρίβρομος 'refers most naturally
to the noise of the waterfall, though the gorge was
full of echoes, the roar of the wind, the rumble of
thunder (v. 11), the rattling of chariots, the tumult
of the people.'[1]   There has been built for Xenocrates,
says Pindar, 'a treasure of song in the vale of Apollo
rich in gold, which neither wintry rain-storm coming
from strange lands, an implacable array from a
thunderous cloud, nor wind, shall carry away into
the recesses of the sea, pounded by the mass of rubble
sweeping along' (10-14).   In the Ninth Pythian the
maiden Cyrene is said to have been carried off by
Apollo 'from the wind-echoing dells of Pelion' (5),
which probably suggested to Swinburne his 'clefts
hoarse with wind.'   Of the Symplegades he says:

'The pair were living things, and rolled along more
swiftly than the files of the loud-thundering winds.'
(Pyth., iv. 209-10.)

In Greek drama the preoccupations of a seafaring
race have left deep marks.   The posture of men's
affairs, their mental and moral dispositions are often
expressed in terms of weather conditions.   A state of
soul is a wind, and a change of mood, of purpose, or
of fortunes is a counter-gale.   Iphis says to Evadne:

τέκνον, τίς αὔρα ; τίς στόλος ;

as if she were setting out on a voyage (Supplices, 1048).
Constant Antigone is said to be moved by the same
blasts as formerly (Antigone, 929).   Agamemnon's
resolve to sacrifice Iphigeneia is a change of spirit, a
veering gale, unblest and unholy (Agam., 217-220).[2]

---

[1] Professor Gildersleeve.
[2] For a few examples out of many, see Aeschylus, S.C.T., 707;
Sophocles, Trach., 827; Electra, 652; Euripides, Andromache, 148, 791;
Electra, 1147.

Of the sufferings at Troy through the inclemencies of the weather we do not hear much. There is but one brief indication in the *Odyssey*. Odysseus, in need of a coat, and made bold by wine, plays a beggar's part with spirit. He describes his sorry plight on the occasion of a night ambuscade under the walls of Troy. He and his comrades lay among the reeds in marshy ground, protected only by their shields. Through windless air the snow came down in the form of frozen crystals, and ice gathered on their arms (xiv. 468-82). In the Sixteenth Book of the *Iliad*, and in a manner indirect yet beautifully simple and natural, Homer reminds us that even Achilles was but as other men, and that shining armour and heavenly halos were not his only wear. Seeking a cup wherewith to make a libation, he went to his hut and opened the lid of a fair coffer that silver-footed Thetis placed on board of the ship which brought him to Troy, 'and she filled it well with tunics and cloaks to keep the wind from him (ἀνεμοσκεπέων) and thick rugs' (221-224). The Herald in the *Agamemnon* recites a tale of woe—bad quarters on board, on land rain and dew damaging clothes irretrievably and matting the hair till men looked like beasts, from Ida's snows bird-killing cold, and at midday intolerable heat (555-66). Clytemnestra imagines the Greek victors lodging in the captured houses of the Trojans, free at last from the frosts and dews of the open (334-36). The Chorus in the *Ajax* long for home; the thick dews on the hair never allow them to forget that they are still in dismal Troy-land (1206-10). In the *Rhesus* Hector reproaches the Thracian for his tardy appearance on the scene; many have already found graves there; the rest

135

endure hardships under arms—chill blasts and a parching sun (411-19).

In the above passages dew is seen in an unfavourable light. But it is not always so in Greek poetry. That which brings hardness into the peculiar life may be a blessing in the midst of a people. Odysseus, his life-force spent in battling with the waves, fears the θῆλυς ἐέρση of early morning, but he knows it will cheer the growing grass and springing corn in his native Ithaca. Dew is a symbol of tender life and youthful freshness.[1] Homer calls young lambs ἔρσαι (*Ody.*, ix. 222), Aeschylus speaks of lions' whelps as δρόσοι (*Agam.*, 141), and Sophocles uses the term ψακαλ-οῦχοι for mothers with young (*Fr.*, 962). The cheering property of dew is a favourite figure with Pindar. When he celebrates great deeds he is sprinkling them with the soft dew of his songs' outpouring (*Pyth.*, v. 97-100). He showers Alcmaeon's grave with the dew of song (*Pyth.*, viii. 57). To bring the glory of victory to one's clan is to water it with the delicious dew of the Graces (*Isth.*, v. 64).[2] When Menelaus received the mare from Antilochus, 'his heart was gladdened, and it was as the refreshing of dew round the ears of growing corn, when the fields are bristling' (*Il.*, xxiii. 596-600). In a similar figure in Arnold's *Sohrab and Rustum* the gladness is shown by movement:

> 'As, in the country, on a morn in June,
> When the dew glistens on the pearled ears,
> A shiver runs through the deep corn for joy—
> So, when they heard what Peran-Wisa said,
> A thrill through all the Tartar squadrons ran
> Of pride and hope for Sohrab, whom they lov'd.'

[1] 'The morn and liquid dew of youth.' (*Hamlet*, i. 3.)
[2] Cf. *Nem.*, viii. 40; *Isth.*, vii. 55.

The following figure expresses the devilish glee of Clytemnestra after the murder of her husband:

κἀκφυσιῶν ὀξεῖαν αἵματος σφαγὴν
βάλλει μ᾽ ἐρεμνῇ ψακάδι φοινίας δρόσου,
χαίρουσαν οὐδὲν ἧσσον ἢ διοσδότῳ
γάνει σπορητὸς κάλυκος ἐν λοχεύμασιν.

(*Agam.*, 1389-92.)

'Breathing out a quick spurt of the blood of his slaughter, he smites me with a dark splash of gory dew, and I rejoiced in it as a cornfield in the heaven-sent rain, what time the ear is coming to birth.'

On the charms of the winter season Greek poetry is silent. In epic and tragedy the point of view is that of the man in the trenches or the rustic or the sailor. The poets handicapped themselves by their choice of heroic themes in preference to contemporary experiences, which meant continual archaising. The ordinary Athenian probably preferred an hour or two in the gymnasium to a solitary 'constitutional.' In the more occasional and seasonal lyrics winter is man's mortal enemy, synonymous with storm, bringing discomfort and depression, and full of unpleasant associations. Winter delights are what Cowper calls 'intimate,' found indoors. In wintry weather, when Ζεὺς ὕει, Alcaeus calls for fuel and honey-sweet wine:

κάββαλλε τὸν χείμων᾽ ἐπὶ μὲν τίθεις
πῦρ, ἐν δὲ κίρναις οἶνον ἀφειδέως
μέλιχρον.

(*Bergk*, 34.)

Horace followed this recipe, and so did the Scottish poet Henryson:

'I mend the fyre, and beikit me about,
Than tuik ane drink my spreitis to confort.'

137

A character in Sophocles finds it pleasant to lie cosy and listen to the rain upon the roof:

$$\text{ὑπὸ στέγῃ}$$
$$\text{πυκνῆς ἀκοῦσαι ψακάδος εὑδούσῃ φρενί.}$$

(Nauck, *Fr.* 574.)

Tibullus is like-minded:

Aut, gelidas hibernus aquas cum fuderit Auster
Securum somnos, imbre juvante, sequi.

(I. i. 47-48.)

Wordsworth was an out-of-doors man, yet he could say:

'How touching, when, at midnight, sweep
Snow-muffled winds, and all is dark,
To hear—and sink again to sleep!'

For a description of the winter season we have to go to Hesiod, and we find it in the passage of the *Works and Days* (504-63) which characterises the month Lenaeon (December-January). The days of this month are all evil, 'cattle-flaying days'—κάκ' ἤματα βουδόρα πάντα. It is the hardest month for man and beast:

$$\text{χειμέριος, χαλεπὸς προβάτοις, χαλεπὸς δ' ἀνθρώποις.}$$

The sun is short-lived, the morning chill, and by evening you may look out for a soaking. Boreas is regent, and he makes earth and forest bellow. Beasts shudder and put their tails beneath their legs. Hair and fur are no protection; only the thick fleece of the sheep can withstand Boreas. He makes the old man, probably already battered by the elements into premature shrunken age, 'curved like a wheel' (if that be the meaning of τροχαλόν). The piece is a transcript, direct and vigorous, from the experience of one living in an upland environment, whose happiness and very existence depend on nature's moods. It has been very favourably compared with Virgil's description of winter (*Georg.*, iii. 349-83), which Landor says is 'a disgrace to the *Georgics*.' It is hardly that, and when Landor praises Cowper and Thomson in comparison, he overlooks the fact that in nearly half of his description of Siberia the latter is only adapting Virgil. Virgil's mistake lay in deserting Italy and Mantua for Scythia. For Hesiod's wild beasts of the woods shivering and seeking for shelter from the snow in hollows and caves, Virgil substitutes the deer and Thomson the bear, 'sourer as the storms increase.' But neither Virgil nor Cowper nor Thomson is in so direct a line of descent from Hesiod as is Gawain Douglas. In the Prologue to the Seventh Book of his translation of the *Aeneid*, he fills in, with wider perspective and excessive particularity, Hesiod's sketch. Farther along the line comes Burns, who, in a stanza of his *Winter Night*, adds appropriate sentiment to Hesiod's objectivity in his notice of animal life:

> 'List'ning the doors an' winnocks rattle,
> I thought me on the ourie cattle,
> Or silly sheep, wha bide this brattle
>   O' winter war,
> And thro' the drift, deep-lairing, sprattle,
>   Beneath a scaur.'

In some parts of Greece boys may have made sport with 'mockery kings of snow,' and ὁ παῖς τὸν κρύσταλλον was a proverb. But the island poets, who would have been most likely to find in snow a theme for song, probably had little experience of snowstorms. In Greek poetry there is no contemplation of falling snow, at once pleasing the eye and touching the heart, such as we find in Ecclesiasticus (xliii. 17, 18):

As birds flying down He sprinkleth the snow;
And as the lighting of the locust is the falling down
    thereof;
The eye will marvel at the beauty of its whiteness,
And the heart will be astonished at the raining of it.'

Besides using snow to illustrate number, and lightness, and softness (*Il.*, xix. 357; xv. 170; iii. 222), Homer has two pictures of falling snow. A shower of stones is compared to snowflakes which 'a violent wind, whirling the shadowy clouds, rains down thick on all-nurturing earth' (xii. 156-58). The other simile, though less appropriate, is a piece of patient workmanship: 'As the flakes of snow fall thick on a winter day, when Zeus, the All-wise, has set himself to snow, displaying his arrows to men; lulling the winds, he pours the snow steadily till he has covered the peaks of lofty mountains, and the jutting head-lands, and the grassy plains, and the fruitful works of men; and it is spread over the havens and beaches of the hoary sea, and the incoming wave holds it back, but all things else are overlaid, when the storm of Zeus is heavy; so thick flew the stones from both sides' (xii. 278-87). It is a picture of perfect stillness and ceaseless activity. This kind of snow has no bite; it is too quiet for drift and too damp to be powdery; but its fall is beautiful to see. Chapman has been more successful with the simile than Pope. The latter makes the sea

'Drink the dissolving fleeces as they fall.'

He makes the addition

'Bent with the weight the nodding woods are seen,'

which recalls Horace's

> *Nec iam sustineant onus*
> *Silvae laborantes.*
>
> *(Odes,* i. 9, 2-3.)

With their generalising statements both Pope and Horace miss the finest feature—the rich disguise and fairy-like drapery of individual trees. In the *Romaunt of the Rose* a maiden's throat is compared to new-fallen snow on a branch:

> 'La gorgete ot autresi blanche
> Cum est la noif desus la branche
> Quant il a freschement negié.'
>
> (545-47.)

Chaucer's (?) translation is

> 'Hir throte, al-so whyt of hewe
> As snow on braunche snowed newe.'

CHAPTER VII

MISCELLANEOUS

In his Third Olympian Pindar tells the story of the Finding of the Olive by Heracles. Pursuing the hind with golden horns, the hero came to the land of Ister, 'the land that lies behind the blast of the chill northwind. There he halted and wondered at the trees; and sweet desire for them took hold upon him, that he might plant them about the post which chariots double twelve times.' 'Hitherto no fair trees had flourished in the glens of Kronian Pelops, and for lack of such it seemed to him that the garden was at the mercy of the fierce rays of the sun.' And so Heracles made another journey to the Hyperborean folk, and from them 'he begged a plant to be a shade to all-comers and a crown for valorous deeds' (13-34). The story emphasises Greek appreciation of trees as a means of shade and also the spirit in which athletes strove for the palm of victory, content to receive as 'a far-seen splendour' nature's γλαυκόχροον κόσμον ἐλαίας placed on the head.

In Pindar's myth the olive is of the wild variety—κότινος. But the Athenians had an olive tradition of their own, proudly claiming the plant 'self-created and inviolable' as the gift of Athena to Attica. To understand the depth of Athenian veneration for the olive and its economic importance, we have but to read the famous Stasimon of the *Oedipus Coloneus*.[1]

[1] See also *Troades*, 498.

Round the altar of Athena in the Academy there was a group of sacred olive-trees (μορίαι), under the protection of Ζεὺς Μόριος, and supposed to have been propagated from the original olive on the Acropolis. Many olive-trees were the property of the State, and heavy penalties were attached to sacrilegious interference with these, even the stumps being regarded as sacred.[1]

In the Old Testament, in the light of monotheism, all trees are 'the trees of the Lord.' But among the polytheistic Greeks particular trees and plants were sacred to special deities. The oak was sacred to Zeus, the black poplar to Persephone, the white poplar to Heracles, the stone-pine to Cybele, the laurel to Apollo, while the vine and the ivy were associated with Dionysus. Plant mythology, however, is almost unknown to Homer, though he assigns the oak to Zeus and calls the olive ἱερά. Nor does he know much about tree-worship. Odysseus is said to have gone to Dodona 'to hear the advice given by the high leafy oak-tree of the god' (Ody., xiv. 327-28); and the Σελλοί, the interpreters of the meaning of the movements among the oak-leaves, are mentioned once (Il., xvi. 234).[2] The palm was held sacred in connection with the labour of Leto and the birth of Apollo (Theognis, 5; Homeric Hymn To Delian Apollo, 117; Callimachus, Hymn To Delos, 210). To the palm Euripides adds a laurel (Hecuba, 458; Ion, 919), and to these an olive (Iph. in T., 1097-1102). The same poet calls the palm πρωτόγονος, as having been created for the occasion. But, though Odysseus is said to have seen a palm growing by the altar of Apollo in Delos, it is not called sacred nor is there any reference to the birth of the god.

[1] See the oration of Lysias entitled Περὶ τοῦ σηκοῦ.
[2] See also Aeschylus, P.V., 831; Sophocles, Trach., 165-68.

The catalogue of trees and shrubs usually mentioned in Greek poetry is not far from complete in the Homeric poems. The elm (πτελέη), the white poplar (ἀχερωΐς), the evergreen oak (φηγός), the plane (πλατάνιστος) are named in the *Iliad* but not in the *Odyssey*. The pine (πίτυς) is found in both poems, but the πεύκη in the *Iliad* only. The wild fig-tree (ἐρινεός) occurs in both, but the cultivated variety (συκῆ) in the *Odyssey* only. The alder (κλήθρη) is peculiar to the *Odyssey*. The olive (ἐλαία) is named but once in the *Iliad*, while it is of frequent occurrence in the *Odyssey*. The laurel—or bay—(δάφνη), the cypress (κυπάρισσος), the cedar (κέδρος, perhaps a species of juniper), the citrus (θύον), the palm (φοῖνιξ) are found in the *Odyssey* only, and each but once. They seem to have been rare in Homer's experience. The laurel shades the cave of Polyphemus (ix. 183); the cypress, cedar, and citrus are mentioned in the description of Calypso's island (v. 60, 64).

Compared with that of other early epics Homer's list of trees is a lengthy one.[1] In the *Chanson de Roland*, for example, the pine, olive, laurel, and eglantine exhaust the list. The contrast is accounted for, partly at least, by difference of circumstances and of plan, Homer's art of simile and the character of the story in the *Odyssey* being in his favour. But in Homer no special tree is the object of popular veneration, like the mountain-ash, the birch, and the oak among the ancient Celts and Teutons. On the whole the oak seems to have been the tree most admired by Homer. He has placed two on the battlefield at Troy, one near the Scaean gate, the other farther out on the plain. These are φηγοί, less tall and sturdy than the δρύες. Height and leafiness are always attractive to him.

[1] The Indian epics excepted, of course.

The δρῦς is lofty-crested and high-foliaged (ὑψικάρηνος, ὑψίκομος). The silver-fir shoots up to heaven (οὐρανο-μήκης). Sleep is said to have alighted on 'a very tall fir, the loftiest that then on Ida rose through the mists to the upper air' (*Il.*, xiv. 287-88). His olive has wide-stretching leaves (τανύφυλλος). The mountains Neriton and Pelion are said to be 'quivering with leaves' (εἰνοσίφυλλον); the mountain of Phthires is ἀκριτόφυλλον, the leaves being so closely blended as to be indistinguishable. His poplar is tall and water-nourished (ὑδατοτρεφής), and its leaves are ever-tremulous, 'with their noise of falling showers,' [1] if we are to find in movement the point of the simile in which the industrious maidens in the house of Alcinous are compared to leaves on the poplar (*Ody.*, vii. 105-6).

Homer refers to the white blossom of the olive (*Il.*, xvii. 56), but he never uses the epithet γλαυκή, so often found in later poetry, denoting the greenish-gray colour of its leaves. Among poets, after Homer, Euripides is the most observant in the matter of trees. He applies the Homeric epithet ὑψίκομος to the silver-fir, ἐλάτη (*Alcestis*, 585). In the *Bacchae* he gives a picture of the Maenads sitting beneath the green firs—χλωραῖς ὑπ' ἐλάταις—on the roofless rocks (38). Later in the play he is careful to distinguish between the silver-fir and the stone-pine. The Maenads sit in a ravine shaded by pines—πεύκαισι συσκιάζον—(1052). Dionysus catches a fir-tree slip by the top and drags it down to the earth, till it becomes arched like a bow or a curving wheel that has its circumference marked out on a lathe (1064-67). In his notes to the play Paley remarks—'The stone-pine grows like our Scotch fir, with spreading boughs forming a wide and

---

[1] Tennyson. See also Sophocles, *Frag.* 24.

dense crown, totally unlike the spiry pyramidal
outline of the silver-fir. . . . The silver-fir, which has
a tall, straight, and flexible stem like the spruce-fir,
was well adapted for bending downwards. It was
from the same use of the same tree that Sinis the
robber obtained the name of πιτυοκάμπτης.'

In Greek poetry we find no forest-sentiment,
nothing worthy to be called forest-description, nothing
that can be set alongside of the episodes of Ráma in
the forest of Panchavati in the *Rámáyana* and of Nala
in the *Mahábhárata*, where vast and varied panoramas
of sylvan scenery are not only described but con-
templated. Homer probably knew something of
forests. In many of his similes in the *Iliad* he takes us
to the wooded mountains; but they are the scene of
the woodman's labours or of the ravage caused by
fire or wind or wild animals. Not one of these figures
gives sure proof that the poet had ever wandered in
a forest. Nor is the case much altered when we turn
to the *Odyssey*. The island off the harbour in the land
of the Cyclopes is wooded, and it abounds in wild
goats. The heroes roam over it all 'wondering.'
Kindly nymphs start the goats and soon they have
game in plenty. The wood itself inspires neither joy
nor fear. At the cave of Polyphemus Odysseus sees
a few laurels and pines and oaks, but to these he is
indifferent. There are other caves and 'windy
heights' in the vicinity, but there is no reference to a
forbidding forest. In Circe's island a copse surrounds
the witch's halls, and the phrase διὰ δρυμὰ πυκνὰ καὶ
ὕλην used to denote it is an Homeric commonplace.
The glades are 'sacred,' owing to the presence of the
goddess; but I doubt whether the word ἱεράς will
bear to be translated by our 'uncanny' or 'eerie,' or
any such word suggesting mystery or danger. The

trees round Calypso's grotto inspire wonder, and even
the most sceptical must accept them as ornaments.
In the account of his wanderings Odysseus has nothing
to say of the 'waving shadows of the woodlands'—
horrentibus umbris—noted by Virgil (*Aen.*, i. 311; iii.
230). Men do not 'tremble before wood and rock'
(viii. 350). In the *Odyssey* there is not, as in *Beowulf*,
'a joyless wood of mountain-trees leaning over a hoar
rock.' [1] Odysseus is not, like Aeneas, a Man of
Destiny, who reaches the Promised Land, and at
dawn sees a mighty wood, through which a pleasant
stream swirls seawards, the haunt of fluttering birds
that charm the air with their song (*Aen.*, vii. 29-36).
When Homer's hero comes out of the sea and looks
about him on Scheria, he sees a wood on the hillside.
He thinks of his own cruel need, not of beauty to please
the eye. He fears wild beasts, but he must have a
place of shelter, and he finds a perfect one. 'So he
crept in beneath two bushes growing from one root,
one a lentisk, the other an olive. Neither the force
of the moist winds blew through these, nor did the
beaming sun strike on them with its rays, nor did the
rain pierce right through, so closely intertwined did
they grow. Under them went Odysseus, and quickly
did he heap together with his hands a broad couch,
for there was a fall of leaves in great plenty, enough
to draw over two or three men in winter time, even
if the weather were very hard' (v. 476-85).

> 'Feather-beds are saft,
> Pented rooms are bonnie,'

but here is Mother Nature's own cosiness. A wild
beast may have been the previous occupant. So

---

[1]   Fyrgen-bēamas
    Ofer hārne stān helonian funde,
    Wyn-lēasne wudu.   (1414-16.)

Homer must have thought, for he utilises four of the lines, with very slight change, in his description of the lair of a boar (xix. 440-43). How unerringly has Homer interpreted the needs and instincts of a man whose portion, for the time, is with the beasts; no lendings to unbutton, 'the thing itself, a poor, bare, forked animal,' to quote Lear's words! Let him sleep on for twenty-four hours. Then he will awake, see Nausicaa, and compare her to a young palm at which he once marvelled.

Neither the elegiac nor the lyric poets bring us to close quarters with woods. Of the extant dramas the *Bacchae* is the only one that gives much opportunity for the observation of woodland scenery. The Maenads are said to be roving among the dark shady hills (218); but an unbroken mass of forest would not have suited their revels and dances. They do not range far from the upper boundary of the cattle-pastures. The herdsmen hide among bushes (722). Probably pines and firs 'fledge the wild-ridged mountain' here and there. In the dells overhanging trees form a denser shade, and there the women are seen (1051). There are grassy glades too (1048). Parts of the body of Pentheus are said to lie 'among the leafage of the thick wood' (1138). Cadmus finds them lying 'in the impenetrable wood' (1221). And the mention of ὕλη brings us to another consideration.

The Greeks had no word for *forest* in the modern sense, as distinct from a *wood*. When Homer wishes to give us the impression of a vast extent of wooded ground, he uses the term ἄσπετος ὕλη. But ὕλη itself does not always mean a collection of tall trees; it often means bushes, or brushwood. It may have that meaning in the above quotations from the

Bacchae.[1] Τάρφος is a thicket of low growth; a lion's den is in βαθείης τάρφεσιν ὕλης (*Il.*, v. 555). Δρυμά, originally a collection of oaks, is a coppice of any kind of trees; ῥωπήϊα πυκνά is thick undergrowth. When two boars are said to snap the ὕλην by the roots (*Il.*, xii. 148), the smaller growths only must be understood. The boar of Calydon lays low row upon row of tall trees (*Il.*, ix. 541), but they are fruit-trees. In Ovid the same animal overturns a whole grove (*Met.*, viii. 340). He was a miraculous sort of brute, 'a mighty sight of a pig.' The term ἀγρία ὕλη is found in Archilochus and Sophocles, meaning a collection of uncultivated trees, as opposed to ἥμερα. It might be translated by our 'wild wood.' But there is nothing in Greek poetry that quite corresponds to the expanse of moor, heath, and forest, beyond the *mark* of the *tun*, the home of black wood-elves and other uncanny creatures which struck dread into the hearts of our English forefathers.

It was the ἄλσος that made the most pleasant appeal to the Greeks. The word, however, has more than one meaning. When Aphrodite is said to love the ἄλσεα σκιόεντα (Homeric Hymn *To Aphrod.*, 20), and when Hippolytus is said to pursue wild beasts, in the company of Artemis, χλωρὰν δ᾽ ἀν᾽ ὕλην (*Hipp.*, 17), ἄλσος and ὕλη would seem to be synonymous. So in Latin *nemus* and *silva* are sometimes interchangeable. But when such places are spoken of, in general language, as the haunt of Nymphs, the word used is always ἄλσος (Homeric Hymn *To Aphrod.*, 97; Homer,

---

[1] 'Euripides needed to go to Macedonia to find forests high enough to make a dignified procession for Orpheus' (M. A. E. Zimmern in *The Greek Commonwealth*). He adds, 'There is nothing of German forest sentiment (*Wald-Zauber*) in the description of the Maenads on the mountains. The two things are as wide apart as is the Parthenon from a Gothic cathedral.' That needed saying. There has been too much sentimental writing on the *Bacchae*.

Il., xx. 8; *Ody.*, x. 350), denoting *woodland* rather than *wood* in the strict sense. Sometimes ἄλσος is a spot planted with trees and sacred to some deity, such as the grove of Athena in Scheria (*Ody.*, vi. 291-92). One in Ithaca contained an altar to the Nymphs (*Ody.*, xvii. 208-11). The presence of trees is sometimes emphasised; Maron, the priest of Apollo, dwells ἐν ἄλσεϊ δενδρήεντι (*Ody.*, ix. 200). Sometimes, again, ἄλσος stands for the whole sacred enclosure—τέμενος (Pindar, *Oly.*, iii. 18, etc.). Homer calls Onchestus the ἄλσος of Poseidon (*Il.*, ii. 506); Thebes is the ἄλσος of Thebe (*Antig.*, 845). The sea is πόντιον ἄλσος (*Persae*, 111). The grove of the Eumenides described by Sophocles is a dense plantation and forbidden ground; those in Scheria and Ithaca are situated by the public road and open to wayfarers. Groves, prized by Greeks, were banned by orthodox Hebrews as affording opportunities for idolatry. Backsliding Israelites burned incense 'under oaks and poplars and elms, because the shadow thereof is good' (*Hosea*, iv. 13). 'Ahab made a grove' (1 *Kings*, xvi. 33). Good Hezekiah 'removed the high places, and brake the images, and cut down the groves' (2 *Kings*, xviii. 4).

Fire in a forest provides Homer with several analogies. The sheen of bronze is like the gleam of fire in a huge wood (*Il.*, ii. 455-58). Trojan heads fall like saplings burned to the roots by the flame of a furious fire in an unthinned wood—ἐν ἀξύλῳ ὕλῃ (xi. 155-59). Hector rages as a deadly fire among brushwood (xv. 605-6).[1]

Warriors are likened to trees. Polypoetes and Leonteus standing at the gate are like 'oak-trees with

---

[1] In Icelandic verse fire is called 'the forest-bane,' 'the birch-pest,' 'the wood-wolf,' etc.

lofty crests, that endure wind and rain continually, firm-set with roots great and far-spreading:

ῥίζῃσιν μεγάλῃσι διηνεκέεσσ᾽ ἀραρυῖαι

(xii. 131-34).

Four words! What a line![1] A similar figure— really a double figure—is finely and patriotically handled by Virgil, who makes Pandarus and Bitias, born in a grove and now tall as their native pines or mountains, stand on each side of the gate, with fluttering plumes:

> Quales aëriae liquentia flumina circum,
> Sive Padi ripis Athesim seu propter amoenum,
> Consurgunt geminae quercus, intonsaque cælo
> Attollunt capita, et sublimi vertice nutant.

(ix. 679-82.)

Falling or fallen warriors also turn Homer's thoughts to trees. Crethon and Orsilochus fall like lofty firs (*Il.*, v. 560). Young Imbrius falls like an ash seen from far on a mountain crest, which is cut by the axe, and brings to the ground its tender foliage (xiii. 178-81). Ever practical, the poet knows that, though a good tree fall, its end is not yet. The oak or white poplar or pine to which Arius and Sarpedon are compared is to serve as ship-timber (xiii. 389-92; xvi. 482-91). The fall of Simoisius with his lofty crest recalls to Homer's mind the sight of a poplar growing in a fen, bushy a-top with shoots. A wheelwright,[2] in need of a felloe for a beautiful chariot, comes with his gleaming blade and cuts it down; it now lies drying by a river-bank (iv. 482-89). But the most beautiful of all such

---

[1] Besides suggesting by its sound clasp and clamp and serpentine spread, the line shows how the poet can take advantage of varying dative endings.

[2] Fastidious Pope calls him 'an artist,' by which he may mean *artisan*.

similes is that in which Euphorbus 'whose hair was like the hair of the Graces' is likened to an olive: 'As when a man rears a goodly olive shoot in a lonely spot, where plenteous water moistens it, a plant fair and flourishing; and the breath of all the breezes shakes it, and it bourgeons thick with white blossom; but suddenly a wind comes with a mighty hurricane and wrenches it from its trench and stretches it out upon the earth: in such wise Euphorbus, son of Panthus, of the good ashen spear, did Menelaus, son of Atreus, slay and strip of his armour' (xvii. 53-60). The simile was a favourite with Pythagoras, who had a ghostly proprietary interest in it.

The figure of youth growing up like a plant and the metaphorical use of ἔρνος, θάλος, ῥίζα, etc., are too common to require illustrative comment.[1] As a reminder of the gardener-instinct spoken of in a previous chapter nothing is more striking than the remark of Athena to the Eumenides in the play of Aeschylus:

στέργω γάρ, ἀνδρὸς φιτυποίμενος δίκην,
τὸ τῶν δικαίων τῶνδ' ἀπένθητον γένος.

(911-12.)

'For, like a gardener, do I love the stock of this just people freed from grief.' And in the same play the usefulness of trees, and especially of the olive, is emphasised in part of the prayer of the Chorus calling down blessings on Attica:

'May no tree-blighting blast of damage blow.'

(938.)

For stateliness Odysseus compares Nausicaa to a palm; but in classical Greek poetry there are no examples of the surpassing excellence of a hero or a

---

[1] See Homer, *Ody.*, xiv. 175, etc.; Sophocles, *Trach.*, 144-150; *Ajax*, 558; *Antig.*, 599; Pindar, *Nem.*, vi. 38; *Oly.*, vi. 68; Aeschylus, *S.C.T.*, 755; Euripides, *Iph. in T.*, 610, etc.

heroine being compared to the superiority of one tree over another, such as are found in the Icelandic *Elder Edda*. For instance, the following is part of Sigrun's lament over Helgi in the *Lay of Helgi*:

'As high above all lords did Helgi bear him
As the ash-tree's glory from the thorn ariseth.'

Nor are trees used as emblems of destitution as in the *Lay of Hamdir*:

'All alone am I now as in holt is the aspen;
As the fir-tree of boughs, so of kin am I bare;
As bare of things longed for as the willow of leaves
When the bough-breaking wind the warm day
    endeth.' [1]

In moralising Pindar there are some examples of tree and plant analogies. 'In a short time the delight of mortals grows up, and so in a little it falls to the ground, shaken by an adverse doom' (*Pyth.*, viii. 92-94). 'Excellence grows, exalted among men wise and just, as when a tree watered by fresh dews shoots up to the buxom aether' (*Nem.*, viii. 40, 41). But in moral figures drawn from trees Greek cannot compare in richness with Hebrew. One has but to recall the beautiful thirty-first chapter of *Ezekiel*, from the third verse to the end: 'Behold, the Assyrian was a cedar in Lebanon,' etc. Or *Isaiah*, xiv. 7, 8, addressed to the King of Babylon:

'The whole earth is at rest, and is quiet: they
    break forth into singing.
Yea, the fir-trees rejoice at thee, and the cedars of
    Lebanon, saying, Since thou art laid down, no
    feller is come up against us.'

[1] Magnússon and Morris's translation. Lucan's comparison of Pompey to an aged oak (*Phars.*, i. 136-143) has been kept in remembrance by the words—*stat magni nominis umbra*.

Or the apostrophe in *Zechariah*, xi. 2:

> 'Howl, fir-tree; for the cedar is fallen; because the mighty are spoiled; howl, O ye oaks of Bashan; for the forest of the vintage is come down.'

The Greeks of the classical period do not apostrophise trees. Hesiod did not treat of trees, and Virgil's sentiment is his own when he prays that it may be his, unknown to fame, to love the woods, and calls for one to lay him in the cool dells of Haemus, beneath the shade of giant boughs.

Comparisons between men and leaves are common in all literatures. Homer compares the Greeks standing in their multitudes on the plain of Scamander to leaves and flowers (*Il.*, ii. 467-68). In vi. 146-49 the reference is to the rise and fall of particular families:

οἵη περ φύλλων γενεή, τοίη δὲ καὶ ἀνδρῶν.
φύλλα τὰ μέν τ᾽ ἄνεμος χαμάδις χέει, ἄλλα δέ θ᾽ ὕλη
τηλεθόωσα φύει, ἔαρος δ᾽ ἐπιγίγνεται ὥρῃ,
ὣς ἀνδρῶν γενεὴ ἡ μὲν φύει, ἡ δ᾽ ἀπολήγει.

'Even as the generation of leaves so also is that of men. Some the wind sheds on the ground, but others the wood flourishing puts forth, and they come on in the season of spring; so with the race of men, one is fruitful and another dies away.' [1] Simonides calls this simile 'the fairest saying of the Chian bard.' Mimnermus generalises the sentiment, applying it to the passing of youth (*Bergk*, 2). Bacchylides gives a new turn to the figure, and also localises, when he speaks of Heracles' visit to the lower world: 'There, by the streams of Cocytus, he perceived the souls of

---

[1] Cf. Aristophanes, *Birds*, 685.

hapless mortals like the leaves which the wind makes
to tremble on the gleaming headlands of Ida where
flocks graze' (v. 63-67). Virgil adds a touch in comparing the ghosts to leaves that fall 'at the first chill
of autumn frost' (*Aeneid*, vi. 309-10). Dante adds
another and another. The souls drop into Charon's
boat 'as in autumn the leaves lift themselves off, one
after other, until the branch sees on the earth all its
spoil':

> *Come d' autunno si levan le foglie*
> *L' una appresso dell' altra, infin che il ramo*
> *Vede alla terra tutte le sue spoglie.*
>
> (*Inf.*, iii. 112-14.)[1]

Leaves play small part in Greek metaphor.
Clytemnestra declares that the return of Agamemnon
is the reappearance of leaves on the old tree, to be a
shade in the scorching days of the Dog-star (*Agam.*,
966-67). 'The very-aged (ὑπεργήρων : Chaucer's
for-old, which unhappily has not survived), when his
leaf is in the sere (φυλλάδος ἤδη κατακαρφομένης),
walks the three-foot ways' (*Agam.*, 79-81). That is
Aeschylus's version of Shakespeare's

> 'My way of life has fallen into the sere,'

and

> 'That time of year thou may'st in me behold
> When yellow leaves, or none, or few, do hang
> Upon those boughs which shake against the cold.'

Lacking opportunity, Pindar says, the glory of the
swift feet of Ergoteles would have shed its leaves

[1] Cf. Seneca, *Oedipus*, 600; Milton, *P.L.*, i. 351; Byron, *Destruction of
Sennacherib*; Arnold, *Balder Dead*, i. ; Swinburne, *Atalanta in Calydon*:—

> 'Nor she in that waste world with all her dead,
>   My mother, among the pale flocks fallen as leaves.'

Conversely, in his *Ode to the West Wind*, Shelley compares leaves to
ghosts.

(*κατεφυλλορόησε*), unhonoured and unsung (*Oly.*, xii. 15).

'From leaf to flower and flower to fruit.'

The love of flowers is so widespread as to seem the earliest and most purely instinctive form of the sensuous feeling for nature. Yet in literature flower-feeling has beginnings and its story is one of growth, so that it may be treated chronologically from Homer onwards. It is notable that in the Eden of Scripture there are no flowers. The word 'flowers' occurs first [1] in the Old Testament in the instruction given for the gold-work ornamentation on the candlestick of the Tabernacle (*Exod.*, xxv. 31). Homer too has basins and cups adorned with flower-work (*Il.*, xxiii. 885; *Ody.*, iii. 440; xxiv. 275). Andromache embroiders a cloak with variegated flowers—*θρόνα* (*Il.*, xxii. 441). 'Flowery meadows,' which are so common in Greek poetry, make their first appearance in Homer; in the Catalogue Pyrasus is 'flowery.' The simple metaphor *ἥβης ἄνθος* occurs first in *Iliad*, xiii. 484. But Homer names very few flowers. He compares the Greeks streaming out from huts and ships to bees issuing from a rock and flying in clusters among 'the flowers of spring' (*Il.*, ii. 88-90). In Virgil, the souls on the banks of Lethe are likened to bees in sunny summer settling on the many-coloured flowers of the meadow; but the poet adds:

> *et candida circum*
> *Lilia funduntur.*
>
> (*Aen.*, vi. 707-9.)

As a couch for Zeus and Hera on Gargarus the earth puts forth 'fresh grass, and dewy lotus, and crocus,

---

[1] Not necessarily first in the order of composition.

and hyacinth, thick and soft' (*Il.*, xiv. 347-49).[1] The λωτός was a kind of clover with yellow flower, much appreciated by horses. The ὑάκινθος is said not to have been our flower of that name, but whether iris or larkspur or gladiolus botanists have not yet determined. It is supposed to be different from the later flower of Ajax, which was probably the scarlet gladiolus. When the locks of Odysseus are compared to the hyacinth flower (*Ody.*, vi. 231; xxiii. 158) the reference may be either to colour (dark) or to the clustering curls. The κρόκος, saffron-flower, does not occur elsewhere in Homer; the epithet κροκόπεπλος is found only in the *Iliad*. The poppy, μήκων, is named once, in a simile, but it is a cultivated species—ἥ τ᾽ ἐνὶ κήπῳ—(*Il.*, viii. 306). As yet it has no connection with Demeter. In Calypso's meadow only one flower is represented, the violet, ἴον, a dark-coloured flower. The sea is ἰοειδής, iron is ἰόεις, and wool ἰοδνεφές. The meadows of Hades are covered with asphodel bloom (ἀσφοδελός) or king's spear, a white flower. The roots of the plant were eaten by the poor, as Hesiod suggests (*W.D.*, 41), and its presence in the lower world may be accounted for by the primitive notion that the shades of the dead needed sustenance, though Homer may not have been conscious of such an explanation. Neither the rose nor the lily is named by Homer; they were late in arriving from Persia. But Homeric epithets assume knowledge of them; ῥοδοδάκτυλος is an epithet of Dawn, and the oil with which Aphrodite anoints the dead body of Hector is ῥοδόεις, 'rose-scented' (*Il.*, xxiii. 186). The epithet λειριόεις is applied to the voice of the cicada

---

[1] This gave Milton his cue for the couch of Adam and Eve:—

'Pansies, and violets, and asphodel,
And hyacinth, Earth's freshest softest lap.' (*P.L.*, ix. 1040-41.)

(*Il.*, iii. 152), a sound loved by the Greeks.[1] It may mean *shrill* or *clear* or *delicate*. The same epithet is used of the skin in *Iliad*, xiii. 830; of the singing of the Muses in Hesiod's *Theogony*, 41; of the eyes of young men and maidens in Bacchylides, xvi. 95; of the chant of the Sirens in Apollonius Rhodius, *Argon.*, iv. 903.

Homer, therefore, has little flower-sense. Not a single epithet of form or of colour is attached to any flower. Calypso's violets are left uncharacterised. Crocuses and hyacinths form a bed thick and soft— πυκνὸν καὶ μαλακόν. The poet makes no allusion to the fragrance of flowers. They are not spoken of sentimentally as associated with human joy or sorrow, nor regarded as significant symbols. Our wonder at this will be less if we consider how small a part flowers play in other European heroic poetry. In the *Chanson de Roland* Charles comes to a meadow 'full of flowers, which are red with the blood of his barons' (2871, 72). 'The holy flowers' of Paradise are referred to (1856). The hair of the Emir is 'white as a flower in summer' (3162). His beard is 'as white as a flower' (3173). Not one flower is named.[2] In the *Nibelungenlied* Siegfried falls among the flowers (xvi. 988). Rüdiger's heart bears virtues 'as the grass blooms with flowers in May' (xxvi. 1639). There are no flowers in *Beowulf*.

The Hesiodic poems are almost destitute of flowers. There are flowers in the garlands put by Athena on the head of the maiden, 'the beautiful evil' formed by Hephaestus (*Theog.*, 576). The epithet ῥοδοπήχυς occurs in *Theogony*, 247 and 251; there is a crocus in

---

[1] The sound is really made by the action of the wings.

[2] In some of the Chansons de Geste there is found the expression *Par Deu, qui fist la rose en mai*—'God, who made the rose in May.' See L. Gautier's edition of the *Chanson de Roland*, p. 17.

the Hesiodic Catalogue, 19. Archilochus is the first to mention 'the fair flower of the rose-bush'—ῥοδῆς τε καλὸν ἄνθος (*Bergk*, 29). The epithet ἰοστέφανος, so well known later, is applied to Aphrodite in Solon (*Bergk*, 19, 4), and to the Muses in Theognis (250). The longest flower passage in classical Greek poetry is in the Homeric Hymn *To Demeter*. Persephone was playing with the daughters of Oceanus and gathering flowers in a meadow on the plain of Nysa, 'roses and crocuses and beautiful violets, irises (ἀγαλλίδας) too and hyacinths, and a narcissus which Earth made to grow by the counsel of Zeus to please Polydectes, a snare for the flower-bud [1] girl, a flower wondrous and radiant. A thing of awe it was for all to see, both immortal gods and mortal men. From the root of it there grew a hundred heads, and most sweet was its fragrance, and all the wide heaven and the whole earth and the salt sea wave laughed. Then the girl amazed stretched forth both hands to seize the lovely plaything' (6-16). Later in the poem lilies are added to the list (426-28). There too the narcissus is said to be 'like a crocus,' so that the yellow *tazetta* species may be meant. The narcissus was sacred to Demeter and Persephone, but its derivation from νάρκη, the numbness of death, is problematical.

Of the lyric poets, and indeed of all Greek poets, Sappho takes first place as a lover of flowers. 'All nature sings with her. The flowers, the grass, the sea, the rain, the dew, the moon, the stars sing in her song. The world within is projected through her, so to speak, into the doings and phenomena of surrounding nature, and nature seen with her eyes is all colour and all light.' [2] Some of her comparisons drawn from

---

[1] 'Queen rose of the rosebud garden of girls.' (Tennyson, *Maud*.)

[2] Fraccaroli, *Lirici Greci, Poesia Melica*, p. 199.

nature exist only in phrases—ῥόδων ἀβροτέρα, 'finer than roses'; ὕδατος ἀπαλωτέρα, 'more delicate than water.' (123.)   Passion makes her 'more pale-green than grass':

$$\chi\lambda\omega\rho\sigma\tau\acute{\epsilon}\rho\alpha\ \delta\grave{\epsilon}\ \pi\sigma\acute{\iota}\alpha\varsigma$$
ἔμμι.   (2.)

Ἔστι μοι κάλα πάϊς, χρυσίοισιν ἀνθέμοισιν
ἐμφέρην ἔχοισα μόρφαν, Κλῆϊς ἀγαπάτα.

(85.)

'I have a fair child with a form like golden flowers, beloved Cleïs.'   Cretan women dance round an altar 'trampling the tender soft bloom of the grass':

πόας τέρεν ἄνθος μάλακον μάτεισαι.[1]   (54.)

In a Bridal Song an unmarried girl is compared to 'a hyacinth on the mountains which the shepherds tread underfoot, and the purple flower lies on the ground':

Οἴαν τὰν ὑάκινθον ἐν οὔρεσι ποίμενες ἄνδρες
πόσσι καταστείβοισι, χάμαι δέ τε πόρφυρον ἄνθος.

(94.)

The companion lines liken a virgin-bride to 'a sweet apple that reddens on the top of the bough, a-top of the topmost bough; the gatherers forgot it; nay, they did not forget it, but they could not reach it':

Οἶον τὸ γλυκύμαλον ἐρεύθεται ἄκρῳ ἐπ' ὕσδῳ
ἄκρον ἐπ' ἀκροτάτῳ· λελάθοντο δὲ μαλοδροπῆες,
οὐ μὰν ἐκλελάθοντ', ἀλλ' οὐκ ἐδύναντ' ἐπίκεσθαι.[2]

(93.)

---

[1] Cf. Homer, *Ody.*, ix. 449.
[2] Cf. Catullus, lxii. 39-58; xi. 21-24; Ariosto, *O.F.*, i. 42:
    La verginella è simile alla rosa.

A vulgar woman 'has no share in the roses of Pieria':

οὐ γὰρ πεδέχεις βρόδων
τῶν ἐκ Πιερίας.

She shall wander obscure even in the house of Hades.
(68.)

Here we may set down the anonymous Flower-song of children, arranged in the form of question and answer:

A. Ποῦ μοι τὰ ῥόδα, ποῦ μοι τὰ ἴα, ποῦ μοι τὰ καλὰ σέλινα ;
B. Ταδὶ τὰ ῥόδα, ταδὶ τὰ ἴα, ταδὶ τὰ καλὰ σέλινα.

(19.)

Bacchylides has not much of interest on this head. He is fond of using conventional epithets. Ἰοστέφανος is applied to Persephone (iii. 2), to the Muses (v. 3), and to Thetis (xii. 122), but without any mystic significance. The rare epithet καλυκοστέφανος, 'crowned with flower-buds,' is used of Artemis (v. 98), appropriately enough, Artemis being a vegetation goddess, and it is applied also to the daughters of Proetus (x. 108), who had been aided by Artemis. When Theseus descended into the sea, Amphitrite gave him a mantle of gleaming purple and put on his head 'a choice wreath dark with roses, which guileful Aphrodite had given her in days of old on her marriage' (xvi. 112-116). This associates the rose with Aphrodite, and the passage shows Bacchylides' love of colour and colour-contrast.

In Pindar's Sixth Olympian, which blazes with colour, there is a notable flower passage. In the dark shade of a thicket violet-tressed Evadne put aside her silver pitcher and crimson girdle, and her child was born. He was left there, but was nursed by two

L   161

gleaming-eyed serpents: 'But he was hidden among rushes, in a boundless brake, the tender body bathed in the golden and deep-purple rays of violets'[1] (53-56). From ἴον the boy was called Ἴαμος. There is an adaptation of the scene in Swinburne's *Atalanta in Calydon*:

> 'White or duskier violet,
> Fair as those that in far years
> With their buds left luminous
> And their little leaves made wet,
> From the warmer dew of tears,
> Mother's tears in extreme need,
> Hid the limbs of Iamus.'

Pindar has many flower metaphors. Youth and wealth and songs are flowers. The flower of youth bourgeons (κυμαίνει). 'Once more, after the wintry gloom of changeful months, the happy hearth of the Cleonymidae blossoms, as the earth with red roses, by the counsels of the gods' (*Isth.*, iii. 18). To Sogenes the poet says, 'Even honey palls and the delightful flowers of Aphrodite' (*Nem.*, vii. 51, 52). But for him 'the Muse is fastening together gold and white ivory and the delicate flower (white coral) taken from beneath the dew of the sea' (77-79). Dr. Bury quotes from Swinburne's *A Forsaken Garden*: 'The foam-flowers endure when the rose-blossoms wither.'

For mention of specific flowers Aeschylus is drawn blank, and we must content ourselves with 'the children of all-fruitful earth' which Atossa carries to the tomb of Darius:

> ἄνθη τε πλεκτά, παμφόρου γαίας τέκνα.
>
> (*Persae*, 618.)

---

[1] Violets, or pansies, or irises, or gillyflowers, or wall-flowers—what you and your botanist will.

There is almost equal dearth in Sophocles. The narcissus and the crocus flourish at Colonus:

> θάλλει δ' οὐρανίας ὑπ' ἄχνας
> ὁ καλλίβοτρυς κατ' ἦμαρ ἀεὶ
> νάρκισσος, μεγάλαιν θεαῖν
> ἀρχαῖον στεφάνωμ', ὅ τε
> χρυσαυγὴς κρόκος.
>
> (*Oed. Col.*, 681-85.)

The narcissus, as 'the flower of imminent death,' is consecrated to Demeter and Persephone; the epithet καλλίβοτρυς implies a flower with many spikes. Euripides enumerates no flowers in the coronal which Hippolytus culls from the virgin meadow in honour of Artemis (*Hipp.*, 73-83). Roses and hyacinths bloom in the meadow on Ida where the goddesses contend for the prize of beauty (*I.A.*, 1297-99). Apollo finds Creusa gathering golden crocuses (*Ion*, 887-90). When carried off by Hermes Helen was among the roses (*Helena*, 242-45). The child Archemorus met his death when plucking flowers, ἕτερον ἐφ' ἑτέρῳ (*Hypsipyle*, Nauck, Frag. 754). The meadows of the Μύσται in Aristophanes' *Frogs* are bright with roses:

> χωρῶμεν ἐς πολυρρόδους
> λειμῶνας ἀνθεμώδεις.
>
> (448-49.)[1]

In the *Peace* Trygaeus wishes to be back at the farm, among the figs and olives, to see 'the violet-bed by the well' (577-78).[2] Simple words on rustic lips,

---

[1] Cf. Propertius—
> Mulcet ubi Elysias aura beata rosas.   (iv. 7, 60.)

Tibullus adds perfume—
> Totosque per agros
> Floret odoratis terra benigna rosis.   (i. 3, 61, 62.)

[2] Cf. Virgil—
> Irriguumque bibant violaria fontem.   (Georg., iv. 32.)

but they mean much to the modern reader. Aristophanes is the only classical Greek poet who explicitly associates memories of home with flowers. Chaeremon puts side by side bright-beaming roses and white lilies:

ῥόδ᾽ ὀξυφεγγῆ κρίνεσιν ἀργεννοῖς ὁμοῦ.
(*Thyestes*, Frag. 8.)

He calls the rose 'the finest nursling of the spring':

τιθήνημ᾽ ἔαρος ἐκπρεπέστατον.
(*Odysseus*, Frag. 13.)

Thus the rose is the queen of flowers, and ῥόδα may sometimes stand for flowers in general. Wild roses of various kinds grew in some parts of Greece. Matthew Arnold may not have been far out when he embalmed Oeta in the fragrance of an English June:

'O villages of Oeta
With hedges of the wild rose!'
(*Merope*.)

The rose, the flower of Aphrodite, Alamanni's

Amorosa, gentil, lodata rosa,

is the flower of passion, yet how coolly and dispassionately Greek poets speak even of it! Homer has but one flower simile, properly speaking, that in which the bowed head of Gorgythion is likened to a poppy heavy with fruit and the showers of spring (*Il.*, viii. 306-308). European poetry can show a long list of flower figures used to heighten the pathos of untimely death, most of them expressed more tenderly and exquisitely than Homer's example. We have but to think of Virgil's Pallas (*Aen.*, xi. 68-71), of his Euryalus (ix. 435-38), of Ovid's Hyacinthus (*Met.*, x. 190-95), of Ariosto's Brandi-

164

marte (*O.F.*, xliii. 169), of Camoens' Ignaz de Castro (*Os Lus.*, iii. 134), of Arnold's Sohrab.

> 'Most can raise the flowers now,
> For all have got the seed.'

Their seedsman was Homer, and they knew it. Undoubtedly Greek heroic feeling prized the plant and the sapling above the flower. The conservative tragedians were full of the Homeric spirit, and some of their flower images have been stigmatised as harsh; such as that in Aeschylus:

$$\mathrm{\dot{o}\rho\hat{\omega}\mu\epsilon\nu\ \dot{a}\nu\theta o\hat{\nu}\nu\ \pi\acute{\epsilon}\lambda a\gamma o\varsigma\ A\mathring{\iota}\gamma a\hat{\iota}o\nu\ \nu\epsilon\kappa\rho o\hat{\iota}\varsigma}$$

(*Agam.* 659),

and that in Euripides:

$$\mathrm{\dot{\omega}\varsigma\ a\mathring{\iota}\mu a\tau\eta\rho\dot{o}\nu\ \pi\acute{\epsilon}\lambda a\gamma o\varsigma\ \dot{\epsilon}\xi a\nu\theta\epsilon\hat{\iota}\nu\ \dot{a}\lambda\acute{o}\varsigma.}$$

(*I.T.*, 300.)

But in interpreting ἀνθεῖν, its derivatives and compounds, 'don't press' may be as salutary advice as in golf. It is in monodic lyric that one expects to find more marked expression of feeling for flowers. Had we possessed fuller remains of Bridal-songs, we should probably have found further models for the lines of Catullus:

> *Uxor in thalamo tibi est,*
> *Ore floridulo nitens*
> *Alba parthenice velut*
> *Luteumve papaver.*

(lxi. 185-88.)

After all, it is none so far a cry from the Cleïs of Sappho and the 'flower-bud' Persephone of an anonymous Greek poet to the Troubadour convention of comparing a lady to an Easter rose, to Chaucer's Emily,

> 'that fairer was to sene
> Than is the lilie upon his stalke grene,'

165

or to Milton's

> 'Proserpin gathering flow'rs
> Herself a fairer flow'r.'

Yet we have only to recall Dante's Rose and the very title of the *Roman de la Rose* to appreciate the difference between Greek naturalism and the allegorical conceptions of mediaeval theology and chivalry.

A population largely industrial is apt to be forgetful of the earth as the sustaining mother of men. It needs a bloody war to rouse us to a fitful sense of sanctity in corn-bearing land and the precious fruits brought forth by the sun. Heiring the legacies of long ages of civilisation so-called we reserve our wonder for the discovery or invention of yesterday; the Chorus in Sophocles' *Antigone* marvel at the ingenuity of the ploughman. The Greeks lived nearer to the earth than we, and sentiments close to their hearts sound to us very far off. The trail of the plough is over all their poetry. Hence an insistent interest in the cycling of the seasons in relation to the needs of man. In earlier times the seasons were three: ἔαρ, spring; θέρος and ὀπώρα, early and late summer; χεῖμα, winter. Homely practical Hesiod is the poet and preceptor of field-work, which he regulates according to the rising and setting of stars, and other signs in nature. Some of his observations may serve as a means of approach to the chief topic of poetic interest under this head. Midwinter has been spoken of already, and from it we can go backwards.[1]

'When the Pleiades, daughters of Atlas, are rising (May), begin your harvest, and your ploughing when

---

[1] Parallels and contrasts between Hesiod and Virgil have been so fully drawn by Sellar and others that they need not be noted here. Professor A. W. Mair's article on *The Farmer's Year in Hesiod*, in the Addenda to his translation, is valuable.

they set (November).' 'Take heed when you hear the voice of the crane uttering her yearly cry from the clouds above. It gives the sign for ploughing (and sowing) and shows the season of rainy winter.' (*W.D.*, 383-84; 448-51).[1] The same cry brings grief into the heart of Theognis, for his fields have passed into the hands of others (1197-1202). October is the time for felling timber. 'Then the wood cut with the axe is less liable to be worm-eaten when it sheds its leaves on the earth and ceases to sprout' (*W.D.*, 420-21).

The vintage-time is in September. 'When Orion and Sirius come into mid-heaven and rosy-fingered Dawn looks upon Arcturus, then, O Perses, pluck and bring home all thy grapes' (609-11). It is the later days of ὀπώρα, the fruit-time, τεθαλυῖα ὀπώρα. In the vintage scene on the Shield of Achilles in the *Iliad*, a boy is singing a Linus-song, a lament for departing summer (xviii. 570). The word ὀπώρα can stand for fruit itself. Danaus warns his daughters that 'tender fruit (τέρειν' ὀπώρα) is not easy to guard. . . . When the orchard gate is open, every passer-by shoots at the charms of virgin beauty a winning arrow of the eye' (Aeschylus, *Supp.*, 1003-1005). The season is specially associated with the vine. When the master is about the house, says Clytemnestra, there is coolness 'at the time when Zeus is making wine from the sour sap of the grape' (*Agam.*, 970-72). Pindar calls the soft down on a young man's cheek and chin τέρειναν ματέρ' οἰνάνθας ὀπώραν—'summer, the tender mother of the vine-bud' (*Nem.*, v. 6). It is also 'the time most sweet that turns the mind to thoughts of Aphrodite' (*Isth.*, ii. 4, 5).

[1] Cp. *Iliad*, iii. 3; Aristophanes, *Birds*, 710.

July, when Orion appears, is the time for winnowing (*W.D.*, 507 ff.). The hottest part of summer is when 'Sirius parches head and knees, and the skin is dry through heat' (June-July). The artichoke is in bloom and the cicala pours forth his shrill song continually. Then Hesiod would sit in the shade, feast on delicacies, and drink wine (582-96). At that season the cicala is θεσπέσιος and ἡλιομανής—'inspired' and 'mad with delight in the sunshine,' says Aristophanes (*Birds*, 1096). Alcaeus is like-minded with Hesiod:

Τέγγε πνεύμονα Ϝοίνῳ· τὸ γὰρ ἄστρον περιτέλλεται.
(*Bergk*, 39.)

Theognis thinks him a fool that does otherwise (1039). Then, too, the grapes are colouring (*Shield of Heracles*, 399); and the countryman, perplexed with leisure, regards them long and critically (Aristophanes, *Peace*, 1159-63). When the snail (φερέοικος, house-carrier) climbs up the plants from the ground, to escape the Pleiades, trenching about the vines should be finished, and preparation made for the grain-harvest of May (571-81). Laertes was trenching when Odysseus visited him (*Ody.*, xxiv. 227), and so was the old man of Onchestus whom Hermes bribed (Hymn *To Hermes*, 90).

The vines should be pruned before the arrival of the swallow (February-March). It comes 'when Arcturus rises in his brilliance at evening dusk' (564-70). This is the beginning of spring, 'gray spring'—ἔαρ πολιόν—the buds being yet in the husk. Then you sell your overcoat and buy a light suit (Aristophanes, *Birds*, 716). Boys went about singing the swallow-song (χελιδόνισμα) in hopes of a gratuity:

῍Ηλθ’ ἦλθε χελιδών,
καλὰς ὥρας ἄγουσα,
καλοὺς ἐνιαυτούς, κ.τ.λ.

(*Bergk*, 41.)

Young scamps, like the Sausage-Seller in Aristophanes’ *Knights*, utilised the occasion for practical jokes:

‘Then, there were other petty tricks I practised as a
    child,
Haunting about the butchers’ shops, the weather
    being mild.
“See, boys,” says I, “the swallow there! Why,
    summer’s come, I say,”
And when they turned to gape and stare, I snatched
    a steak away.’ [1]

In March the cuckoo ‘first utters his note among the leaves of the oak and makes men glad over the boundless earth’ (Hesiod, *W.D.*, 486, 87). English poets have trustfully regarded the cuckoo’s earliest cries as marking the beginning of summer:

    ‘Sumer is icumen in;
    Lhude sing, cucu!’

In Old English poetry ‘the mournful note’ of the cuckoo inspires *Wanderlust* and makes men think of the sea.[2] In the Finnish *Kalevala* and in Celtic poetry the cuckoo is *the* bird.

Spring, so uncertain and trembling with us, is the sure and pleasant season in Greece, and beloved of the poets. Nevertheless they indulge in no lengthy conglomerate descriptions of the features of spring such as we find in the opening of Lucretius or in the *Georgics*, ii. 315 ff. Alcaeus feels the approach of

---

[1] Frere’s translation. *Summer* should be *Spring*—ὥρα νέα in the original.
[2] Catullus, eager to set out from Phrygia, sings:
    Jam mens praetrepidans avet vagari,
    Jam laeti studio pedes vigescunt. (xlvi.)

flowery spring, and how soft is the sound of its coming in his line!

῾Ηρος ἀνθεμόεντος ἐπάϊον ἐρχομένοιο.

(*Bergk*, 45.)

In a dithyramb Pindar says: 'In Argive Nemea the bard overlooks not the time when the chamber of the bright-robed Hours is opened and the nectarous plants feel the fragrant spring' (*Bergk*, 45).[1] It is the time of the vernal Dionysia at Athens when 'lovely violet-tufts are spread over the everlasting earth and roses are twined in the hair.' φοινικάνθεμον ἔαρ Pindar calls it elsewhere (*Pyth.*, iv. 64); in Latin *purpureum ver*; 'the purple year' of Pope and Gray. Spring wakens Love; Eros leaves Cyprus and goes abroad among men, says Theognis (1275-78).[2] Then in the gardens of the Academy the plane-tree whispers to the elm—πλάτανος πτελέᾳ ψιθυρίζῃ (Aristophanes, *Clouds*, 1008).[3] Herald melodies are heard, and the nightingale and swallow have pride of place. In the *Odyssey* Penelope beautifully compares the close-thronging cares that beset her heart to the often-changing note of the nightingale sitting among the thick leafage of the trees in early spring (xix. 518-21).[4]

---

[1] Cp. Coleridge:
> 'Amid the howl of more than wintry storms,
> The halcyon hears the voice of vernal hours
> Already on the wing.'

[2] Cp. Lucretius, v. 737: *It ver et Venus*, etc.

[3] Imitated by Claudian in his *De Nuptiis Honorii et Mariae*:
> *Populeo suspirat populus ictu;*
> *Et platani platanis alnoque assibilat alnus.*   (67-68.)

[4] Coleridge comes nearest Homer in describing the nightingale's song:
> ''Tis the merry nightingale
> That crowds, and hurries, and precipitates
> With fast thick warble his delicious notes.'

Coleridge does not associate melancholy with the song of the bird nor does he make the female sing, contrary to the dictates of a mythology which has tyrannised over most poets from Homer till now.

To Simonides nightingales are 'the much-warbling, fresh-and-full-throated birds of spring':

Δεῦτ' ἀηδόνες πολυκώτιλοι
χλωραύχενες εἰαριναί.

(*Bergk*, 73.)

And the swallow is 'the shrill herald of fragrant spring':

Ἄγγελε κλυτὰ ἔαρος ἁδυόδμου,
κυανέα χελιδοῖ.

(*Bergk*, 74.)

'Spring's messenger, the lovely-voiced nightingale' is a one-line fragment of a poem by Sappho:

Ἦρος ἄγγελος ἱμερόφωνος ἀήδων.

(*Bergk*, 42.) [1]

We may take farewell of Sappho by quoting the following fragment of a spring or summer scene of *dolce far niente* in a garden:

Ἀμφὶ δὲ ψῦχρον κελάδει δι' ὔσδων
μαλίνων, αἰθυσσομένων δὲ φύλλων
κῶμα καταρρεῖ.

(*Bergk*, 4.)

'Around there is a cool murmur through the apple-boughs, and as the leaves quiver slumber slides down.'

The Greek seasons are well marked off from one another, and the year presents no such gradual and almost imperceptible transitions as we experience in our northern insular climate. Spring comes with a bound—ἔαρ ἐξαπίνας, Theocritus calls it—and its reign is short. A long and dry summer follows; then the rains begin and winter sets in. There is no autumn in our sense of the word, a time with which English poets generally associate a pensive sadness.

[1] The original, probably, of Ben Jonson's 'Dear good angel of the Spring.'

Nothing could be less Greek than the apostrophe which Morris puts into the mouth of Medea when about to slay her children, beginning:

> 'But ye—shall I behold you when leaves fall,
> In some sad evening of the autumn-tide?'

The collective Horae are personified and endowed with moral attributes, but not the individual seasons. For a tentative procession of the seasons we have to wait till Lucretius (v. 735-48), whose *crepitans dentibus algor* is the forerunner of Spenser's

> 'Lastly, came Winter cloathed all in frize,
> Chattering his teeth for cold that did him chill.' [1]

Twelve Attic months were officially recognised, but their rather unmanageable names make no figure in poetry. Each of our months has its own special features, so that Tennyson can without exaggeration say:

> 'The daughters of the year,
> One after one, thro' that still garden pass'd:
> Each garlanded with her peculiar flower
> Danced into light, and died into the shade.'

His own periphrasis for March is a good example:

> 'The roaring moon of daffodil and crocus.' [2]

In Greek we find no 'drear-nighted Decembers,' no 'proud-pied Aprils,' no lines like

> 'Three April perfumes in three hot Junes burned.'
> 'All the buds and bells of May.'
> 'Flashing like the dogwood crimson in October.'

---

[1] The Seasons are pictured as attendants on the Sun in Ovid's description of the Palace of the Sun (*Met.*, ii. 27-30). Cp. Horace, *Epode*, ii. 17, 18.

[2] Tennyson's 'roaring moon' is a translation of the Old English name for March, *hlȳd-mōnath*, noisy month.

Ἔαρος νέον ἱσταμένοιο, says Homer;

> 'Bytwene Mershe and Averil,
>   When spray beginneth to springe,'

says a nameless Early English poet. For personification the Greeks go to mythology. Where an English poet speaks of

> 'The tall wheat coloured by the August fire,'

a Greek calls up the figure of Demeter φοινικόπεζα, 'whose steps make red the corn.' Spenser brings on the stage

> 'October full of merry glee;
> For yet his noule was totty of the must';

a Greek poet shows the form of a god 'ever fair and ever young,' 'whose is the gift of the grape's gladness,' and who comes 'from the ivy-mantled slopes of Nysa's mountains and from the shore green with many-clustered vines.'

It is interesting to note some Greek conceptions of paradisal bliss and the characteristics of places where favoured mortals dwell. The Elysium of the *Odyssey* is in the far west, at the world's end. Menelaus is to live there, in the body, it being ordained that he shall not die. 'There life is most easy for men. No falling of snow is there, nor any great storm, nor rain; but always does Ocean send forth breezes of the shrill-blowing West Wind for the refreshing of men' (iv. 563-68). Similar paradises have been imagined by many poets, some of them conscious Homeric adaptations; they are found in Lucretius, in Dante, in the anonymous Old English *Phoenix* (borrowed from the Latin *Carmen de Phoenice* attributed to Lactantius), in the *Romaunt of the Rose*, in Tennyson, in Swinburne. The enchanted gardens of Politian,

Ariosto, Tasso, Spenser, etc., can be traced back to Claudian and other Roman poets, and even to Homer's gardens of Alcinous. The Islands of the Blest are first mentioned in Hesiod's *Works and Days* (167-73). Happy heroes live there, 'by the banks of deep-eddying Ocean; and for them the grain-giving earth bears honey-sweet fruit which flourishes thrice a year.' In a scolion (*Bergk*, 10) Harmodius dwells there, and there are Achilles and Diomedes:

'It may be we shall touch the Happy Isles,
    And see the great Achilles, whom we knew,'

says Tennyson's Ulysses.

Pindar gives a more detailed account of the fortunes of men after death. He believes in a system of rewards and punishments. Those who have kept pure through a series of probationary stages dwell for ever in bliss. In that place the night is as the day, there is no toil by land or sea, and there are no tears. But it is a habitation for good aristocratic heroes only; the others (τοὶ δέ) are to be found elsewhere. 'Round the islands of the blest Ocean airs are breathing, and there flowers of gold are glowing, some on the fair trees of the land, some nourished by the waters; garlands thereof they twine for hands and head' (*Oly.*, ii. 70-74).

In a threnos (*Bergk*, 95) the same poet describes the place of the good in a department of Hades. It may be compared and contrasted with Virgil's Fortunate Groves in *Aeneid* vi. 'For them the strength of the sun shines below while in this world it is night; and round their city are meadows abounding in red roses and frankincense-trees and golden fruits. Some in horses and feats of body, some in dice, some in the music of the lyre take delight. Among them all the

flowers of bliss are blooming, and fragrance fills the
lovely land, all manner of incense mingling in a far-
seen blaze on the altars of the gods continually.' But
better than any bald prose translation, or mistransla-
tion, is Tennyson's transfusion in *Tiresias*:

> 'These eyes will find
> The men I knew, and watch the chariot whirl
> About the goal again, and hunters race
> The shadowy lion, and the warrior kings,
> In height and prowess more than human, strive
> Again for glory, while the golden lyre
> Is ever sounding in heroic ears
> Heroic hymns, and every way the vales
> Wind, clouded with the grateful incense-fume
> Of those who mix all odour to the Gods
> On one far height in one far-shining fire.'

CHAPTER VIII

THE SENTIMENTAL (I)

THE title of this chapter is perhaps open to the charge of having been selected on the famous principle of *lucus a non lucendo*. In truth, Greek writers can rarely be said to view nature in the modern sentimental manner. If in some instances an approach seems to be made to our sentimental attitude, closer examination will reveal a difference. The sentimental, moral and spiritual views of nature which constitute the very breath and spirit of the poetry of Wordsworth and other nineteenth-century poets were unknown to the Greeks.

To the Greek there seemed to be a bond of sympathy between man in his innocence and the elemental powers of nature, which he regarded as ἀγνοί and ἱεροί. Man breaks this sacred bond. When he stains his hands with kindred blood, he dare not look heaven in the face, he desires to hide his guilt from the all-seeing, all-nourishing, and holy sun. This is the wish of the hero in *Hercules Furens*, when he says to Theseus:

τί δῆτά μου κρᾶτ' ἀνεκάλυψας ἡλίῳ ;

(1231.)

Theseus, however, does not believe that a mortal can pollute what belongs to the gods:

τί δ'; οὐ μιαίνεις θνητὸς ὢν τὰ τῶν θεῶν.

(1232.)

176

In *Medea*, the Chorus, after praising the climate of Attica, lay stress on the purity and sanctity of the waters of Cephisus, and ask the murderess how she can hope for a place of refuge in Athens (846 ff.). In *Oedipus Tyrannus*, Creon says that the sun must not see Oedipus; the holy rain will not fall upon him; neither earth nor the pure light can suffer his presence (1424-29). The Second Messenger, impressed by the enormity of the guilt of Oedipus, declares that neither Ister nor Phasis—representative rivers—can wash the house clean again (1227-30).[1]

In such instances the sentiment has a sacred and religious basis. The fact that the individual can put himself beyond the pale of nature's sympathy, in other words, can outrage nature, supplies us with the key to the explanation of the feeling. It does not attach itself to the picturesque shows of nature, nor does it depend upon personal susceptibilities. It is communal, and it has its roots in the early elemental stage of Greek religion.

In times of trouble the Greeks would address earth and air and sun, unburdening their woes. The Servant in *Medea* says she is so utterly miserable that she must tell to heaven and earth the sad fortunes of her mistress (56-58). Such occasions generally paved the way for soliloquies, which, especially in Euripides, tend to pall on the reader. They are ridiculed by Plautus. Before the murder of the children by Medea, the Chorus appeal to the earth and the sun (1251-57). Here the apostrophe to the sun is specially appropriate in the light of Medea's parentage, and the same is true of the address of Creusa in *Ion*, 881 ff.

The griefs and terrors of the night are also told to

[1] Cp. Aesch., *Choeph.*, 983-85; Eur., *I.T.*, 1207.

the bright sun and the clear sky of morning. Iphigeneia resolves to do so, though she doubts if it can afford any relief:

ἃ καινὰ δ' ἥκει νὺξ φέρουσα φάσματα,
λέξω πρὸς αἰθέρ', εἴ τι δὴ τόδ' ἔστ' ἄκος.

(*I.T.*, 42, 43.)

In Euripides' play, Electra comes from the house, habited like a menial and bearing a pitcher on her head, to show herself thus degraded to the gods and to utter to the ether laments for her father (58, 59). Sophocles' Electra issues from the abode of pollution to tell the sorrows of the night to the holy light and the air that canopies the earth (86-95). Scared by fearful visions, Hecuba addresses the dazzling light of Zeus, gloomy night, and earth, 'mother of black-winged dreams' (68 ff.).

Earth, the Mighty Mother, is often invoked. She is appealed to by the Chorus in *Philoctetes*:

ὀρεστέρα παμβῶτι Γᾶ, μᾶτερ αὐτοῦ Διός.

(391.)

'There is special appropriateness,' says Campbell, 'in the invocation of the primal power of nature upon a desert shore, where no temples were to be seen, as the Great Mother was at the same time one of the most universal of deities. Wherever Earth was she might be assumed to be.' Ἰὼ Γαῖα μαῖα, says the Chorus affectionately (*Choeph.*, 45); ὦ μᾶ Γᾶ, cry the Danaids, like lisping children (*Supp.*, 890).

One apostrophe deserves special mention. It is the appeal of Prometheus when he breaks silence after the departure of his tormentors. He calls on divine ether, the swift winds, the river-fountains, the innumerable laughing waves of the sea, earth, the

universal mother, and the all-seeing sun, to witness
what a god suffers at the hands of gods:

ὦ δῖος αἰθήρ, καὶ ταχύπτεροι πνοαί,
ποταμῶν τε πηγαί, ποντίων τε κυμάτων
ἀνήριθμον γέλασμα, παμμῆτόρ τε γῆ,
καὶ τὸν πανόπτην κύκλον ἡλίου καλῶ·
ἴδεσθέ μ', οἷα πρὸς θεῶν πάσχω θεός.

(88-92.)

Chained to a rock in the lonely Scythian waste, this
survivor of an older race of gods is beyond the hearing
and help of man, so he calls on the elements that form
the theatre of his sufferings. The sublimity of the
appeal matches the majesty of the scene. All the
same, the lines should not be quoted as evidence of a
love for solitary communion with nature on the part
of the Greeks.

These passages may be sufficient to show the nature
of the sentiment. It is devotional and sacramental.
The speaker addresses natural phenomena as sacred, as
ministering to and intimately associated with the life of
man, as everlasting spectators of the successive dramas
played by generations of mortals on the world's stage.[1]

Parenthetically it may be worth noting that in
his non-Christian plays Shakespeare now and again
gives us reminders of the primitive feeling. For
instance, in *Cymbeline*, Belarius, Guiderius, and
Arviragus are living in a cave. Belarius says:

'Stoop, boys: this gate
Instructs you how to *adore the heavens,* and bows you
To a morning's holy office: the gates of monarchs
Are arch'd so high that giants may jet through
And keep their impious turbans on, without
Good morrow to the sun. Hail, thou fair heaven!'

[1] For other examples see the dramatists *passim*. They abound.

NATURE IN GREEK POETRY

Guiderius and Arviragus follow suit with—'*Hail, heaven!*' (iii. 3). Mark the words in italics. The whole of King Lear's oath:

'By the sacred radiance of the sun,
  The mysteries of Hecate and the night,
By all the operation of the orbs
From whom we do exist and cease to be,
Here I disclaim all my paternal care,
  The name and all the additions to a king'—
                               (i. 1)

might have been written by a Greek. In *Antony and Cleopatra*, iv. 9, the words of Enobarbus—'O thou blessed moon!'—might perhaps pass as Greek, but his continuation—'O sovereign mistress of true melancholy!'—is Shakespeare.

Such apostrophes, however, are not always appeals by those in trouble. In her joy at the murder of Aegisthus, Euripides' Electra addresses the light of the sun, earth, and night (866-67). In *Antigone*, the Chorus hail 'the eye of golden day,' fairer in seeming than ever before, which saw the rout of the Argive host (100-8). Sometimes there is a call for active sympathy. Electra watching by Orestes' bed, the Chorus call upon 'majestic night, giver of sleep,' to come to the house of Agamemnon (*Orestes*, 176-79). The breezes are asked to waft Agamemnon's son to Athens (*I.T.*, 1487 ff.). In the song of triumph raised by the Chorus in *Hercules Furens*, after the death of Lycus, the appeal is mainly local: 'Crown thyself with garlands, O Ismenus; dance, ye stately streets of the city of the Seven Gates; fair-flowing Dirce, with the nymphs, the daughters of Asopus, leave the water of your father, and come to celebrate with us the glorious victory of Heracles. Wooded Pytho, and ye dwellings of the Muses of Helicon, sing a joyful song in honour of our city and our walls' (781-93).

To the Greeks, for whom βλέπειν was a synonym for life itself, it would have seemed ungrateful to forget the beneficent sun in the anguish of farewell. 'Les Grecs exprimaient cette faiblesse humaine avec un inconcevable charme. Non pas comme les Allemands en formules philosophiques; leurs personnages ne disaient pas comme l'Egmont du célèbre Goethe: "Adieu la douce habitude de l'existence et de l'action!" Les attributs de la vie, les objets de la nature, trouvaient place dans leur discours naïfs, et s'y montraient sous des formes d'une simplicité et d'une grâce enchanteresses. Le jour, surtout, le jour, l'air, la lumière du soleil, ces biens universels qu'on regrette dans tous les temps et par tous pays, étaient sans cesse rappelés dans ces adieux suprèmes.

' " Aux regards d'un mourant le soleil est si beau!" a dit éloquemment un des plus grands poètes de notre âge, l'auteur des *Méditations*. Mais, on le sent, c'est surtout dans la Grèce, cette terre favorisée du ciel, où l'air est si limpide, la lumière si pure, les horizons si riches et si éclatants; c'est à Athènes, où la vie n'était pas ôtée au condamné avant la coucher du soleil . . . c'est, dis-je, dans la Grèce et à Athènes que ces images devaient s'offrir d'elles-mêmes à la poésie. Aussi reviennent-elles sans cesse dans la tragédie d'Eschyle, de Sophocle, d'Euripide, et en relèvent-elles les douloureux tableaux par le contraste touchant de la sérénité de la nature avec le malheur de l'homme. . . . Ce soleil, insensible témoin de nos maux, n'était pas seulement présent à l'imagination dans les spectacles de la Grèce; mais, par la disposition des théâtres ouverts à la lumière du jour, il revêtait de son riant éclat les tristes tableaux de la scène tragique; il brillait aux yeux d'Ajax qui l'invoquait, de tous ces spectateurs qui suivaient involontairement vers le ciel le regard, le geste du héros, et que ce mélange singulier des fictions du drame avec la vivante décoration de la nature, transportaient réellement, dans des instants d'une illusion complète, parmi ces fabuleuses aventures et dans ces temps reculés.' [1]

Sophocles' presentation of the last hours of Ajax has a fascinating interest. His proud spirit yet unbroken, as the cloud of madness lifts, the hero calls upon the darkness of the nether world to receive him who would not look on the face of man again (394-400). He addresses the rushing waters of the narrow seas, the caves by the shore, the wooded promontory, the near streams of Scamander (412-28). He falls into a reflective mood, musing on the significance of his name—Aἴας—and how it suits with his fortunes—αἰαῖ (430-33). When the sword is set for the deed of self-destruction, he prays to Zeus, Hermes, and the Eumenides (831-44). He looks to the sun, now mounting the steep of heaven, and bids him check his golden rein when Salamis is reached, and tells his fate to aged father and mother (845-51). He addresses Death, soon to be his familiar in the other world. Again he turns to the sun for the last time. He calls on Salamis, the seat of his fathers; on Athens and the Athenians; and once again on the springs and rivers and plains around, that have nourished him (854-63).

No one can fail to appreciate the pathos of this farewell. But one feature in it is noteworthy. He says to the waters of Scamander:

[1] Patin, *Études sur les tragiques grecs : Sophocle*, i.

οὐκέτ' ἄνδρα μὴ
τόνδ' ἴδητ', ἔπος
ἐξερέω μέγ', οἷον οὔ τινα
Τροία στρατοῦ δέρχθη χθονὸς μολόντ' ἀπὸ
Ἑλλανίδος· τανῦν δ' ἄτιμος
ὧδε πρόκειμαι.

(421-27.)

'Ye shall not look on this man any more—a mighty
word will I utter—such an one of the host as Troy
has not seen come from the land of Greece; but now
I am laid thus low in dishonour.' These words are
very different from those of a sentimentalist, full of a
sense of man's littleness in the presence of nature.
They ring with the egoism of a proud man. He does
not say—'*I* shall not look on *you* any more.' He is
dishonoured, but he is not humbled. Ajax dies
Ajax; but he dies 'in the light.'

Alcestis, at the point of death, speaks to the sun and
the clouds scudding across the sky (243-44). Oedipus,
whose eyes 'roll in vain,' addresses the light, now
lightless but once his:

ὦ φῶς ἀφεγγές, πρόσθε πού ποτ' ἦσθ' ἐμόν.

(*O.C.*, 1549.)

'Put me not to death untimely,' says Iphigeneia to
her father, 'for it is sweet to see the light':

μὴ μ' ἀπολέσῃς ἄωρον· ἡδὺ γὰρ τὸ φῶς
λεύσσειν.

(*I.A.*, 1218-19.)

And again:

τὸ φῶς τόδ' ἀνθρώποισιν ἥδιστον βλέπειν.

(1250.)

Her last words are:

χαῖρέ μοι, φίλον φάος.

(1509.)

In *Antigone* the heroine has placed herself in the

183

position of an enemy to civic order. The Chorus give her cold comfort, for they are old men and cannot countenance rebellion. In her isolation she calls on Dirce and the precinct of Thebe to bear witness to her unjust condemnation:

ἰὼ Διρκαῖαι κρῆναι Θήβας τ'
εὐαρμάτου ἄλσος, ἔμπας
ξυμμάρτυρας ὔμμ' ἐπικτῶμαι
οἷα φίλων ἄκλαυτος, οἵοις νόμοις
πρὸς ἔρμα τυμβόχωστον ἔρχομαι
τάφου ποταινίου.   (844-49.)

She who has set at naught the laws of the city in order to obey those unwritten ordinances which no man brought into being, now appeals from the ephemeral units in the city to the eternal scene around. Her sentiment is that of the citizens who form the community of Thebes. The tie is local; it unites the citizen with the *genii loci*, so to speak. In *Oedipus Coloneus*, Polynices adjures Oedipus by the same waters of Dirce, when both are at Athens, not at Thebes (1333, 34). Similarly the Trojans swear by Ida—'Ιδαία μᾶτερ (*Orestes*, 1452). When in Egypt Helen calls on Eurotas, green with rushes (*Helena*, 348-51). Cassandra, soon to sing her prophecies beside Cocytus and Acheron, thinks of Scamander, of whose stream her fathers drank and on whose banks she was reared (*Agam.*, 1157-59). Hippolytus takes farewell of Athens and Troezen:

'Fare ye well, O land
And city of old Erechtheus! Thou, Troezen,
What riches of glad youth mine eyes have seen
In thy broad plains! Farewell! This is the end,
The last word, the last look!'   (1094 ff.)[1]

[1] Professor Gilbert Murray's translation.

The Chorus in *Ajax* are somewhat selfish and peevish; they are homesick. They think of their native Salamis, throned on her happy seat among the waves, while they spend countless months on the meadows of Ida, with no prospect but black Hades (596-608). They curse the inventor of war, who has caused them to forgo the joys of society, the garlands and wine-cups, the sweet sound of the flute, the joys of love. Far from these they lie, while the nightly dews falling on their hair remind them that they are still in dismal Troyland (1185-1210). Fain would they be where the wooded cape overhangs the sea at Sunium, that so they might greet sacred Athens (1217-22). Note the expression given to the social instincts, so marked a feature of Greek poetry.

There are two notable passages of similar import in *Iphigeneia in Tauris*. The Chorus of captive Greek maidens, attendants of Iphigeneia, would hail with delight news of their deliverance from bondage. O to be at home in the fatherland, even in dream, to share in the joys of song (452-55)! They address the halcyon that sits on the rocks by the sea, singing a mournful strain for its lost mate. Wingless, they long for the assemblies of Hellas, or to be in Delos, where are the palm and the laurel and the olive of Artemis. Iphigeneia will sail for home without them. Would that they could soar through the air and fold their wings when above their chamber-roof! Would that they were once more joining in the mirth of the bridal, circling in the dance with their companions of other days, and vying in the contest of beauty and costly array (1089-1151).

No writer has expressed more pithily than Tacitus the difference between the alien and the native feeling for the natural aspects of a country. '*Quis porro, praeter periculum horridi et ignoti maris, Asia aut Africa aut Italia relicta Germaniam peteret, informem terris, asperam caelo, tristem cultu aspectuque, nisi si patria sit'* (*Germania,* 2). Homer's Odysseus says, 'I can see nothing else sweeter than one's own country' (*Ody.,* ix. 27, 28). He looks at the homeland from the point of view of the chieftain and warrior. Ithaca is 'rugged, but a good nurse of heroes' (*Ody.,* ix. 27). It has always a supply of rain and abundant dew, all kinds of wood and never-failing watering-places (*Ody.,* xiii. 245-47). No sooner is he made comfortable in Scheria than he implores his entertainers to bestir themselves by break of day so as to conduct him home, adding—'May even my life leave me when I have had sight of my possessions, my bondmen, and my great and lofty abode' (*Ody.,* vii. 224-25).

As we have seen, rivers and fountains, being κουροτρόφοι, were held in special regard. Pindar is proud of drinking Dirce's pleasant water while he weaves a hymn for warriors (*Oly.,* vi. 86-87). 'Dolt is he who hath not in continual remembrance the waters of Dirce that nurtured him' (*Pyth.,* ix. 87-88), is his version of Scott's

> 'Breathes there the man with soul so dead,
>   Who never to himself hath said,
>   This is my own, my native land!'

Edie Ochiltree, however, was not thinking of nourishment when he said, '*Me* no muckle to fight for, sir?—isna there the country to fight for, and the burnsides that I gang daundering beside?'

The *Septem contra Thebas* is 'full of Ares.' The enemy are at the gates, and the Chorus pray to a whole hierarchy of gods. This is their final appeal—

'What better land than this shall you get in exchange, if you give up to the enemy our deep-soiled earth and the water of Dirce most nourishing to drink— εὐτραφέστατον πωμάτων' (304-309). Earth and water rear trusty shield-bearers—ἀσπιδηφόρους πιστούς— and when these fall they are said to pay the nurture-price—ἀποδοῦναι τροφεῖα. The sentiment is paralleled in Shakespeare's *Richard II.*, when Gaunt eulogises England as

'This nurse, this teeming womb of royal kings,'

and Bolingbroke says:

'Sweet soil, adieu;
My mother and my nurse, that bears me yet!'

On the other hand, in *Marmion*, the exclamation of Fitz-Eustace:

'Where's the coward that would not dare
To fight for such a land!'

is inspired by a picturesque panorama seen from Blackford Hill. The sentiment is very modern and Scott's own.

When the exile has again reached home after a long absence, how is he affected? Homer's Odysseus, when he is assured by Athene that his feet are at last on his native soil, 'was glad, rejoicing in his own land, and he kissed the grain-giving earth' (*Ody.*, xiii. 353-54). Besides being a natural sign of feeling the kissing of the land is a religious ceremonial. 'Grain-giving,' ζείδωρον, is a colourless epithet for such an occasion. He takes no note of any well-known features of the land, but he offers up a shrewd prayer to the indwelling deities, the Naiads. In the *Odyssey*, Agamemnon 'kissed his fatherland as he touched it, and many hot tears fell from him, for well pleased

was he to see it' (iv. 522-23). In Aeschylus' play he
merely addresses Argos and the gods of the land who
had helped him to capture Troy and reach home
(*Agam.*, 810-13). The herald is more effusive, magni-
fying his office. He apostrophises his paternal soil,
the sun, Zeus, Apollo, the gods who helped to gain
the victory, Hermes, the palace, the royal seats in
front of it, the statues of the gods facing the sun
(503-24).

The *Hippolytus* of Euripides is probably unique in
the dramatic use it makes of the surrounding scene
in a story of passionate love. Phaedra and the
Nurse are on the stage, and the love-sick Queen
expresses a wish for a draught of water from some
dewy spring and to rest reclined on the grassy meadow
beneath the poplars (209-12). The Nurse is alarmed
and entreats her not to utter such mad words in the
hearing of the crowd. But Phaedra breaks out again.
She will go to the mountain, to the pine-trees where
hounds pursue the dappled stags (215-18). What
has she to do with the chase, asks the Nurse. Why
wish for a flowing spring when water can be had
from a hill hard by? But Phaedra will not be silenced.
She longs to go to the stadium at neighbouring Limna
to curb Venetian steeds. Some god must have
distracted her, says the Nurse, and the Queen admits
that so it must be (224-49).

There is a fine tragic irony in the situation, for the
spectators are privy to a secret unknown to the Nurse.
All the Queen's longings are to be in places associated
with Hippolytus. The modern reader, unlike the
ordinary Athenian, sees nothing wild in Phaedra's
wishes; he is glad to be transported for a moment
from a stifling atmosphere to the healthy air of
mountain and sea.

The *Philoctetes* of Sophocles is notable for another reason. Philoctetes has spent ten years of lonely misery on Lemnos. There is no one near to minister to him, no one to greet him with the language of voice or eye. Pain and hunger are his companions. The only sounds he hears are the echoes that answer his wails, and the lashing of the waves on the rocks. It is small wonder if he has learned to unburden his soul to the beasts and inanimate objects around. One of these invocations is specially significant. When Neoptolemus turns away from him and refuses to answer, Philoctetes addresses the landing-place, and the rocks, and his wild companions of the hills. The words:

> ὑμῖν τάδ᾽, οὐ γὰρ ἄλλον οἶδ᾽ ὅτῳ λέγω
> ἀνακλαίομαι—
>
> (938-39.)

'I make this lament to you, for I know none other to whom I may speak,' show us that his communion with nature is not spontaneous. Well might this Greek Crusoe have exclaimed:

> 'O solitude! where are the charms
> That sages have seen in thy face?'

It is quite to misapprehend the situation to say that 'Sophocles in the *Philoctetes* approaches even the feeling of Wordsworth.'

When he is about to leave the island, he takes farewell of the sights and sounds that time has rendered so familiar to him—the cave ('sole comrade of my watch'), the water-nymphs of the meadow, the deep voice of the sea-beaten cape, the springs, the Lycian fount. It is pathetic certainly, yet one may be permitted to doubt whether a disinterested feeling

189

alone prompts his words. Does not the introduction sound stagey?—φέρε νυν στείχων χώραν καλέσω—

'Come now, let me address the land as I depart.'

(1452.)

It marks the performance of a ceremonial. Two other passages seem to be in keeping with this view. When Philoctetes is eager to depart—for Scyros, as he thinks—he suggests to Neoptolemus that they should first say farewell to his home which has been no home:

ἴωμεν, ὦ παῖ, προσκύσαντε τὴν ἔσω
ἄοικον εἰσοίκησιν.

(533-34.)

Here, however, as the hero himself says, the desire is partly that Neoptolemus may gain a clearer conception of the wretchedness from which he is about to deliver him. But the words of Neoptolemus in line 1408 are evidently the inculcation of a duty—στεῖχε προσκύσας χθόνα. To omit such a formality when leaving a friendly land, and not to be greeted in return by those left behind, was a bad omen. Philoctetes expects Lemnos to send him a fair breeze 'to his heart's content' (ἀμέμπτως).

That there is a close connection between the nature of the soil and climate of a country and the general mental characteristics of its inhabitants the Athenians firmly believed, so far as they themselves were concerned, and they were not slow to attribute their nimble wits to the virtues of the clear air of Attica.[1] Euripides patriotically flatters the descendants of earth-born Erechtheus,

ἀεὶ διὰ λαμπροτάτου
βαίνοντες ἀβρῶς αἰθέρος,

[1] 'Pure the air and light the soil,' says Milton.

and puts a new interpretation on the myth by attribut-
ing the physical beauties and mental glories of the
people to the effects of the fine climate (*Medea*,
824-45). But of belief in the power of nature to
comfort the heart, to subdue the passions, and to
speak peace to the souls of men we find no trace in
Greek poetry. Greek sentiment does not endorse
the words of Cowper—'The spleen is seldom felt
where Flora reigns.' The Greeks did not take nature
medicinally. Inert matter having no moral life of
its own could give no moral impulse. But though
a landscape could not be a moral factor, natural
objects might be moral exemplars, appealing to the
intellect if not to the affections. There are some
examples of direct lessons drawn from nature. One
is Pindar's parable of the lopped oak, by which he
hints to Arcesilas of Cyrene the expediency of re-
calling the exiled Damophilus. 'If a man with sharp-
edged axe lop the branches of a mighty oak and shame
its comely form, even though the fruit thereof fail,
it yet gives proof of its worth, if it come at last to the
winter fire, or stayed with upright lordly columns
it perform dreary service, leaving its own place
desolate' (*Pyth.*, iv. 263-69). In the *Antigone*, Haemon
is imploring his father to listen to reason, and he uses
this illustration—'You see how, beside the rush of
wintry torrents, the trees that yield save even their
twigs, while those that resist perish root and branch'
(712-14). Ajax, schooling himself to bend to the
authority of the Atreidae, finds patterns in nature—
'Things most strong and terrible yield to office.
Thus winter whose track is marked by snow gives
place to fruitful summer; thus night's dreary round
makes way for day with her white steeds to shed her
light; the blast of dreadful winds lets rest the groan-

ing deep; yea too, all-powerful sleep sets free whom he has bound, nor always holds him fast' (669-76). In a famous ῥῆσις of the *Phoenissae* Jocasta pleads with Eteocles to observe the law of equal rights. Do not sun and moon fairly measure out their yearly round, one not envying other?

νυκτός τ᾽ ἀφεγγὲς βλέφαρον ἡλίου τε φῶς
ἴσον βαδίζει τὸν ἐνιαύσιον κύκλον,
κοὐδέτερον αὐτῶν φθόνον ἔχει νικώμενον.

(543-45.)

CHAPTER IX

THE SENTIMENTAL (II)

To Ruskin the use of the terms 'objective' and 'subjective,' when speaking of 'the difference between the ordinary, proper, and true appearances of things to us, and the extraordinary, or false appearances, when we are under the influence of emotion, or contemplative fancy,' was anathema. He preferred to use the term 'pathetic fallacy,' which has become popular and is useful.[1] It is a question-begging term, and it implies some confusion between the provinces of poetry and science. It cuts at the very root of imagination. There is truth of passion as well as truth of fact; passion is creative:

'The poets in their elegies and songs
  Lamenting the departed, call the groves,
  They call upon the hills and streams to mourn,
  And senseless rocks; nor idly; for they speak,
  In these their invocations, with a voice
  Obedient to the strong creative power
  Of human passion.'[2]

Ruskin is not consistent in his explanation of the term, and some of his examples of the so-called fallacy might figure as instances of what he elsewhere calls 'imagination penetrative.' He says that 'the

---

[1] *Modern Painters*, Part IV.
[2] Wordsworth, *The Excursion*, Book I.

greatest poets do not often admit this kind of falseness.' He puts Shakespeare in the first rank; yet where can you find finer examples of the fallacy than in Shakespeare? Though a fallacy, he says, it denotes a noble state of mind or body, 'according to the force of the emotion which has directed it.' 'There is a point at which all feverish and wild fancy becomes just and true.' It becomes untrue 'the moment the mind of the speaker becomes cold.' 'An inspired writer, in full impetuosity of passion, may speak wisely and truly of "raging waves of the sea foaming out their own shame"; but it is only the basest writer who cannot speak of the sea without talking of "raging waves," "remorseless floods," "ravenous billows," etc.; and it is one of the signs of the highest power in a writer to keep his eyes fixed firmly on the *pure fact*, out of which if any feeling comes to him or his reader, he knows it must be a true one.' Keeping the eyes fixed on the pure fact is not a bad way of defining that quality of Greek poetry, and of all poetry, which most of us call objective.

Apart from a few exceptions, the Greek poet does not speak of nature as coloured by his own feelings or in terms of his own passions; he does not see in her the reflection of his own moods. In connection with the sea, however, Homer has been credited with a sentimental love of nature, 'that love of nature which discerns a correspondence, and as it were a sympathy between its appearances and changes, and the vicissitudes of human feeling and passion. Chryses, after his entreaties have been denied, walks ἀκέων παρὰ θῖνα πολυφλοίσβοιο θαλάσσης, where the murmur of its waves responds to his feelings, and stirs him to pour them forth in prayer to Apollo.

In like manner, Achilles, when Briseis is taken from him, sits apart by himself:

> θῖν᾽ ἐφ᾽ ἁλὸς πολιῆς ὁρόων ἐπὶ οἴνοπα πόντον.

The epithet οἴνοπα, denoting the dark gloom, perhaps the purple grape-colour of the distant sea, while it was dashing and foaming at his feet, brings it into harmony and sympathy with Achilles. A bright, blue sea would have been out of keeping.' [1] At first thought this seems plausible. But, as regards the first quotation, common sense suggests that the priest needs no incitement to pray to Apollo; that is his natural resource. As regards the second, it so happens that there is another reading—ἐπ᾽ ἀπείρονα instead of ἐπὶ οἴνοπα. Ameis adopts the alternative and thinks that the expression 'boundless' or 'infinite' sea intensifies the feeling of desolation and despair. Thus, no matter which reading we prefer, Homer seemingly remains sentimental.

Let us examine further examples from the *Iliad* and the *Odyssey*. When Achilles, standing by the pyre of Patroclus, sorely troubled, addresses the river Spercheius, he looks over the 'wine-dark' sea:

> ὀχθήσας δ᾽ ἄρα εἶπεν ἰδὼν ἐπὶ οἴνοπα πόντον.
>
> (*Il.*, xxiii. 143.)

This suits Hare's notion excellently, for is not the sea responding to the feelings of the hero? When his companions have gone each to his tent to take his rest, Achilles lies groaning on the beach of the 'loud-sounding' sea:

> Πηλείδης δ᾽ ἐπὶ θινὶ πολυφλοίσβοιο θαλάσσης
> κεῖτο βαρὺ στενάχων.
>
> (*Il.*, xxiii. 59, 60.)

[1] *Guesses at Truth by Two Brothers* (Hare).

Are we to suppose that Achilles and the sea are in concert? On another occasion, when the same hero wanders wildly by the beach of the sea, we find no epithet at all: δινεύεσκ' ἀλύων παρὰ θῖν' ἁλός (*Il.*, xxiv. 12). So it is also in *Iliad*, xix. 40, 41, when he goes along the shore uttering shouts terrible to hear. A 'loud-sounding' sea would have been in keeping. When Ajax and Odysseus go on an embassy to Achilles, they walk by the shore of the 'loud-sounding' sea, praying earnestly to the Earth-shaker that they may prevail on Achilles (*Il.*, ix. 182-84). Is the great natural organ intoning in unison with the prayers? Agamemnon sends Talthybius and Eury-bates to the tent of Achilles, to bring away Briseis. They go unwillingly along the beach of the 'barren' sea:

τὼ δ' ἀέκοντε βάτην παρὰ θῖν' ἁλὸς ἀτρυγέτοιο.

(*Il.*, i. 327.)

Have they a presentiment that their errand will prove fruitless? In Ogygia Odysseus sits on the rocks weeping and looking over the 'barren' sea (*Ody.*, v. 158). Would not οἴνοπα have shown more sympathy and ἀπείρονα have intensified the feeling of desolation and despair? Some, however, think that ἀτρύγετος may mean 'restless.' In that case the sea may be in keeping with the turmoil in the hero's breast. Again, we find Odysseus on the shore of Ithaca weeping, and at the same time

ἑρπύζων παρὰ θῖνα πολυφλοίσβοιο θαλάσσης.

(*Ody.*, xiii. 220.)

As for οἶνοψ, it is used always of πόντος only, not of θάλασσα or of ἅλς. It indicates an effect of distance; its use is not due to consideration for the feelings of the person looking over the sea (*Il.*, v. 771), and

196

ships have no feelings to be considered (*Il.*, ii. 613). Πολύφλοισβος is an epithet of θάλασσα only. Ἀτρύγετος is attached to πόντος, θάλασσα, and ἅλς, and is therefore in great request.

Some lines in the *Attis* of Catullus may be useful here. Attis, on the morning after his frenzy, descends from Ida and makes his way to the shore. He looks over the Aegean towards Greece, his home, which he addresses in words full of regret:

> *Animo aestuante rursum reditum ad vada tetulit.*
> *Ibi maria vasta visens lacrimantibus oculis,*
> *Patriam allocuta maestast ita voce miseriter.*

(47-49.)

Vasta attached to *maria* implies distance. Somewhere by the same shore Achilles stands. He looks over the sea in the direction of the river Spercheius, whom he apostrophises. The poet thinks of the stretch of water and says πόντον. To that word he prefixes οἴνοπα, which he considers to be a suitable epithet for something implying distance. Neither *vasta* nor οἴνοπα is used to be in keeping with a state of soul.

The use of such epithets is too narrow a foundation for a sentimental theory. It is probably not far from the truth to say that, while Homer is not altogether careless in his employment of epithets, those called *recurring* are not intended to echo the mood of the person concerned from time to time. Not altogether careless, I say, advisedly. For instance, in the line descriptive of a stormy sea:

κύματα παφλάζοντα πολυφλοίσβοιο θαλάσσης,

I think I understand why Homer should prefer πολυφλοίσβοιο to ἀτρυγέτοιο, metrical considerations excluded. But, when I read that the companions of *Odysseus* 'uncovered their heads on the shore of the unharvested sea, and gazed at the stag, for a very big beast was he':

ἐκ δὲ καλυψάμενοι παρὰ θῖν' ἁλὸς ἀτρυγέτοιο
θηήσαντ' ἔλαφον· μάλα γὰρ μέγα θηρίον ἦεν—
(*Ody.*, x. 179-80)

I am not so sure about ἀτρυγέτοιο. A friend may say to me, 'Don't you understand that the sea contrasts with the stag as famine with plenty?' I answer, 'Perhaps.' I do not know, and I do not inquire why Homer says παρὰ θῖν' ἁλὸς ἀτρυγέτοιο instead of contriving to say παρὰ θῖνα πολυφλοίσβοιο θαλάσσης, as in *Iliad*, i. 34. Had he done so, the picture would not have vanished; it would have been slightly altered, but, I think, improved. Sense with the context would have been there still, and music would have been there. In either case a vivid statement musically made moves me. In either case the epithet is a general one, and it is of value less in itself than as part of a musical and pictorial phrase. The phrase may have suggested one thing to Homer's hearers, to my friend it may suggest another, to me yet another. To Homer's objectivity we moderns may make subjective additions, to the thing we may add reflection on the thing. In our age that is inevitable. And is it not a tribute to what we call Homer's universality?

At the risk of being tedious, let us contrast a modern poem, in one of its aspects, with Homer. Suppose we select Morris's *Life and Death of Jason*, a poem on a Greek theme. Great part of the pleasure derived from its perusal is in distinguishing the interwoven ancient, mediaeval, and modern strands. Speaking of Morris's seascapes, Mr. Noyes says, 'We have in Morris a series of conventional drawings of a singularly limited range. In the most part his waves are "green," a little less frequently they are "blue"; and beyond that he has—in energetic moments—"white" and "tumbling" and perhaps two or three words more, all of which he uses over and over again. In less energetic moods he is usually content with the quaint inversion "the water wan," which occurs some hundreds of times in the course of his works, and certainly scores of times in *Jason* alone.' Very well; Morris, like Homer, makes great use of conventional epithets. But in his frequent use of 'green' and 'blue' he shows a stronger colour-sense than Homer. Οἶνοψ has already been discussed. Ἰοειδής appears three times (*Il.*, xi. 298; *Ody.*, v. 56 and xi. 107). In none of these places is there any special reason for its use. Γλαυκή occurs once, in *Iliad*, xvi. 34. Patroclus is rebuking Achilles:

οὐκ ἄρα σοί γε πατὴρ ἦν ἱππότα Πηλεύς,
οὐδὲ Θέτις μήτηρ· γλαυκὴ δέ σε τίκτε θάλασσα
πέτραι τ' ἠλίβατοι, ὅτι τοι νόος ἐστὶν ἀπηνής.

The notion of colour is faint in the word. If it mean 'glancing,' 'glittering,' it has not been selected to suit the sentiment. If it mean 'gray,' with a suggestion of *bleakness*, it comes nearer to being a word of reproach. In the following lines Morris calls the sea 'green' for pictorial effect, to contrast with Pelias's 'cup of ruddy gold' and the rising sun striking on the figure of the god with his crystal rod, whereas Homer indulges in no such colour-schemes:

'And now may ye behold
The broad new-risen sun light up the God,
Who, holding in his hand the crystal rod
That rules the sea, stands by Daedalian art
Above his temple, set right far apart
From other houses, nigh the deep green sea.'

199

But there is more in Morris's style than this.
When we read of Orpheus:

> 'And glad they were indeed that he should be
> Their mate upon the *bitter tuneless* sea,'

we understand that 'bitter' and 'tuneless' are used
because the sweet music of Orpheus is to alleviate in
some measure the hardships of the voyage, the sea's
music being harsh. In the following 'trackless' has
been carefully selected to be in keeping with the fact
that Argo is to traverse unsailed and uncharted seas:

> 'There ask for one
> Who now gets ready a great race to run
> Upon a steed whose maker thou shalt be,
> And whose course is the bitter *trackless* sea.'

In this couplet 'doubtful' is due to the fears and un-
certainty of the heroes:

> 'While clashed their armour to the minstrelsy
> That went before them to the *doubtful* sea.'

In the protestation of Medea to Jason:

> '"Nay, sweet," she said, "let be;
> Wert thou more fickle than the *restless* sea,
> Still should I love thee"'__

'restless' echoes 'fickle.' In the following the epithet
'changeful' is chosen for contrast:

> 'Think rather of a peaceful land,
> The changeless land where ye may be
> Roofed over by the *changeful* sea.'

When the perilous expedition has come to a successful
end, Morris writes:

> 'From time to time in pleading song and prayer,
> Swept by the wind about the summer air,
> Clear rung the voices of the Minyae
> Unto the dashing of the *conquered* sea.'

In these instances—and there are many more—Morris is neither Homeric nor conventional. He changes his epithets to suit the sentiment and the occasion, which Homer does not. Sometimes, however, Homer can give the force of Morris's epithet by adding an explanatory clause. For example, I can imagine a Homeric equivalent of the last quotation running somewhat on the following lines: 'There on the beach of the loud-sounding sea Odysseus made prayer to Athena, for that he had come in safety to his own land, after suffering much sorrow of heart in passing through the grievous waves.'

Homer speaks of 'grievous waves'—ἀλεγεινὰ κύματα—but I do not find him speaking of 'heedless waves,' like Morris:

'But, O poor king, thy corpse shall not be hurled
Hither and thither by the *heedless wave*.'

He makes Telemachus say that the white bones of his father 'lie rotting in the rain on land, or the wave rolls them about in the sea.' Similarly Milton says in *Lycidas*:

'Ay me! whilst thee the shores and sounding seas
Wash far away, where'er thy bones are hurl'd.'

Neither Homer nor Milton expressly attributes feeling or lack of feeling to the wave, but they present us with a concrete picture of a wave in action. As we read we are moved, and we add the associated feeling. Thus, once more, Homer's objectivity explains his universality.

Some sentences by an Italian writer bear so closely on this point that I take the liberty of quoting them: 'Tra la cosa ed il simbolo, tra il particolare e l' universale deve esser rapporto di suggestione e non di ragionamento, e una suggestione costantemente voluta e conscientemente fatta notare non è più suggestione, ma persuasione. Il simbolo, come l' allegoria, sarà fonte di poesia vera fino a che resta in una certa indeterminatezza e vaporosità che basti a far sentire l' analogia tra le cose avvicinate. Ma chi vi insiste troppo e richiama la riflessione e la ragione sopra di esso, costui mette in vista non i rapporti di analogia, ma le disformità tra i due concetti, e per lo meno limita, definendoli, i detti rapporti. Achille sulla spiaggia del mare, come lo rappresenta l' Iliade, è più poetico e insieme più vero di quello del nostro commento, che l' anima d' Achille era in tempesta come il mare, o che il suo dolore era infinito come il mare, o che so io: ciascuno di questi commenti contiene del troppo e del falso, poichè l' equazione è manchevole assai e per misura e per qualità, inquanto il determinato è sempre più breve dell' indeterminato e tra questi termini contradittori non è possibile parificazione.' [1]

As it is with the sea so is it with the earth. To suppose that Homer becomes sentimental when, in the account of a fight, he calls the earth *black*, is to shut the eyes to the distinction between that which is all-important and that which is nugatory, from the point of view of feeling, in the phraseology of all early poetry. If, in such a case, Homer employs the expression γαῖα μέλαινα, may it not be that he is thinking much about the fight and very little about the earth, so little that instead of bestowing upon it an epithet that will associate it 'with scenes of death and bloodshed,' he uses one which he conceives to be literally true and useful on any occasion whatsoever? Homer can speak of μέλαν αἷμα—black or dark-red blood—as

[1] G. Fraccaroli: *L' Irrazionale nella Letteratura*, cap. xii.

202

well as of γαῖα μέλαινα. Two friends are to 'redden the same earth' (*Il.*, xviii. 329); the earth is 'reddened with blood' (*Il.*, x. 484); the earth is 'wet with dark (πορφυρέῳ) blood' (*Il.*, xvii. 360-61); 'the black earth runs with blood' (*Il.*, xx. 494). Nowhere in Homer are *black* earth and *red* blood brought into contrast. On the other hand, when Bacchylides says:

> ἐναριζομένων
> δ' ἔρευθε φώτων
> αἵματι γαῖα μέλαινα,　(xii. 151-53)

the contrast is probably intended, as that poet has a lively colour-sense. Similarly, when we read that Oedipus 'ruled the Cadmaeans in pleasant Thebes, while he suffered pain owing to the baneful counsels of the gods':

> ἀλλ' ὁ μὲν ἐν Θήβῃ πολυηράτῳ ἄλγεα πάσχων
> Καδμείων ἤνασσε θεῶν ὀλοὰς διὰ βουλάς,
> (*Ody.*, xi. 275-76)

we are not bound to suppose, with one commentator, that the poet hints at the aggravation of human misery by reason of its contrast with beautiful surroundings. It is all a question of whether we are to emphasise πολυήρατος or to regard it as a humble drudge-horse epithet.

Perhaps no two lines in Homer are better known than those in which he replies to Helen's surmises regarding Castor and Polydeuces, whom she misses from the number of the Greeks on the Trojan plain:

> ὣς φάτο, τοὺς δ' ἤδη κατέχεν φυσίζοος αἶα
> ἐν Λακεδαίμονι αὖθι, φίλῃ ἐν πατρίδι γαίῃ.
> (*Il.*, iii. 243-44.)

They were used by Ruskin in illustration of Homer's

practice of limiting his expression to bare fact. 'Note here,' he says, 'the high poetical truth carried to the extreme. The poet has to speak of the earth in sadness, but he will not let that sadness affect or change his thoughts of it. No; though Castor and Pollux be dead, yet the earth is our mother still, fruitful, life-giving. These are the facts of the thing. I see nothing else than these. Make what you will of them.' It is amusing to note the irony of the situation when one reads Matthew Arnold's criticism of this explanation in his essay, *On Translating Homer.* According to Arnold, Ruskin, by stressing the epithet φυσίζοος, 'life-giving,' and supposing that Homer used it in order to relieve the gloom, has really made the poet sentimental. One infers that Arnold regarded φυσίζοος as a no-account epithet. Professor Gilbert Murray, on the other hand, considers it to be 'steeped in primitive mysticism. Ruskin's error was that, not having the clue, he did not go far enough. His feeling about the word was right; but he stopped short at sentiment, whereas the word really connoted religion. The 'life-giving' earth is that most ancient goddess who is the cause not only of the quickening of seeds but of the resurrection of man. We are familiar with the thought from St. Paul's use of it as a metaphor. But the conception is far older than St. Paul, and lies in the very roots of Greek religion, as may be seen in Dieterich's *Mutter Erde.'* [1] The word is used only twice elsewhere in Homer, in *Iliad,* xxi. 63 and *Odyssey,* xi. 301. While the passage in the *Odyssey* refers to the alternate resurrection of the pair, neither passage in the *Iliad* contains the notion. The sense of the whole episode in *Iliad,* xxi., is strong on Arnold's

---

[1] *What English Poetry may still learn from Greek,* in *Essays and Studies by members of the English Association,* vol. iii.

side of the argument. Achilles wonders how Lycaon
has escaped from the day of destiny, though sent as a
slave to Lemnos. He is facetious, and pretends to
fear that the Trojans whom he has slain may rise up
again, seeing that this fellow has come back across
the sea, the grave of many. He is to make Lycaon
taste of his spear-point, that he may see whether he
shall come even from there as well (as from Lemnos),
'or whether the life-giving earth shall hold him down,
she that keeps hold of a man however strong he be.'
Are the lines in *Iliad* iii. and xxi. any more mystical
than those in Aeschylus:

καὶ Γαῖαν αὐτήν, ἣ τὰ πάντα τίκτεται
θρέψασα τ' αὖθις τῶνδε κῦμα λαμβάνει,
(*Choeph.*, 127-28)

or than the line in Lucretius:

Omniparens eadem rerum commune sepulchrum,
(*D.N.R.*, v. 259)

or than the lines in Shakespeare:

'The earth that's nature's mother is her tomb;
What is her burying grave, that is her womb'?
(*Romeo and Juliet*, ii. 3, 9-10.)[1]

There are, however, in Homer and other Greek
poets, examples of what may be called pathetic fallacy,
when nature is represented as sympathising with or
being otherwise moved by the lot of the living, human
or divine. In the *Iliad*, at the moment when the ships
of the Greeks are endangered, Poseidon mounts his
chariot at Aegae and drives over the waters to visit
the scene of action. The sea-monsters are aware of

[1] The point is: Did Homer *feel* the word φυσίζοος to be mystic?
If not, it is a mere ornamental epithet.

their lord and frolic at his coming, and the sea joy-
fully divides:

ἄταλλε δὲ κήτε' ὑπ' αὐτοῦ
πάντοθεν ἐκ κευθμῶν, οὐδ' ἠγνοίησεν ἄνακτα,
γηθοσύνῃ δὲ θάλασσα διίστατο.   (xiii. 27-29.)

Again, when the same god mingles in the fray, the
sea dashes up to the huts and ships of the Greeks:

ἐκλύσθη δὲ θάλασσα ποτὶ κλισίας τε νέας τε
'Αργείων.   (*Il.*, xiv. 392-93.)

On the same plane must be put the passages in the
Hymn *To Delian Apollo*, when Delos smiles just before
the god is born—μείδησε δὲ γαῖ' ὑπένερθεν (118), and
'a dark wave on either hand, driven on by shrill
winds, rolled to the land' (27-28).   On the same
occasion according to Theognis:

πᾶσα μὲν ἐπλήσθη Δῆλος ἀπειρεσίη
ὀδμῆς ἀμβροσίης, ἐγέλασσε δὲ γαῖα πελώρη,
γήθησεν δὲ βαθὺς πόντος ἁλὸς πολιῆς.   (8-10.)[1]

In the *Prometheus* of Aeschylus, on the other hand,
nature mourns in sympathy with the Titan:

βοᾷ δὲ πόντιος κλύδων
ξυμπίτνων, στένει βυθός,
κελαινὸς Ἄϊδος ὑποβρέμει μυχὸς γᾶς,
παγαί θ' ἁγνορύτων ποταμῶν
στένουσιν ἄλγος οἰκτρόν.   (431-36.)

On the morning of birth and the noon of marriage
the all-seeing sun was supposed to look down,
either in joyous sympathy with mortals beginning
a prosperous existence, or with a gloom that presaged
disaster (Euripides, *Phoen.*, 1-6; *Supplices*, 990-999).

[1] Cp. *Theogony*, 193-94; Homeric Hymn *To Athena*, 9-16; Pindar,
Oly., vii. 38; Euripides, *Ion*, 1079-86; Bacchylides, xvi. 124-28.

The perpetration of a deed fraught with momentous consequences might be accompanied by a disturbance in the natural order of the universe. When Thyestes got possession by fraud of the lamb with the golden fleece, Zeus changed the course of the sun, which travelled from west to east (Euripides, *Electra*, 726-46).[1] But Euripides makes the Chorus avow their disbelief in such stories, which are useful, however, in promoting worship of the gods through fear. Similar, but not identical, are the dramatic omens of the *Iliad* when Zeus thunders, or sheds bloody rain-drops on the earth, as a sign that many men are to be sent down to Hades; 'pieces of mysterious wildness,' like the vision of Theoclymenus in the hall of Odysseus; and the storm, thunder, and mysterious voices that signalise the passing of Oedipus in Sophocles.

Some of these, however, in so far as they form part of the popular belief of the time in the permanent possibilities of nature and are not due merely to the personal emotion of the poet, Ruskin would not have called pathetic fallacies. Moderns, who recognise a dualism in nature, would call them supernatural and regard them as poetic machinery. Radically, of course, the same principle accounts for both kinds; mythology is the pathetic fallacy of the Greeks.

In later epics there are many parallels to one or other of the above passages. In Virgil's *Aeneid*, at the crisis in the passion of Aeneas and Dido:

> *Prima et Tellus et pronuba Juno*
> *Dant signum : fulsere ignes et conscius aether*
> *Conubiis, summoque ulularunt vertice Nymphae.*
> *Ille dies primus leti primusque malorum*
> *Causa fuit.*
>
> (iv. 166-70.)

[1] There are variants in the legend. See also *Orestes*, 1001-07; *Iph. in T.*, 192-202.

207

Contrast with this the joyance of all nature when Adam and Eve enter the nuptial bower (*P.L.*, viii. 509-20). At the expulsion of the rebel angels, 'Disburdened Heaven rejoiced' (vi. 878). In Tasso's *Gerusalemme Liberata*, all the world is glad when the evil spirits are sent to Hell:

> *Liberato da lor, quella sì negra*
> *Faccia depone il mondo, e si rallegra.*
>
> (ix. 66.)

In Milton, when Eve had tasted of the forbidden fruit:

> 'Earth felt the wound, and Nature from her seat
> Sighing through all her works gave signs of woe,
> That all was lost.'
>
> (ix. 782-84.)

When Adam also shared the sin:

> 'Earth trembl'd from her entrails, as again
> In pangs, and Nature gave a second groan;
> Sky lower'd, and muttering thunder, some sad drops
> Wept at completing of the mortal sin
> Original.'
>
> (ix. 1000-04.)

And again:

> 'At that tasted fruit
> The Sun, as from Thyestean banquet, turn'd
> His course intended.'
>
> (x. 687-89.)

'Mute signs in nature' portend a further change for Adam and Eve (xi. 181-207). In Dante's *Purgatorio* the mountain trembles when a soul is purified (xxi.)

Homer calls a stone 'shameless' ($\dot{a}\nu a\iota\delta\dot{\eta}s$); Aeschylus calls iron 'savage-minded' ($\dot{\omega}\mu\dot{o}\phi\rho\omega\nu$) and a mountain-peak 'proud in its isolation' ($o\dot{\iota}\dot{o}\phi\rho\omega\nu$). Homer makes the earth 'laugh':

γέλασσε δὲ πᾶσα περὶ χθὼν
χαλκοῦ ὑπὸ στεροπῆς.

(*Il.*, xix. 362-63.)[1]

Aeschylus has his

ποντίων τε κυμάτων
ἀνήριθμον γέλασμα.

(*P.V.*, 89, 90.)

Odysseus longed for his island home, but he did not speak of 'the sobbing crags of Ithaca.' Night after night, for a whole year, the Watchman in the *Agamemnon*, couched on the house-top of the Atreidae, gazes on the concourse of the stars. But they are not the 'patient stars' of Keats:

ἄστρων κάτοιδα νυκτέρων ὁμήγυριν,
καὶ τοὺς φέροντας χεῖμα καὶ θέρος βροτοῖς
λαμπροὺς δυνάστας, ἐμπρέποντας αἰθέρι.

(4-6.)

Neither Homer nor Aeschylus would have made one speaker say to another, as Celia to Rosalind in *As You Like It*:

'By this heaven, now at our sorrows pale,
Say what thou canst, I'll go along with thee.'

(i. 3.)

There is nothing in Homer like the comment on the prodigies in the *Song of Roland*, cxii. Wind, rain, hail, thunder and lightning, earthquake, trouble all the realm of France. There is geat darkness at noon-day. Some say, 'It is the end of the world.' 'They do not know; they speak not true,' says the author:

C'est la granz dulurs pur la mort de Rollant.

Homer has words of pity for fallen warriors, but he does not send a hero into the fight and at

---

[1] The original meaning of γελᾶν was *shine*, and it may mean so here.

the same time lament his doom, after the manner of Virgil:

Te nemus Angitiae, vitrea te Fucinus unda,
Te liquidi flevere lacus.

(*Aeneid*, vii. 759-60.)

Homer did not originate pastoral conventions.

The *Hyperion* of Keats is Greek in subject, but how un-Greek are the opening lines! Not only is the figure of the god sunk in and dwarfed by nature; the landscape is infected by his presence, and this infected landscape strengthens the sentiment of nerveless despair. In the first line the note of modernity is struck by the word 'sadness,' and all the details aid the general impression. Contrast with this the opening of the *Prometheus Vinctus*, where the chained figure imports nothing into the native wildness of the scene. Tennyson's *Mariana* is perhaps the finest among many fine instances of that poet's skill in picturing the objects in a landscape as they are seen by a person dominated by a single overmastering emotion. The scene is made to suggest a painful story, and every epithet responds to the sensibilities of a woman deserted and utterly miserable. In the opening of *Maud* too nature blabs and provides a clue. It is difficult to find an analogous situation in Greek poetry, but the apostrophe of Oedipus to the scene of his father's murder affords the rudiments of a contrast. The dell, the coppice, and the narrow pass where three roads meet stand out in the vividness of naked reality. The spot is addressed as sentient, it is true, and even that is something remarkable in Greek; but not a single epithet is employed to betray the emotion of the self-blinded wreck (*Oed. Tyr.*, 1398-1403).

In Beaumont and Fletcher's *Maid's Tragedy* Aspatia criticises her maid's piece of needlework, in which is represented the story of Theseus and Ariadne:

'These colours are not dull and pale enough
To show a soul so full of misery
As this sad lady's was. Do it by me,
Do it again by me, the lost Aspatia;
And you shall find all true but the wild island.
Suppose I stand upon the sea-beach now,
Mine arms thus, and mine hair blown with the wind,
Wild as that desert; and let all about me
Tell that I am forsaken. Do my face
(If thou had'st ever feeling of a sorrow)
Thus, thus, Antiphila: strive to make me look
Like Sorrow's monument; and the trees about me,
Let them be dry and leafless; let the rocks
Groan with continual surges; and behind me,
Make all a desolation.'   (ii. 2.)

The prescription is peculiarly modern, unknown to the Greeks and the Romans, to Catullus and Ovid. Only in allegorical descriptions, such as Ovid's House of Sleep and Claudian's Cyprian Grove, is there an approximation to this method of treating natural backgrounds.

In modern poetry nature is often used as a means of relief or contrast, but Greek examples are not numerous. Gladstone has spoken of Homer's art in introducing the following peaceful scene into one of the combats in the *Iliad*: 'So long as it was morning and the sacred day was growing, so long did the spears of both sides reach their mark and the people fell; but just when a woodman gets ready his dinner in the mountain glades, when he has tired his hands cutting tall trees, and weariness comes on his spirit, and desire of sweet food takes hold on his heart, then did the Greeks by their valour break the battalions, as they called on their companions throughout the ranks' (xi. 84-91). No doubt Gladstone's praise is deserved. Some critics, however, have been less discriminating in eulogising Homer's art in his mountain similes. In the *Iliad* he is continually illustrating action by reference to familiar rustic operations and animal life. But we are not to suppose that the mere mention of a natural feature in the course of a simile implies intended relief or contrast and a feeling for nature. For his woodmen, boars, jackals, wolves, lions, forest fires and mists, the poet must go to woods and mountains. It is his necessity, not his choice. Thus words and phrases like οὔρεσι, ὄρεσφι, οὔρεος ἐν βήσσῃς, ὄρεος κορυφῇσι, οὔρεος ἐν κορυφῇς are Homeric commonplaces. We may, if we choose, snatch a double pleasure, and give the poet goodwill and royalty for it. But it is certain that we are prone to find in Homer's work now more, now less than he put there.

Nor do the tragic poets make much use of the calm of nature as a set-off to the action and passion of man. There are two unique lines at the crisis of the *Bacchae*, before the burst of Bacchic fury. Dionysus is heard calling on the Maenads to come and take vengeance on Pentheus, the mocker at their rites. All the air is hushed, every leaf in the forest-glade is still, and no sound of living thing can be heard:

σίγησε δ' αἰθήρ, σῖγα δ' ὕλιμος νάπη
φύλλ' εἶχε, θηρῶν δ' οὐκ ἂν ἤκουσας βοήν.

(1084-85.)

The Chorus, it is true, especially in Euripides, sing songs which relieve the tension and 'bring in, as it

were, the ideal world, to heal the wounds of the real.'
But these songs are not like Shakespeare's irresponsible
snatches. The Chorus are not entirely free agents,
and in the midst of their roamings on sea, mountain,
and plain, they are never disobedient to the call of
the city or the gods. The stasimon of the *Oedipus
Tyrannus* which precedes the catastrophe carries us
away in thought to Cithaeron and Cyllene, to the
haunts of the nymphs, Pan and Dionysus. In the
Bacchae, when the supposed minister of Dionysus has
been captured and imprisoned, the Chorus sing of
their god and his band revelling on Nysa, or on the
Corycian heights, or among the woody solitudes of
Olympus, where of old trees and beasts were spell-
bound by the music of Orpheus. The most beautiful
song of all, beautifully translated into verse by Dr.
Gilbert Murray, is not an exception. The land of
the heart's desire is the country of common fable.
The lines form part of an ode in the *Hippolytus* (732-74),
sung when Phaedra has left the stage bent on self-
destruction. The sentiments are those of the Psalmist:

'Fearfulness and trembling are come upon me, and
    horror hath overwhelmed me.
And I said, Oh that I had wings like a dove! for then
    would I fly away, and be at rest.'

'O that God would set me as a bird among the
winged tribes in the hiding-places of the hills! Might
I fly to the Adriatic shore, to the banks of Eridanus,
into whose clear waters the weeping sisters of Phaethon
drop amber-gleaming tears! Might I win to the land
where the Hesperian maidens sing round the apple-
laden tree, past the heaven-appointed end of man's
utmost sail over reddening seas, beyond the holy
bound of Atlas! There, in the garden of the divine

213

espousal, ambrosial waters are ever welling, and sacred Earth, the life-giver, yields to the Immortals bliss abounding more and more.'

Mainly modern too is the thought that nature is wholly indifferent to man, or smiles at his tears, or rebukes his ceaseless effort. There are a few instances in which Greek lyrists draw a contrast between nature's calm and man's unrest; but the contrast is merely predicated; there is no rebellion or remonstrance as in Burns's *Bonnie Doon*. In the following fragment Ibycus contrasts nature's recovery of freedom in spring with his heart's bondage to love:

Ἦρι μὲν αἵ τε Κυδώνιαι
μαλίδες ἀρδόμεναι ῥοᾶν
ἐκ ποταμῶν, ἵνα παρθένων
κῆπος ἀκήρατος, αἵ τ᾽ οἰνανθίδες
αὐξόμεναι σκιεροῖσιν ὑφ᾽ ἔρνεσιν
οἰναρέοις θαλέθοισιν· ἐμοὶ δ᾽ ἔρος
οὐδεμίαν κατάκοιτος ὥραν, ἅθ᾽ ὑπὸ στεροπᾶς φλέγων
Θρηΐκιος Βορέας, ἀΐσσων παρὰ Κύπριδος ἀζαλέαις
μανίαισιν ἐρεμνὸς ἀθαμβής,
ἐγκρατέως παιδόθεν φυλάσσει
ἀμετέρας φρένας.   (*Bergk*, I.)

'Truly in spring Cydonian apple-trees watered by streams from rivers, where is the unmown garden of the Nymphs, and the buds sprouting, beneath the shadowing vine shoots flourish; but with me love is at no hour at rest, love which, like the Thracian North Wind that rages midst the lightning, darting from the side of Cypris with parching madness, stern and fearless, from earliest youth keeps my heart in fast hold.' Greek poetry is here in touch with Provençal and Renaissance literature; with Petrarch and his

Zephiro torna, e 'l bel tempo rimena,

and with Surrey's 'Description of Spring, wherein each thing renews, save only the Lover.'

Alcman's night-piece, with its echoes of Homeric phraseology, is probably also a contrast, but unfortunately the human side of the picture has not been preserved:

Εὕδουσιν δ' ὀρέων κορυφαί τε καὶ φάραγγες
πρώονές τε καὶ χαράδραι,
φῦλά τε Ϝέρπεθ' ὅσα τρέφει μέλαινα γαῖα,
θῆρές τ' ὀρεσκῷοι καὶ γένος μελισσᾶν
καὶ κνώδαλ' ἐν βένθεσι πορφυρέας ἁλός·
εὕδουσιν δ' ὀϊωνῶν
φῦλα τανυπτερύγων.   (Bergk, 60.)

'Asleep are the mountain-tops and the clefts of the hills, cliffs, and ravines, all creeping things that black earth feeds, wild beasts that haunt the mountains, the race of bees, and the monsters in the depths of the purple sea; asleep too are the bird-tribes long of wing.' Compare and contrast Goethe's

Über allen Gipfeln
Ist Ruh',

and the section of Tennyson's *In Memoriam* beginning

'Calm is the morn without a sound." [1]

We have already seen how the form of Greek drama handicaps the introduction of external nature as an emotional element. Further illustrations may be given here without too much irrelevancy. The use of nature as a means of relief or contrast must be rare in plays which, with few exceptions, admit of

[1] Cp. in long line, Apollonius Rhodius, *Argon.*, iv. 744; Virgil, *Aen.*, iv. 522; Ovid, *Met.*, vii. 184; Statius, *Silvae*, v. 4; Dante, *Inferno*, ii. 1; Ariosto, *O.F.*, viii. 79; Tasso, *G.L.*, ii. 96.

no change of place. In *Macbeth*, the conversation of Banquo and Duncan as they approach Macbeth's castle (i. 6) 'gives that repose so necessary to the mind after the tumultuous bustle of the preceding scenes, and perfectly contrasts the scene of horror that immediately succeeds.' It reveals character and it is full of irony. With a stretch one could imagine such a colloquy between Orestes and Pylades in either of the *Electras*, were not Pylades a κωφὸν πρόσωπον, or in the *Choephoroe*. The scene between Orestes and Clytemnestra in the *Choephoroe*, when the former asks admittance to the palace, reverses the situation in Shakespeare. The murderer is without and the victim within; and the irony comes from the other side of the gate, when Clytemnestra says that the house holds every comfort for guests, 'hot baths' included, so that she can 'provide for' Orestes as she had done for Agamemnon. But the garden-scene in *Richard II.* (iii. 4), which shows the disposition of the commonalty towards the king, would be impossible in a play which preserved scenic unity. The representation of a career of crime and freedom from the trammels of a chorus render possible the recurrence of such soliloquies and apostrophes as we find in *Macbeth* (i. 5; ii. 1; iv. 2). Previous to a battle Greek dramatists have no room for promiscuous camp talk among groups of combatants. Shakespeare has scenes in which leaders discuss weather prospects, and even read their fortunes in the conscious sun and conspiring heavens, as in *Henry IV.*, Part I, v. 1. We hear similar speculations in *Richard III.*, v. 3, where Shakespeare has boldly staged the tents of Richard and Richmond simultaneously. Romantic love finds no place in Greek tragedy or comedy, and so there can be nothing there analogous to the moonlight scene in

The Merchant of Venice or the balcony scene in *Romeo and Juliet*. Scenes such as those in *Macbeth*, *Julius Caesar* and *King Lear*, in which nature is an active background intensifying emotion, illuminating character, and making a symphony with human action and passion, are outside the economy of Greek drama. Shakespeare and the Athenian dramatists alike wrote for the average spectator and kept in touch with popular beliefs or superstitions. Shakespeare brings ghosts upon the stage; Aeschylus shows a sisterhood of Furies with snaky hair and bloodshot eyes dogging the steps of Orestes. But so strong was the force of mythology that neither in Aeschylus nor in Euripides do we hear from the lips of Orestes words like those of Alonzo in *The Tempest*, iii. 3:

'O, it is monstrous, monstrous!
Methought the billows spoke and told me of it;
The winds did sing it to me, and the thunder,
That deep and dreadful organ-pipe, pronounced
The name of Prosper: it did bass my trespass.
Therefore my son i' the ooze is bedded, and
I'll seek him deeper than e'er plummet sounded,
And with him there lie mudded.'

CHAPTER X

ALEXANDRIAN POETRY

'I‍L a fait par ses vers plus de mal que de bien.' These are words of the French historian Burnouf, writing of Theocritus. It is a mistaken criticism which thus regards Theocritus merely as a pastoral poet, and proceeds to attribute to him, as the father of pastoral poetry, all the shortcomings of his literary descendants. Besides rural idylls, Theocritus wrote short heroic poems, or epic moments, as they may be called, dramatic dialogues, and occasional poems. There is no reason to suppose that, disgusted with life at the court of Ptolemy Philadelphus, he turned to the delineation of a mode of life charming in its simplicity, and setting at defiance all the conditions of a rural existence. His work was not inspired by sentiments like those of Lady Wishfort, for example, in Congreve's *Way of the World*, who, feeling the tedium of a life of constant intrigue, a tedium which not even occasional quotations from 'the natural, easy Suckling' can dispel, thinks of turning shepherdess, of retiring 'to deserts and solitudes, and feeding harmless sheep by groves and purling streams.' Theocritus' pictures of rural life are not the dreams of an Alexandrian citizen, but transcripts from reality. They paint life as he saw it for himself in the land of Sicily, the ideal country for shepherds, presenting a striking contrast to the cold surroundings of northern rustics. The singing-match, the banter, the love-ditty, the dirge, the country legend the poet had himself heard in boyhood and treasured in his memory till the time came to use them for purposes of art. The objections urged by Fontenelle and English eighteenth-century critics against the sentiments and graces of his shepherds and herdsmen are best answered, as is shown by Mr. Lang in the introduction to his translation of this poet, by the fact that the folk-songs of modern Greece have exactly the same characteristics. Further, if Theocritus represents every shepherd with his pipe and the gift of song in some measure, the shepherds none the less remain shepherds, and the coarser country features peep out from time to time. His characters utter their *opprobria rustica* with an ease and a heartiness that Virgil failed to imitate. A rival is not always hailed as 'a sweet mouth of the Muses'; he is sometimes a scoundrel and a thief, and even worse. While our ears are charmed by the Doric music of the songs, we cannot close them to the country 'clash' (to use an expressive Scots word), any more than we can shut our eyes to some rough wooing. If, in the ninth Idyll, Daphnis and Menalcas sing the joys of the shepherd's life, in the fourteenth Aeschines bemoans the caprices of a light o' love, and vows—the last resource of a rascal rustic in our own north at the present time—to enlist. That Theocritus has sometimes idealised his pictures may be freely admitted. Daphnis and Menalcas, for instance, exhibit none of the satyr-like instincts of Comatas and Corydon. Idealisation is a prerogative of poetry, and as Theocritus himself has said, 'Whatever the Muses touch they make altogether beautiful': ὧν γάρ χ' ἅψησθε θεαί, καλὰ πάντα ποεῖτε.

The rural poems of Theocritus do not merit the

219

title of 'cold pastoral.' They are redolent of the soil, full of a pulsing life and a warm humanity. Coldness arises from the loss of reality consequent on the attempts of Virgil, and of Italian, French, and English poets to transfer the scenery of Sicily to alien lands, and to moralise and allegorise their subjects. Our Hobb and Sandy have indeed their pipes, but with a difference; and Gay pointed out the true lines on which a native English pastoralism might have progressed, had the time not been past for such a phase of literary art, when in his *Shepherd's Week* he made Lobbin Clout wager, instead of the orthodox delicately-carven cup, a tobacco-pouch. That pastoral must inevitably prove cold in which a Priest of Pan takes part in a May-day function, when the guise of shepherds but dimly conceals the features of wrangling Catholic and Protestant, and when 'Pan and his son and fair Syrinx' typify James the Second, his Queen, and the Old Pretender.

Nor is it correct to refer to Theocritus much of what is called 'pastoral melancholy.' That came in with Virgil in whose work we constantly hear a sad undertone. Rarely does his piping take a troubled sound. 'His reflections are frequent, but seasonable; soon over, like the shadows of spring clouds on flowery meadows, and not hanging heavily upon the scene, nor depressing the vivacity of the blithe antagonists.' Vivacity, that is the word which best describes the conduct of the shepherd, who, when awarded the prize of victory, claps his hands and leaps skyhigh. Theocritus does not grieve for the mere luxury of grief, nor, like Pope, does he

'with melodious moan
Teach rocks to weep, and make the mountains groan.'

220

But, when his genius turned to pure poetry the rural dirge for the ideal shepherd Daphnis, he produced the model—a dangerous one as it has proved—for those elegies in which later poets have consecrated their hour of grief for 'the inheritors of unfulfilled renown.'

That Theocritus knew country life at first hand, and as no mere townsman ever knows it, is clear from many of his lines. The stroke with which he indicates the time of sundown in Idyll xiii. could have been given but by one who had been about a Sicilian farm in the evening: it is the time when the hen flaps her wings on the smoke-blackened beam and the chickens look up to the perch:

ὑπόκ' ὀρτάλιχοι μινυροὶ ποτὶ κοῖτον ὁρῶεν,
σεισαμένας πτερὰ ματρὸς ἐπ' αἰθαλόεντι πετεύρῳ.

(xiii. 12, 13.)

He has spied the air of pride with which Master Chanticleer officiously clarions the morning, raising his finely-feathered neck the while—ἀνασχὼν εὔτριχα δειράν (xviii. 57). He has watched the swallow come flying with food for her little ones in the nest under the eaves, and swiftly set out for more (xiv. 39-41). He may have received a rather too fierce welcome from a faithful farmyard dog, or seen the same animal dozing with nose on fore-paws, thinking of 'brose' or hunting in his dreams (xxi. 44, 45). He has seen a ewe painfully limping in the rear of the flock by reason of a thorn-pricked foot (x. 4). Walking along a narrow country road in the cool evening he has had to step aside till a drove of kine has passed on the way to the homestead, and then instinctively hurried his pace (xvi. 92, 93).

Along with a knowledge of rural life there is in Theocritus a conscious appreciation of the charms of

221

Nature. In this respect, however, it is possible to overvalue him, and without doubt some writers have made too much of his intimacy with Nature. Our interest in his characters is never distracted by attention to details of scenery. His prime interest is in humanity, and most of all in youth; in young men with beards like the golden ivy-flower, or in shepherds, like Lycidas, with twinkling eyes and smiling lips, in maidens with bright ringlets rippling down the beautiful neck, or with 'the charm of married brows' (σύνοφρυς). Such figures lend life and beauty to a landscape. Milton knew this when he animated his towers 'bosom'd high in tufted trees' by imagining within them some beauty, 'the cynosure of neighbouring eyes,' and when he made the breathing presence of Eve enhance in the eyes of the Tempter the charms of her bower. The simile by which the latter situation is illustrated has more than once been quoted to prove Milton's feeling for Nature —which it does to some extent—but that is not the point of the comparison:

> 'As one who long in populous city pent,
> Where houses thick and sewers annoy the air,
> Forth issuing on a summer's morn to breathe
> Among the pleasant villages and farms
> Adjoin'd, from each thing met conceives delight,
> The smell of grain, or tedded grass, or kine,
> Or dairy, each rural sight, each rural sound;
> If chance with nymph-like step fair virgin pass,
> What pleasing seem'd, for her now pleases more,
> She most, and in her look sums all delight.
> (*P.L.*, ix. 445-54.)

This passage might have been signed by Theocritus and all preceding Greek poets as their confession of faith on the subject of Nature. But, moreover, there is this to be said for Theocritus, that in harmonising his characters with his scenes he stands unsurpassed by any poet.

The descriptions of Nature in Theocritus are thoroughly Greek—slight and eclectic, and rarely independent of the subject. In some of his longer descriptions he has not quite the clearness of outline characteristic of Homer. Unlike Virgil, he neither invents nor embellishes landscape features. Apart from sky and sea he does not deal in large perspectives. In the rustic idylls a few strokes from a sure hand sketch the surroundings of the tiny stage on which his characters enact their little dramas. His shepherds meet in the noonday 'on the long ranges of the hills,' or sit down 'by a well-head' or on some pleasant spot overlooking the laughing Mediterranean, and there commence their discourse or their singing-match. Perfectly happy in their surroundings, they never look beyond the dells and the woods, up to the shadeless peak of Etna where the white clouds play. His herdsmen know the sort of place in which to lie on fleeces 'softer than sleep,' the surroundings amid which one's song sounds more sweetly. In the fifth Idyll Lacon says to his rival: 'More sweetly wilt thou sing, sitting here beneath the wild olive in these groves. Here chill water fills, here grass grows, here is a leafy bed, and here locusts chatter.' But Comatas has a paradise of his own: 'Here are oaks, here is galingale, here the bees hum sweetly round the hives. There are two wells of cold water, on the tree birds warble their songs, and the shade is better far than that where thou art, and the pine from above throws down its cones.' The spot by Propontis where Hylas goes to draw water is a perfect picture of a marshy

223

landscape; a spring, round which there grow in profusion rushes, swallow-wort, maiden-hair, and parsley. Here we meet again our old friends the nymphs, beautiful as ever, with names like very music—'Eunice and Malis and Nycheia with the April eyes (ἔαρ ὁρόωσα)'—dancing in the clear water of the spring. A charming landscape is that in the country of the Bebryces, in the twenty-second Idyll: 'Now they found under a smooth rock a perennial spring filled with pure water, and from the depths below the pebbles showed like unto crystal or silver. Near by there grew tall firs, and poplars, and planes, and cypresses with leafy tops, and therein were all fragrant flowers that bloom in the meadows at the latter end of spring and are dear to the busy, hairy bees.' The former spot was lit up by the fair forms of golden-haired Hylas and the nymphs, but here there is a blot on the landscape—the giant Amycus sitting and sunning his monstrous bulk. In the fourth Epigram we are introduced to a sweet spot quite close to the town. It contains all the favourite sights and sounds of Theocritus, a never-failing stream falling from the rocks, and around the laurel, the myrtle, the cypress, and the vine, where the merles of spring utter their clear and varied chants, and the nightingales answer with honey-sweet notes.

This poet's love of shade and his felicity in describing it reveals itself at every turn. A young man hastens to his friend 'as a wayfarer runs from the fiery sun of noon to the beechen shade' (xii. 8, 9). The old husbandman points out to Heracles the steading of Augeas 'across the flowing river, there where grow abundantly the planes and the green wild-olive:'

φαίνεται εὖ μάλα πᾶσι πέρην ποταμοῖο ῥέοντος,
κείνῃ ὅθι πλατάνιστοι ἐπηετανοὶ πεφύασι
χλωρή τ' ἀγριέλαιος.
(xxv. 19-21.)

This picture haunts us like that of the Reeve's
dwelling in Chaucer's *Prologue*, which has, however,
the additional charm of complete surprise:

'His wonyng was ful faire upon an heeth,
With grene trees y-shadwed was his place.'

And look at his treatment of the old story of Chalcon
who, with a blow of his foot against a rock, produced
the fountain Burine. For Homer and the classical
Greek poets this bare statement of fact would have
seemed sufficient, but Theocritus must linger over
the scene and surround the waters with a leafy grove
of woven, pillared shade:

ταὶ δὲ παρ' αὐτὰν
αἴγειροι πτελέαι τε ἐΰσκιον ἄλσος ὕφαινον,
χλωροῖσιν πετάλοισι κατηρεφέες κομόωσαι.
(vii. 7-9.)

His delight in the sounds of Nature is everywhere
evident. It is noteworthy how often the scene is not
considered perfect without the murmur of water, the
song of birds, or the hum of bees. 'Sweet it is,' says
Daphnis, 'in summer-time to lie beneath the open
sky, beside running water':

ἁδὺ δὲ τῷ θέρεος παρ' ὕδωρ ῥέον αἰθριοκοιτεῖν.
(viii. 7-8.)

And again 'Sweet lows the calf, sweet the heifer, sweet
on his pipe plays the neat-herd, and sweet play also I':

ἁδὺ μὲν ἁ μόσχος γαρύεται, ἁδὺ δὲ χὰ βῶς,
ἁδὺ δὲ χὰ σῦριγξ, χὠ βουκόλος, ἁδὺ δὲ κἠγών.
(ix. 7-8.)

P
225

His lines often echo the delectable sounds of Nature. In the opening lines of the first Idyll we hear the whispering pine:

ἁδύ τι τὸ ψιθύρισμα καὶ ἁ πίτυς αἰπόλε τήνα,
ἁ ποτὶ ταῖς παγαῖσι μελίσδεται, ἁδὺ δὲ καὶ τὺ
συρίσδες.

And here the sound of water falling down from a height:

τῆν' ἀπὸ τᾶς πέτρας καταλείβεται ὑψόθεν ὕδωρ.

(i. 8.)

And in the following the hum of bees:

ὧδε καλὸν βομβεῦντι ποτὶ σμάνεσσι μέλισσαι.

(v. 46.)

Thus *sweetness*, oftener than *beauty*, is the keyword to the Idylls of Theocritus.

For the expression of pure sensuous delight the seventh is the gem of all the Idylls. It recounts the joys of a summer's day spent, with the friends of youth, in the isle of Cos, and viewed through the golden haze of memory. The poet, under the name of Simichidas, accompanied by his two friends, Eucritus and Amyntas, sets out for a harvest feast of Demeter. The poem tells of their walk beneath a burning sun at noon, when

'The lizard with his shadow on the stone
Rests like a shadow,'

of their meeting with the laughing Lycidas, and the generous recognition of each other's genius at that time of life when the clouds of envy have not yet darkened the vision. We hear the songs with which they while away the time, and we smile at the dream of young men, who fancy that their lives can lie under a charm, so that throughout the years none but beautiful things shall come near to them. They part; Lycidas sets his smiling face towards **Pyxa**; the others turn to the farm of Phrasidemus. There they 'drink the spirit of the season,' if ever mortals did. 'There on deep beds of fragrant rush and new-cut vine-leaves we laid us down rejoicing. High overhead waved many a poplar, many an elm, and hard by the sacred water from the cave of the Nymphs made music as it flowed. On shady boughs the brown cicalas kept chirping; far away in dense thickets of thorn croaked the tree-frog. Larks and linnets sang, while cooed the turtle-dove,[1] and round about the springs flitted the tawny bees. All things scented of rich summer, all breathed of fruit-time. At our feet pears, and by our sides apples rolled in plenty, young branches beneath the weight of damsons drooped to the ground; and from the mouth of the wine-jars the pitch of four years was broken.' The poem ends with a picture of Demeter, giver of the grain, standing by a heap of corn, with sheaves and poppies in her hands, and smiling on her votaries. The poem is more than a voice from the grave of a beautiful paganism. It is a revelation of character. The flattering crew round Ptolemy in gay Alexandria had no power to spoil the man who could live over in imagination vanished yesterdays with so little sense of loss. Compare the tone of wistful regret and the old-in-youth spirit which can be detected in Virgil:

> *Omnia fert aetas, animum quoque: saepe ego longos*
> *Cantando puerum memini me condere soles:*
> *Nunc oblita mihi tot carmina.*   (*Ecl.*, ix. 51-53.)

---

[1] 'I heard the cushies croon
Thro' the gowden afternoon.'
     The Bush Aboon Traquair.

For us, amid the complexities and confusions of modern life, it seems a vain endeavour to gain the vantage-ground of Theocritus and remain one with Nature. To find the shade of Melancholy seated near the throne of Beauty,

'To know the change and feel it,'

seems part of our burden brought by the years. Theocritus could find the birds in last year's nest.

Most of the Idylls of Theocritus are of this cheery nature, full of song and sunlight. But one, the twenty-first, is set in a more sombre atmosphere. Throughout we seem to feel the scents of the sea on a summer night just before the dawn. There is no one near; no sound breaks the stillness but the wash of the waves up to a wattled hut, the home of penury, teacher of toil. You can hear it in the words:

ἁ δὲ παρ' αὐτάν
θλιβομέναν καλύβαν τραφερὰν προσέναχε θάλασσα.
(17-18.)

Within are no piping shepherds, merely two battered fishermen. The summer brings them only longer days of labour, and short nights which care fills with a thousand dreams. And yet you hear them speak of 'the beautiful summer'! There is no landscape detail in the Idyll, but, if I mistake not, there is a true feeling for Nature, of the kind that cannot be caught in a classification. It has been already said that the characters and the scenes of Theocritus present a complete harmony. That is no less true here. This grey scene is the only fitting frame for the aged fishermen, round whose lives the shades are gathering.[1]

[1] Some judges say this poem is not the work of Theocritus. It ought to be.

In Theocritus we find, for the first time in Greek literature, that form of the sentimental treatment of the passion of love which connects it with Nature, when love colours all the landscape, and the presence or absence of the loved one has power to change the appearance of the outward world in the eyes of the lover. Listen to what even rustic feet can do. In Idyll VIII. Menalcas says—'There the ewes, there the goats bring forth twins, there the bees fill the hives, and more lofty grow the oaks, where the feet of beautiful Milon tread; ah, if he depart, lean is the shepherd and dry are the pastures!' To this Daphnis replies: 'Spring is everywhere, and everywhere the udders swell with milk and the young are nourished, where fair Nais wanders; ah, if she depart, more parched and thin are herdsman and herds!' This is but the first faint outline of a form of sentiment which has become a convention in modern poetry, more especially in those pastorals where gentles play at shepherds.

In the second Idyll, commonly called the *Pharmaceutria*, love and Nature are united by a bond of a different kind. The girl Simaetha, deserted by her lover, uses charms and incantations to bring him home to her. As she softly sings to the moon, Selene who loved Endymion, and to Hecate, the power of hell, we hear the subdued tones of the girl in the lines:

$$\text{ἀλλὰ Σελάνα}$$
$$\text{φαῖνε καλόν· τὶν γὰρ ποταείσομαι ἄσυχε δαῖμον,}$$
$$\text{τᾷ χθονίᾳ θ' Ἑκάτᾳ, τὰν καὶ σκύλακες τρομέοντι}$$
$$\text{ἐρχομέναν νεκύων ἀνὰ τήρία καὶ μέλαν αἷμα.}$$

(ii. 10-13.)

We feel the contrast between the whirling madness of heart and brain keeping time to the turning of the

magic wheel, and the peacefulness of surrounding
Nature, the calm of the sea, the hush of the winds:

ἠνίδε σιγῇ μὲν πόντος, σιγῶντι δ᾽ ἀῆται·
ἁ δ᾽ ἐμὰ οὐ σιγῇ στέρνων ἔντοσθεν ἀνία.

(38-39.)

Her handmaid gone, she stands alone in the moonlight and pours out all her tale of passion, with the
soft refrain:

φράζεό μευ τὸν ἔρωθ᾽ ὅθεν ἵκετο, πότνα Σελάνα.

(68.)

Her story told, she bids good-night to the listening
Moon and 'the other stars that attend the chariot
of quiet Night,' and a peace like theirs falls upon her
spirit:

ἀλλὰ τὺ μὲν χαίροισα ποτ᾽ ὠκεανὸν τρέπε πώλως,
πότνι᾽· ἐγὼ δ᾽ οἰσῶ τὸν ἐμὸν πόνον ὥσπερ ὑπέσταν.
χαῖρε Σελαναία λιπαρόχροε, χαίρετε κᾶλλοι
ἀστέρες, εὐκάλοιο κατ᾽ ἄντυγα Νυκτὸς ὀπαδοί.

(163-66.)

It is significant of a change in art that Theocritus
can show us the Cyclops Polyphemus in love. To
speak frankly, I do not much care for the exhibition.
As a specimen of robust cannibalism, as the picturesque
scoundrel of Homer's page, Polyphemus was delightful; as a lover he is insipid. We do not care to
fancy that the monster was ever young and lived with
his mother, that he wandered out alone and forgot
the way home, that he shepherded his love with song,
that he held anything dearer than his ram or his
precious one eye. But, if we can forget the Homeric
associations of the Cyclops, we cannot fail to be
struck with the singular grace of many of the lines in
this Idyll. Those in which Polyphemus reminds
Galatea of their first meeting—'O maid, I fell in love

with thee on that day when first thou camest with my mother, desiring to pluck hyacinths from the hill, and I showed thee the way'—were copied by Virgil, who transferred the scene from the free mountain air of Sicily to the richness of an Italian orchard, and, by the addition of a few original touches, fashioned the romance of a boyish love well-known to readers of the *Eclogues*.[1] It is noteworthy that, while the flora of Theocritus is as rich as that of Virgil and others of the Latin poets, he always makes his posies on the spot, and does not ransack the gardens for effect. Polyphemus, indeed, knows a little too much about flowers. After wishing he had been born with fins that he might have visited Galatea in her sea-home, bearing 'either white lilies or the tender poppies with scarlet petals,' he adds, 'but these are flowers of summer, while those are of winter, so that I could not have brought them all at once.' Milton's simple ignorance of times and seasons is preferable to such frigid pedantry as this. But stay; we wrong Theocritus. Is not the poet dramatising and allowing Polyphemus to exhibit his clumsiness? Just as the monster cannot sing, though he thinks he can, so he does not know that human mortals when in love show a lofty disregard of precise truth.

Theocritus does not often bring us into touch with the sea. In the hymn to Castor and Polydeuces a storm at sea is described after the manner of Homer, and with all his art in suggesting sound by the collocation of words:

$$\pi a \tau a \gamma \epsilon \hat{\iota} \ \delta' \ \epsilon \dot{\upsilon} \rho \epsilon \hat{\iota} a \ \theta \acute{a} \lambda a \sigma \sigma a,$$
$$\kappa o \pi \tau o \mu \acute{\epsilon} \nu \eta \ \pi \nu o \iota a \hat{\iota} s \ \tau \epsilon \ \kappa a \grave{\iota} \ \dot{a} \rho \rho \acute{\eta} \kappa \tau o \iota \sigma \iota \ \chi a \lambda \acute{a} \zeta a \iota s.$$
$$(\text{xxii. } 15\text{-}16.)$$

---

[1] See Sellar's *Roman Poets of the Augustan Age: Virgil*.

Contrast with this epic imitation the homely picture of the dog running barking along the shore, while its form is mirrored in the clear water:

ἁ δὲ βαΰσδει
εἰς ἅλα δερκομένα, τὰ δέ νιν καλὰ κύματα φαίνει
ἅσυχα παφλάζοντα ἐπ᾽ αἰγιαλοῖο θέοισαν.

(vi. 10-12.)

But into the mouth of one of his favourites, Menalcas, the poet has put words that reveal the sea as a source of inspiration, words that, as has been said, let us into the secret of his good poetry: 'Not mine be it to own the land of Pelops, nor to possess talents of gold, nor to outspeed the winds; but beneath this rock will I sing, with thee in my arms, looking at our flocks as they feed in company, and gazing on the Sicilian sea' (viii. 53-56).

Many of the similes of Theocritus smack of the farm and the green country. Polyphemus says Galatea is 'whiter than pressed milk, tenderer than the lamb, more wanton than the calf, sleeker than a shiny unripe grape' (xi.). The beard of a husbandman runs round his face 'like ivy round a tree,' and his locks fall about his temples 'like parsley' (xx.). Simaetha, under the fever of love, becomes pale 'as boxwood' (ii.). Some of his figures are framed after Homer's model. The best of this kind is that in which he likens the kine of Augeas coming from the pastures in their thousands, and moving ever onwards, to clouds, countless and ceaseless, rolled on before the winds (xxv.). Sometimes he will take a Homeric simile and give it a new application. Homer had likened the raft of Odysseus, tost by all the winds, to thistle-down swept along the plain; in Theocritus the thistle-down is an image of the wantoning of

Galatea (vi.).[1] Other figures are strikingly original. A countryman, stung by the taunts of a town-girl, becomes 'red as a rose with dew' (xx.). Hylas shoots down into the waters of the spring 'like a star from the sky' (xiii.). No clown of a shepherd could do that. The muscles on the arms of the giant Amycus are compared to stones which have been rounded and smoothed in the eddies of a river (xxii.). Tennyson, in his description of Geraint, adopted the figure:

> 'Arms on which the standing muscle sloped,
>   As slopes a wild brook o'er a little stone,
>   Running too vehemently to break upon it.'

Most original of all, and with something of an Eastern flavour, are those figures which in the *Epithalamium* celebrate the beauty of Helen. A quotation from Calverley's translation may not be amiss:

> 'As peers the nascent morning
>   Over thy shades, O night,
> When winter disenchains the land,
>   And spring goes forth in white;
>   So Helen peered above us,
>   All loveliness and light.
>
> As climbs aloft some cypress,
>   Garden or glade to grace;
> As the Thessalian courser lends
>   A lustre to the race;
>   Such pride had Lacedaemon
>   In Helen's rosebud face.'

Thus it will be seen that Theocritus, with a true dramatic instinct, varies his images with his characters.

---

[1] Cp. the lines of the Cavalier Suckling, beginning:
> 'Hast thou seen the down in the air
> When wanton blasts have tossed it?'

Those employed in the epic idylls are the most imaginative; Lacon and Comatas show a poverty of invention in comparison with Daphnis and Menalcas; the blunt sincerity of Polyphemus proves him a novice in the service of Love.

Perhaps more than enough has here been said about Theocritus. Certainly the subject is a tempting one. His simple, direct, and vivid vision of Man and Nature gives Theocritus a place very near to Homer, whose hand he clasps across the centuries. He has no mission. He is no dedicated spirit. He does not interpret Nature for us. But it is his to pipe, like the shepherd's boy in Sidney's *Arcadia*, 'as though he should never be old,' he offers us to drink from his magic cup 'washed in the well of the Hours.'

The poetry of Theocritus is the brief but beautiful Indian summer of the Greek genius. When we pass to Bion and Moschus we experience a chill. Bion and Moschus, closely as they are associated with pastoralism, are pre-eminently poets of love. 'May the Muses bring Love along' is the prayer of Bion, and at the words up starts a legion of rosy cupids armed with bow and arrow. Rarely do we catch a glimpse of Nature in their works. But the sensuous charms of the seasons are not absent. In Bion (iii.) Cleodamas asks Myrson which of the seasons is most after his heart. It is not difficult to divine the answer. Myrson is pious withal. It does not become mortals, he says, to judge concerning the works of God, for all these things are sacred; yet, if he must speak out, here is his verdict: 'I do not wish for summer, for then the sun roasts me; I do not care for autumn, since ripe fruits bring disease; deadly winter with its frost and snow I dread; but may spring, the thrice-desired, be with me all the year.' Moschus has a kindly word even for the sea, but only when the winds blow softly; when the long waves tower and roar he casts his eyes landwards to the shady woods, where, if the wind be strong, the pine-tree sings her song. Not for worlds would he live the hard life of the fisherman. Be it his to enjoy sweet sleep beneath the thick-leaved planes, or to lie and listen to the near murmuring brook:

αὐτὰρ ἐμοὶ γλυκὺς ὕπνος ὑπὸ πλατάνῳ βαθυφύλλῳ,
καὶ παγᾶς φίλ' ἐμοὶ τᾶς ἐγγύθεν ἆχον ἀκούειν,
ἃ τέρπει ψοφέοισα τὸν ἄγριον, οὐχὶ ταράσσει.

(iv.)

It is in meadows by the sea that Europa and her maiden company wander to cull flowers, taking delight in the sound of the wave no less than in the roses (ii.). The passage descriptive of the flower-gathering is reminiscent of a similar one in the Hymn *To Demeter*. True to Greek feeling, Moschus shows most interest in Europa and the cunning-work on her basket.

In one instance both Bion and Moschus seem to enter into competition with Theocritus. In the dirge for Daphnis, Theocritus has risen into a world ideal and legendary yet subtly connected with the ordinary rustic life of Sicily. The poem is open to a double interpretation. From one point of view, Daphnis is the hero of a tragedy similar to that presented to us by Euripides in his *Hippolytus*, where Aphrodite takes revenge on a youth who has proved cold to the pleasures she has to offer. From another, the poem is founded on the contrast between the littleness of man's individual life and the permanence of Nature. This latter idea, though not primary, is embodied in the myth of Adonis, in honour of whose festival at Alexandria Bion turned out a splendid literary exercise in which he bewailed the plight of Cytherea quite as much as the passing of the lovely youth. The themes of Theocritus and Bion are frankly mythical, but Moschus sings of a human sorrow, and he is thus the true father of what we call pastoral elegy. In the poem of Theocritus the mourning is of the most restrained and artistic character. While the wild beasts and the kine bewail Daphnis, inanimate Nature takes no part in the lament. But in Bion the oaks reply to the 'Woe, woe!' of the mountains, the wells are weeping, and the flowers redden for sorrow. 'Let all things be confounded, for Daphnis is dying,' sings Thyrsis in Theocritus; in Moschus confusion already reigns throughout the kingdom of Nature—the flowers fade, the trees cast down their fruits, the ewes give no milk, and the honey perishes in the wax. In fact, in reading both Bion and Moschus, we suffer ourselves to be led through all the phases of artificial emotion simply because we are enthralled by the beauty and harmony of the verse, just as in the monodies of Milton and Shelley we forget all incongruities by reason of the perfection of the poetry.

One passage in Moschus' elegy is noteworthy, and has been often quoted, for its setting forth of the contrast between the long winter of humanity's tomb and the annual renewal of Nature's life. 'Ah, when the mallows perish in the garden, and the green parsley, and the curling bloom of dill, at a later time they live again and spring for another year; but we men, the great, the strong, the wise, when once we have died, sleep in the hollow earth in silence, a sleep wondrous long, a sleep that knows not end nor awaking.' Compare the lament of Tasso for Corinna, which is less simple and severe, but more soft and tender. 'The white privet falls and springs again, and blooms afresh; and the purple rose when plucked is born again from her thorn, and spreads out her fragrant bosom to the sweet rays; the pine and the beech scatter their leaves on the earth, and the branches are clothed again in their green spoils; the star of love sets and rises; thou, Corinna—oh the hardness of it! hast fallen to rise again no more.'

In one of the sonnets of Wordsworth some words seem to be a reminiscence of Moschus, though it may be but a coincidence:

'Still glides the stream, and shall for ever glide;
The Form remains, the Function never dies;
While we, the brave, the mighty, and the wise,
We men, who in our morn of youth defied
The elements, must vanish;—be it so!
Enough if something from our hands have power
To live, and act, and serve the future hour;
And if, as toward the silent tomb we go,
Through love, through hope, and faith's transcendent
  dower,
We feel that we are greater than we know.'

Perhaps, in these days, any mention of Apollonius Rhodius should be made with an apology. It is his misfortune that, as the writer of a literary epic, he so often brings himself into direct comparison with Homer. In his *Argonautica* he attempted too much. The work lacks unity and is rather a series of episodes than an epic. His archaism has a thin and ghostly effect. The cold and critical light of an unheroic present proves too strong for the glamour of the past. But, when he boldly breaks with tradition and discards mere learning, the result is a psychological study of woman's heart absolutely original and unique in

Greek literature. The episode of Jason and Medea should be read as a prologue to the play of Euripides, and studied in the spirit of the critique by Sainte-Beuve.

The descriptions of Nature in Apollonius exhibit greater sensibility, accompanied by a measure of subjectivity, but they lack the clear-cut grace of Homer's work. That they are generally longer is no recommendation. Too often we are made to feel that they are there of set purpose; they are all in the day's work, so to speak. Apollonius is an anti-quarian eager to utilise his boundless stores of acquired knowledge of geography and mythology. Of his fantastic geography, conspicuous throughout and especially in the long account of the return of the Argonauts, it is not necessary to speak. His descriptions of the island of Thynias, of Acherousia and the cave of Pluto, of the Libyan desert and of Egypt are diffuse and involved. The passage of the Symplegades and of Scylla and Charybdis loses by comparison with the words of Pindar, fit though few, and the clear narrative of Homer. The poet describes the palace and grounds of Aeetes from his knowledge of the island of Calypso and the gardens of Alcinous in the *Odyssey*. The panorama that unfolds itself to the eyes of Eros as he leaves Olympus reminds us of the celebrated passage in the *Clouds* of Aristophanes, quoted in a former chapter. Here it is merely an enumeration, with no note of lyric ecstasy. Similarly, the calm in i. 1154-1155:

$$\dot{\alpha}\mu\phi\grave{\iota} \; \gamma\grave{\alpha}\rho \; \alpha\dot{\iota}\theta\grave{\eta}\rho$$
$$\nu\acute{\eta}\nu\epsilon\mu\circ\varsigma \; \dot{\epsilon}\sigma\tau\acute{\circ}\rho\epsilon\sigma\epsilon\nu \; \delta\acute{\iota}\nu\alpha\varsigma \; \kappa\alpha\tau\grave{\alpha} \; \delta' \; \epsilon\ddot{\upsilon}\nu\alpha\sigma\epsilon \; \pi\acute{\circ}\nu\tau\circ\nu,$$

recalls Aristophanes' $\kappa\acute{\upsilon}\mu\alpha\tau\acute{\alpha} \; \tau' \; \ddot{\epsilon}\sigma\beta\epsilon\sigma\epsilon \; \nu\acute{\eta}\nu\epsilon\mu\circ\varsigma \; \alpha\ddot{\iota}\theta\rho\eta$ (*Birds*, 778).

Of the long descriptions perhaps the most picturesque is the account of the start of Argo. By comparing this with passages in Homer and Pindar we can perceive a decided gain in sensibility to Nature, but at the same time something of loss from the heroic point of view. When Homer sets off Odysseus from Calypso's island he has no time to spend on a farewell scene; he does not linger to paint the aspects of land and sea, but reserves his strength for the coming struggle between the hero and the wrecker Poseidon. Once the vessel has been stored with corn and water and wine, the sails set and the breeze up, Odysseus is off. When Telemachus sets out for Pylos we are told: 'The wind bellied out the sail, and round the cut water of the moving ship the dark wave sounded loudly, and on the vessel sped over the waters, accomplishing her way' (*Ody.*, ii. 427-29). In the fourth Pythian ode Pindar has to send off Argo and her crew. What does he say? Upon the stern he sets the noble figure of Jason with a golden goblet in his hands. The hero calls on Zeus, on the rush of the waves and winds, on the nights and ways of the sea, for a speedy voyage and a safe return. An answer comes from the clouds; thunder peals, lightning flashes. The crew take heart and smite the waters. Anon the south wind wafts them to the mouth of the Axine. Apollonius cannot draw a hero to dominate the scene. But he gives us a picture. He shows us *his* Jason, with eyes full of tears, turning his face to his fatherland. From on high the gods, and from the hills the nymphs, look admiringly on the ship and the crew. Down from the mountain to the water's edge to bid farewell strides Chiron, accompanied by his wife, bearing in her arms young Achilles, whom she holds up before the glad eyes of his father Peleus. 'Then the heroes to the strains of the harp of Orpheus beat with their oars the sounding sea. The waves dashed high, and here and there the dark waters bubbled up into foam, murmuring loudly beneath the might of the strong men. The rigging of the ship as she sped shone in the sun like flame, and the long ways grew ever white as a path seen on a green plain' (i. 540-46). While Homer is clear and business-like, and Pindar is statuesque, Apollonius is picturesque, and so much the worse for his hero. Jason, who ought to have been the observed of all observers, appears as a soft mannikin in a corner of the canvas.

Homer's sunrises and sunsets are facts of daily experience and little more. They are quite independent of locality and landscape effect. He tells us how Dawn of the rosy fingers leaves the streams of Ocean 'to bring light to immortals and to mortal men'; or 'Now the sun set and all the ways were darkened.' In Apollonius the Homeric spirit still lingers, but now and again he takes note of the effect of the phenomenon on the landscape. The following, with its air of utility, is in part Homeric:

ἦμος δ' ἠέλιος δροσερὰς ἐπέλαμψε κολώνας
ἐκ περάτων ἀνιών, ἤγειρε δὲ μηλοβοτῆρας.

(ii. 164-65.)

The following describes the morning when the heroes embarked on Argo:

αὐτὰρ ὅτ' αἰγλήεσσα φαεινοῖς ὄμμασιν Ἠὼς
Πηλίου αἰπεινὰς ἴδεν ἄκριας, ἐκ δ' ἀνέμοιο
εὔδιοι ἐκλύζοντο τινασσομένης ἁλὸς ἄκραι,
δὴ τότ' ἀνέγρετο Τῖφυς.

(i. 519-22.)

And this marks a further advance in sensibility:

ἦμος δ' οὐρανόθεν χαροπὴ ὑπολάμπεται ἠὼς
ἐκ περάτης ἀνιοῦσα, διαγλαύσσουσι δ' ἀταρποί,
καὶ πεδία δροσόεντα φαεινῇ λάμπεται αἴγλῃ,
τῆμος τούσγ' ἐνόησαν αἰδρείῃσι λιπόντες.

(i. 1280-83.)

In Homer the earth laughed with the sheen of armour and spears; in Apollonius it laughs in the bright light of morning:

Ἠὼς δ' ἀμβροσίοισιν ἀνερχομένη φαέεσσιν
λῦε κελαινὴν νύκτα δι' ἠέρος· αἱ δ' ἐγέλασσαν
ἠιόνες νήσοιο καὶ ἐρσήεσσαι ἄπωθεν
ἀτραπιτοὶ πεδίων· ἐν δὲ θρόος ἔσκεν ἀγυιαῖς.

(iv. 1170-73.)

In such passages the poet is Virgilian, not Homeric. A more lively sense of colour is shown in the simile in which the Golden Fleece is likened to 'a cloud which at sunrise is reddened by the glowing rays':

νεφέλῃ ἐναλίγκιον, ἥτ' ἀνιόντος
ἠελίου φλογερῇσιν ἐρεύθεται ἀκτίνεσσιν.

(iv. 125-26.)

Valerius Flaccus adopts and adds to the figure as follows:

*Nubibus accensis similem aut cum veste recincta
Labitur ardenti Thaumantias obvia Phoebo.*

(*Argon.*, viii. 115-16.)

This is not Homeric but Dantesque, a near parallel in Dante being the following:

'Such colour as the sun,
At eve or morning, paints on adverse cloud,
Then saw I sprinkled over all the sky.'

(*Parad.*, xxvii.)[1]

---

[1] Cary's translation.

Again, when we read the lines (imitated by Virgil), in which Lynceus is said to see Heracles afar off 'as when one sees, or thinks he sees all dimly the new moon' (iv. 1479-80), we think of several passages in Dante, such as this:

> 'As at evening hour
> Of twilight, new appearances through heav'n
> Peer with faint glimmer, doubtfully descried,
> So there new substances, methought, began
> To rise in view.'
>
> (*Parad.*, xiv.)

In many of his similes Apollonius imitates Homer, often without regard to the altered situation. Jason advances to the city of the Lemnians 'like a bright star which from their new chambers maidens see rising above the house' (i. 774-776). Again, this hero appears to Medea 'leaping aloft like Sirius from Ocean, which rises beautiful and clear to see, but brings endless evil to the flocks' (iii. 957-59). Both these similes have been suggested by Homer's descriptions of Achilles, but such a weight of glory is too much for his pale shadow Jason. Homer has used bees to illustrate the multitude of the Greeks thronging from the ships and huts to the place of assembly; Apollonius employs them more fantastically. The women of Lemnos coming forth to welcome the heroes are 'like bees when they issue from their hive in a rock and hum loud about the fair lily-flowers, while all around the dewy meadow rejoices, and flitting about they sip now this sweet fruit, now that' (i. 879-882). Here the poet is evidently thinking more about the charm of his picture than the suitability of the image. The comparison of the rout of the Bebryces to the movements of bees that have been smoked from their hive is at once more appropriate and original, and should be compared with the similes of Virgil and Statius which are direct imitations (ii. 130-34).

Homer's similes almost always illustrate *action*, rarely feeling or mental states. In Apollonius, especially in the third book, where the secrets of Medea's soul are laid bare, feelings are often compared to objects and processes in Nature. Medea's fluttering heart is compared, grotesquely enough perhaps, to the light of the sun reflected from moving water in a vessel (iii. 755-60). In a humble way, this marks the beginning of a more accurate scientific observation, for purposes other than didactic. We meet with similar examples in the Latin poets, but it is in Dante that the habit first becomes marked. For instance, when, at the approach of a shining angel, he puts his hands to his face as a screen against the exceeding splendour, he says:

'As when the ray,
Striking on water or the surface clear
Of mirror, leaps unto the opposite part,
Ascending at a glance, e'en as it fell,
Thus with refracted light before me seemed
The ground there smitten.'   (*Purg.*, xv.)

When Jason and Medea meet alone, they stand in silent suspense, till 'the full river of speech' begins to flow at the prompting of Eros: 'And the two stood by each other silent and speechless, like to oaks or tall pines, which close together stand rooted on the mountains, still in breathless calm, but anon again when stirred by the blast of the wind they make a wondrous din' (iii. 965-72). Valerius has put the figure in fewer words:

Abietibus tacitis aut immotis cyparissis
Adsimiles, rapidus nondum quas miscuit auster.
(*Argon.*, vii. 405-406.)

At the speech of Jason, we are told, Medea was glad, 'and her heart melted as round the roses melts the dew when warmed by the morning beams' (iii. 1019-21).

Perhaps the best-known passage in all Apollonius is that in which the fierce struggle between love and filial duty that rages in the breast of Medea, as she tosses in sleepless agony, is contrasted with the calm of Nature: 'Then was Night drawing darkness over the face of earth; and the sailors on the sea were gazing from their ships towards Helice and the stars of Orion; here wayfarer and gate-keeper were now fain of sleep; there slumber deep and unbroken lapped round the mother of children dead; throughout the city no longer was heard bark of dog or echoing din; stillness held the blackening darkness; but on Medea sweet sleep came not' (iii. 744-751). Virgil evidently had this passage in his mind when he described a similar situation in the story of the unhappy, but less passionate Dido, and added the memorable lines:

> *At non infelix animi Phoenissa, neque unquam*
> *Solvitur in somnos, oculisve aut pectore noctem*
> *Accipit.* (*Aeneid*, iv. 529-531.)

These words, in turn, seem to have charmed the Virgilian Tennyson, who has imitated them in *Geraint and Enid*:

> 'She found no rest, and ever fail'd to draw
> The quiet night into her blood.'

And again in *The Princess*:

> 'And twilight gloom'd; and broader-grown the bowers
> Drew the great night into themselves.'

CHAPTER XI

THE GREEK ANTHOLOGY

WHEN we enter the gardens of the Anthology, in addition to much that is merely an accentuation of notes heard before, we find some new features. Of course, part of this collection falls within what we call the classical period, but we are to deal here with the later writers. These short poems are a reflex of the changes that have taken place in man's social environment, and in his intellectual and moral ideals. The intense feeling of national and civic life which preoccupied the minds of Greek citizens, as long as Greece was Greece, has disappeared, and in its place has arisen a family and individual spirit. In the sphere of literary art the glass which had been wont to give so steady a reflection of life is shattered to fragments. The ideals that inspired the writers of epic and drama and lyric are dead, and Romance is not yet fully born. Yet this breaking-up, along with great loss, brings also its compensations. The Anthology is, in its way, a most human document. Now we see, what we had rarely seen before in the days of high art, man in the family, as he lives from day to day, with his individual hopes and fears, and loves and passions. Now we read those 'trivial fond records' of which epic poet and dramatist and lyrist take little or no account, and past which the proud pageant of history imperiously sweeps.

The mission of Hellas among the nations has

245

ended. The Hellene has become a Hellenist, the patriot a cosmopolite. He has broken with the spiritual and heroic past of Hellas; the great gods are senile and topple from their thrones; the deeds of the heroes live but as echoes in the dainty lines of the epigram. He has drunk of the wine of the Orient, but it holds no nepenthe against the thought of death. That thought had always been more or less present to the Greek, but throughout the great period it did not paralyse action. Achilles is the true type of the ancient Greek full of high endeavour in face of death. In the *Iliad* it is just because death may be so very near, because fate is hovering round in a thousand shapes, that Sarpedon calls aloud to Glaucus ἴομεν—'let us on!' Now the cry is 'Why do I labour in vain, seeing the naked end?' At one time 'all is laughter, all is dust, all is nothing'; at another 'all is tears.' Sitting in the shadow of death, men cling helplessly to life and all that makes it dear. Dead to the wider interests of humanity, without country and without faith, they think more of the home, of the love of wife and child, of the little things that fill the narrow round of daily life. This change in feeling colours their conceptions of external Nature, and gives rise to a more sensuous and subjective treatment.

Throughout the complex whole of this collection of epigrams Man's relation to Nature can be treated under a few heads. First, and most prevalent, is the sensuous feeling, when men are concerned about the pleasures of the body and the delights of eye and ear, beyond the smoke and hum of cities. They love comfortable surroundings, the garden and the meadow, the shade and the flowers. They do not paint large landscapes, but vignettes. Their pictures are often set in a framework of mythological symbolism which

246

embodies the spirit of Nature in the forms of god and nymph. The appeal of Nature to Man is made through the deities of hillside, plain, and garden, in the persons of Pan and Priapus. The call is addressed, not to Man's higher nature, but to his senses. We hear, not a stern trumpet-call to duty, but a winning voice inviting man to the enjoyment of boon Nature, this day as every day. Pan is the god to whom are dedicated ἄσπορα τεμένη, 'unsown domains,' where he feeds his 'visionary flocks,' and where he is at last to meet Echo, and end in joy his mad pursuit. By the high-crested pine rustling in the balmy zephyr men sit down beside murmuring water and listen to the sweet piping of Pan till drowsihed comes down on the charmed eye-lids (*App. Plan.*, 13). When he pipes the nymphs dance with joyous feet, then the Dryads' cliff is silent, and the manifold-mingled bleating of the ewes (*Anth. Pal.*, ix. 823). For the foot-sore wayfarer Pan is the willing and trusted pre-scriber: 'Here on the green grass of the meadow fling thyself down, O traveller, and rest thy weak limbs from toil and weariness, for here the pine-tree a-tremble with the breath of the west wind, and the shepherd on the mountains piping at noon-day near the fountain beneath a copse of bushy plane will soothe thee as thou listenest to the tune of the cicala. Escaping the heat of the autumnal dog-star shalt thou cross the height to-morrow. Trust Pan whose good advice this is' (*App. Plan.*, 227). Nor are mortals ungrateful for the attentions of deity. Anyte shows us a shepherd placing under a rock an offering of gratitude to shaggy Pan and the nymphs for support-ing his fainting spirits in the parching summer heat and reaching forth to him in their hands draughts of honey-sweet water (*App. Plan.*, 291). Speaking in person, a wayside fountain, fringed with planes and soft-blossoming laurels, calls the passing pilgrim to draw near and put away weariness and thirst (*Anth. Pal.*, ix. 374).

Readers of Homer will remember what Odysseus declared to be the finest sight in the world. It was to see a whole people making merry and listening to a minstrel in the halls, as they sit feasting at well-laden tables, while a wine-bearer draws off and serves the wine (*Ody.*, ix. 5-11). In contrast with this place the ideal of summer pleasure as expounded by Nicaenetus two hundred years before Christ: 'O Philotherus, I have no desire to feast in the city, but in the country, rejoicing in the west wind's breath; sufficient for me is a couch of strewn boughs beneath my side; for at hand is a bed of osier and willow, the garland of the Carians from of old; but let wine be brought and the gladdening lyre of the Muses, that we may drink to our hearts' pleasure, and celebrate in song the renowned bride of Zeus, our island's queen' (Athenaeus, xv. 673 B).[1] This is a picture of anticipation, corresponding to the *Thalysia* of Theocritus, in which the crown of a summer day's enjoyment has become a pleasant memory.

It might with truth be said that throughout the whole course of Greek poetry the poets had no winter in their year. Their seasonal songs have almost always spring for their theme. By the coast, spring marks the time for putting to sea again. 'A sweet thing it is for sailors, after winter, to see the garland of spring,' says Asclepiades (*Anth. Pal.*, v. 169). Both

---

[1] It is interesting to note how Lucretius contrasts the ideals of Homer and Nicaenetus, in order to inculcate 'plain living and high thinking,' in the passage of Book ii. beginning:

'O miseras hominum mentes, O pectora caeca!' (14.)

Leonidas of Tarentum and Antipater of Sidon celebrate the coming of spring to a seaside community. Priapus bids the sailor take heart and put out to sea, for the gloom has passed from the face of the deep, the waves are silent, the swallow has come to build beneath the eaves, the beneficent west wind gently breathes, and the meadows are laughing with soft leafage (*Anth. Pal.*, x. 1 and 2). But it is in the verses of Meleager, the voluptuous Syrian singer, that the feeling for the sights and sounds of this season rises to something like a real passion. His poem on Spring is one of the longest in the *Anthology*: 'The winds of winter have gone from the sky and the bright season of flowery spring comes smiling in; the dark earth crowns herself with fresh greenery and blooming plants put on new leaves. The meadows laugh as they drink the tender dews of nourishing Morn, and the rose unfolds. In joy on the mountains pipes the shepherd, and the heart of the goat-herd rejoices in his white flock. Now sailors voyage over the wide waves, while the West Wind with harmless breath fills the sails; now men wreathe their hair with the flower of the clustering ivy, and revel in honour of Dionysus who brings the grape's increase. Ox-born bees bethink them of their fair tasks of skill and, sitting in the hive, fashion their white and beautiful works of fresh-flowing pierced wax. Everywhere is heard the song of the clear-voiced race of birds, the halcyons on the wave, swallows beneath the eaves, by river banks the swan, and in the grove the nightingale. Now, if leafy trees rejoice and the earth breaks into bloom, if the shepherd pipes and fleecy flocks are glad, if sailors sail and Dionysus keeps holiday, if birds chirp and bees travail, why should not a poet sing fine songs in spring?' (*Anth. Pal.*, ix. 363.) With something of constraint and artificiality, this lacks the warmth of full-blown romance, and may be contrasted with modern sublimities on the same theme.

Associated with this Spring feeling, and forming a part of simple daily pleasures, there appears a more sympathetic interest in plant and flower life. Moero's lines on an offering to Aphrodite of the Golden House breathe a tender sentiment characteristic rather of Virgil in his *Georgics* than of any Greek writer: 'Thou liest in the golden porch of Aphrodite, O grape-cluster filled with the juice of Dionysus, and never again shall thy mother entwine thee with her beauteous tendril, or above thine head shoot forth her fragrant leaf' (*Anth. Pal.*, vi. 119). Meleager, in consecrating flowers to the service of Love, coins for them new epithets, calling the rose 'lover-loving' (φιλέραστα ῥόδα), and the lily 'full of laughter' (γελῶντα κρίνα). The charms of Zenophila put to shame all the flowers of the meadow: 'Now blooms the white iris, blooms the rain-loving narcissus, and mountain-roaming lilies blow. Now blooms Zenophila, the desired of lovers, timely flower among the flowers, sweet rose of Persuasion. Ye meadows, why that radiant laugh with your leafage, all in vain? Better is the maiden than sweet-breathing garlands' (*Anth. Pal.*, v. 144). Roses blooming in winter suggest the following conceit to Crinagoras: 'Erstwhile we roses bloomed in spring, but now in mid-winter have we opened our bright buds to smile full gladly on this the morning of thy birthday and on the morrow, thy bridal-day. Better is it to be seen on the head of the fairest of maidens than to wait for the sun of Spring' (*Anth. Pal.*, vi. 345).

Besides being associated with the happiness of

birthday and marriage, flowers also adorn the tomb. The dry bones of Anacreon call, not unnaturally, for a libation of wine (*Anth. Pal.*, vii. 26), but on the tomb of Vibius may flowers grow, violet, marjoram, and narcissus, and round him may all be roses (Kaibel, *Epigr. Graec.*, 548). Simmias pays the following tribute to Sophocles: 'Creep gently, O ivy, gently, over the tomb of Sophocles, putting forth thy green tresses, and all about let rose-petals bloom, and let the grape-loving vine spread her soft shoots around, all for the sake of the wise eloquence which was his, the honey-sweet, from Muses and Graces together' (*Anth. Pal.*, vii. 22).

In the moral sphere flowers are employed, as they have been so often since, as reminders of the shortness of life and the passing of youthful beauty. Rufinus sends a garland to Rhodocleia with ungracious advice: 'I send thee, Rhodocleia, this garland, woven of fair flowers by my own hands. Here are lily, and rosebud, and moist wind-flower, soft narcissus, and dark-eyed violet. Garland thyself with these and cease to be high-minded; for even as this garland dost thou flower and fade' (*Anth. Pal.*, v. 74). Readers will call to mind the similar strain of sentiment expressed in English lyrics like Waller's 'Go, lovely Rose!' In fact, as we read parts of the *Anthology* and mark certain characteristics, the emptiness and earthiness, the scampish preoccupation with wine and women, the far-fetched conceits and fantastic griefs of love-in-idleness, we are reminded again and again of the poetry of our lighter Caroline writers.

Along with this increase of interest in inanimate Nature we find a greater sympathy with animal life, due, in part at least, to a sense of the need of companionship to make life fuller and sweeter ere it be lost in the long darkness. The aged ox, worn out with the labour of the plough, is not led to the shambles, but with free neck rejoices in the grass of the meadow (*Anth. Pal.*, vi. 228). Among the many family epitaphs, such as that for the child who has gone to be a flower in Persephone's hair, that for the boy 'who was so beautiful and died,' and that for the black Libyan nurse who was faithful unto death and is at last free in the tomb, yet ready to resume her bonds when the master shall join her in the far-off land, we may read memorials of dumb household pets—dog and bird, and tuneful cricket. 'Thou who passest by this way, if perchance thine eyes light on this monument, do not laugh if it is the grave of a dog; a master wept tears for me and laid me in the dust' (Kaibel, *Epigr. Graec.*, 627). The tame partridge, the prey of the prowling cat, no longer in its wicker home pranks its plumage in the light of bright-faced Dawn (*Anth. Pal.*, vii. 204). The cricket has left the sunlight and the wealthy house of Alcis, to drink dew from the flowers of golden Persephone (*Anth. Pal.*, vii. 189). A swallow carrying off a grass-hopper draws from Evenus a protest against Nature's law of ravin whereby the strong prey upon the weak. The lines have been translated by Cowper:

> 'Attic maid! with honey fed,
>   Bear'st thou to thy callow brood
> Yonder locust from the mead,
>   Destined their delicious food?
>
> Ye have kindred voices clear,
>   Ye alike unfold the wing,
> Migrate hither, sojourn here,
>   Both attendant on the spring.

Ah, for pity drop the prize;
  Let it not, with truth, be said
That a songster gasps and dies,
  That a songster may be fed.'

Pamphilus has an epigram in which he interprets the song of the nightingale—or, as Dr. Mackail says, it may be the swallow, for the two versions of the story are not infrequently confused—in terms of the myth. The Greek poet does not emphasise the hopeless plight of the bird as the English Barnefield does in the lines:

'King Pandion he is dead:
All thy friends are lapp'd in lead.'

Neither does he, like the same poet, think of his own woes and the fickleness of friendship, as in the line:

'Thou and I were both beguiled.'

Neither, as in the sonnet of Milton, is the poet a lover whose heart fills with fresh hope; nor, as in the ode of Keats, is he a young man who listens in the cool dark till 'seems it rich to die.' This Greek's interpretation is on the same lines as the poem of Matthew Arnold who pictures in classico-romantic manner the old-world scene of the tragedy when the change came. 'Why, unhappy daughter of Pandion, dost thou prolong thy wailing notes the live-long day? Has longing seized thee for thy maidenhood of which Thracian Tereus violently bereft thee?' (*Anth. Pal.*, ix. 57.)

Antipater of Sidon in two epigrams makes a happy use of the cry of birds. Telesilla, an industrious maid, dedicates to Athene her shuttle, 'king-fisher of

253

the loom of Pallas,' which made music in the early morning; and Bacchylis offers

> 'The shuttle that doth sing
> A busy nightingale among the thread.'

As regards the former of these Dr. Mackail remarks that the reference may be either to the sound or to the colour, as the shuttle flashes through the loom. An interesting parallel, involving both sound and colour, is found in *Kalevala*, where Osmotar tells Ilmarinen that his Bride of Beauty will

> 'Make for thee the softest raiment,
> Make thy weaver's loom as merry
> As the cuckoo of the forest;
> Make the shuttle glide in beauty,
> Like the ermine of the woodlands;
> Make the spindle twirl as deftly
> As the squirrel spins the acorn.' [1]

Rarely, even in the *Anthology*, is Man made to illustrate Nature. But to an anonymous writer the sight of an eagle soaring above a tomb suggests the aspiring spirit of the great idealistic philosopher of antiquity. The lines are probably best known through Shelley's translation:

> 'Eagle! why soarest thou above that tomb?
> To what sublime and star-ypaven home
> Floatest thou?
> I am the image of swift Plato's spirit,
> Ascending heaven; Athens doth inherit
> His corpse below.'

'Every sea is the sea.' 'The sea's way is the sea's way.' 'As much as a mother is sweeter than a step-

---

[1] Cp. Euripides, *Iph. in T.*, 222—ἱστοῖς ἐν καλλιφθόγγοις.

mother, so much is earth dearer than the grey sea.'
In these words of Antipater we recognise all the old
fear and hatred. And as we read epitaph after
epitaph we begin to realise that now we are face to
face with the full pathos of the tale of the sea. Just
as Mucklebackit in Scott's *Antiquary* curses the boat
which he is trying with fumbling fingers to repair, so
the poet curses the cruel steep of Geraneia on which
the ship struck when the loved one went down (*Anth.
Pal.*, vii. 496). Not even in the days of the halcyons,
when the face of the deep should be as marble, do
men cease to weep for the greed of the waters. Again
and again we read inscriptions beginning 'I am the
tomb of a shipwrecked man,' followed sometimes by
words of encouragement, such as 'We went down,
but other ships sailed on'; sometimes by a prayer,
such as 'God grant thee a more kindly sea.' Even in
the kingdom of the dead the mariner hears in fancy
the hateful roaring of the sea (*Anth. Pal.*, vii. 278).
Often the memorial tells of an empty tomb, for all
the sea is the sailor's grave, and the sea-gull alone
can tell where the white bones lie (*Anth. Pal.*, vii. 285).
Sometimes the tomb of a husbandman adjoins that
of a sailor, for is there not the same Hades beneath
both land and sea? (*Anth. Pal.*, vii. 265). Yet it is
something to be sure of being laid in earth by kindred
hands, so the sailor wishes he had been a happy
shepherd tending his flock on the white and grassy
hillside rather than have dipped an oar in the bitter
brine (*Anth. Pal.*, vii. 636).

Yet, for all its terrors, the sea may become to the
dwellers by its shores, dear as the face of a friend.
In proof, hear the plaint of the Eretrians carried
captive to Ardericca by Darius after the first Persian
war: 'We, who erst left behind the sounding surge of

the Aegean, lie in the middle of the plain of Ecbatana.
Farewell renowned Eretria, once our fatherland;
farewell Athens, the neighbour of Euboea; farewell
dear sea!' (*Anth. Pal.*, vii. 256.) Occasionally, also, we
find expression of the love of an ocean prospect, of the
landscape where land and sea meet, and of gardens
and vineyards by the shore. The following is by
Mnasalcas, in his sharp, austere style: 'Let us stand
by the low beach of the spray-scattering sea, looking
upon the sacred place of Cypris of the Sea, and the
fountain shadowed with poplars, from which the
shrill halcyons draw water with their bills'
(*Anth. Pal.*, ix. 333).

The palace gardens of the Heraeum, opposite
Constantinople, thus commend themselves in the
words of Arabius: 'I am full of waters and
gardens and groves and vines, and the *gladness*
of the neighbouring sea; fisherman and farmer,
from either hand, stretch out to me pleasant
gifts from sea and land; those that stay in me
are cheered either by the song of a bird or the
sweet voice of ferrymen' (*Anth. Pal.*, ix. 667).

It is fitting that Achilles should rest within hearing
of the waves. So thinks our anonymous writer:
'The tomb of Achilles, the breaker of the ranks, which
once the Achaeans reared, a terror even for Trojans
yet to be. It leans sea-ward that so the son of the
sea-nymph Thetis may be honoured by the groaning
of the waters' (*Anth. Pal.*, vii. 142). Compare with
this the grim feeling which inspires the misanthropic
Timon in Shakespeare to make his grave by the
sea:

'Say to Athens,
Timon hath made his everlasting mansion
Upon the beached verge of the salt flood,

256

Who once a day with his embossed froth
The turbulent surge shall cover.'

And the remark of Alcibiades on the same:

'Rich conceit
Taught thee to make vast Neptune weep for aye
On thy low grave, on faults forgiven.'

In the tragic poets we have found instances of appeals to natural phenomena to sympathise with the joy or woe of the speaker. In the *Anthology* these are found generally in poems devoted to the passion of love. In an epigram of Philodemus a lover bids the moon shed her silver light on his love Callistion. 'Happy pair!' surely she will say, for her soul too was once fired by Endymion (*Anth. Pal.*, v. 123). The words of the deserted lover of Marcus Argentarius, 'Golden-horned moon, thou seest this, and ye bright-glowing stars, whom Ocean takes to his bosom, that sweet-breathing Ariste has gone and left me desolate' (*Anth. Pal.*, v. 16), recall the *Pharmaceutria* of Theocritus. Here also we meet with traces of the pathetic fallacy, when Nature is for the occasion endowed with a feeling antagonistic to Man. The grey Dawn goes slowly wheeling round the world when another is with Demo; when she is in the arms of Meleager Dawn makes haste to pour upon them her light *that joys in their grief* — ἐπιχαιρέκακον (*Anth. Pal.*, v. 173).[1] Agathias pictures the sorrows of a lover who has spent the night in tears, and who even at the coming of Dawn cannot sleep for the noise of the swallows. 'Peace! *envious* chatterers,' he cries, 'I did not shear away the tongue of Philomela' (*Anth. Pal.*, v. 237). And again, when the crowing of the cock heralds the *envious* Dawn, the lover

---

[1] Cf. Chaucer's *Troilus and Criseyde*, iii. 1450-1463.

exclaims, 'Curse on thee, most *envious* of birds!'
(*Anth. Pal.*, v. 3.)   Such expressions resemble the
bare rudiments of the art of Shakespeare when he
makes his epithets echo the moods of his characters.
The words of Romeo, when about to leave Juliet,
form a parallel to the above, both in occasion and in
sentiment:

> 'Look, love, what *envious* streaks
> Do lace the *severing* clouds in yonder east!'

'Man knows no second spring,' says Moschus, in
effect, and an unknown author in the *Anthology* has
presented this contrast between Man and Nature,
if less directly, yet with the same tearless calm so
peculiarly Greek: 'Naiads and cold pastures, tell
this to the bees when they come again this way in
spring, how the old man Leucippus died on a winter
night as he snared the bounding hares, and no longer
is it his pleasant task to tend the hives; but the
pastures and the dells sadly miss him who was the
neighbour of the mountain' (*Anth. Pal.*, vii. 717).

We may bring this study to a conclusion with a
quotation from the astronomer Ptolemaeus, who,
as he watches the glories of the heavens, associates the
life of humanity with the Eternal: 'I know that I
am mortal and the creature of a day; but when I
search out the unnumbered circles of the stars, no
longer do my feet touch earth, but by the side of
Zeus himself I have my fill of ambrosia which is the
food of Gods' (*Anth. Pal.*, ix. 577).